T0371767

The Chinese Banking Industry

Banking reform is a prerequisite for continued high economic growth in China and is a crucial element of China's overall economic reforms. Chinese banks, especially state banks, face a wide ranging series of challenges that not only imperil the health of the banking system, but also endanger the stability of the whole economy. This book argues that because banking problems in China are sensitive, involving top political authorities and even government leaders, it is not possible to collect all the necessary information, let alone make it public, and that therefore a good way of analysing present day challenges is to consider how similar challenges arose and were dealt with in the past. The book provides detailed systematic analysis of the historical development of the Chinese banking industry, focusing in particular on the development of the Bank of China (BOC) in the period 1905 to 1949. It addresses important issues in its evolution, including corporate governance, government intervention, foreign competition and white-collar crime, highlighting how these areas continue to be the problem areas today. It evaluates how the challenges in these areas were met, considers the results of its efforts, and draws lessons for policy-making today. Overall, this book analyses the key issues in Chinese banking reform, providing an historical perspective on these challenges by showing how they have been dealt with in the past.

Yuanyuan Peng received an MA in International Finance from the Graduate School of the People's Bank of China, and obtained a PhD in Management Studies from the University of Cambridge. She has professional experience in the Chinese banking sector. Her major research interests include strategy and marketing, banking restructuring and corporate governance.

Routledge Studies on the Chinese Economy
Series Editor
Peter Nolan, University of Cambridge

Founding Series Editors
Peter Nolan, University of Cambridge and
Dong Fureng, Beijing University

The aim of this series is to publish original, high-quality, research-level work by both new and established scholars in the West and the East, on all aspects of the Chinese economy, including studies of business and economic history.

The Theory of the Firm and Chinese Enterprise Reform
The case of China International Trust and Investment Corporation
Qin Xiao

Globalization, Transition and Development in China
The case of the coal industry
Huaichuan Rui

China Along the Yellow River
Reflections on rural society
Cao Jinqing, translated by Nicky Harman and Huang Ruhua

Economic Growth, Income Distribution and Poverty Reduction in Contemporary China
Shujie Yao

China's Economic Relations with the West and Japan, 1949–79
Grain, trade and diplomacy
Chad J. Mitcham

China's Industrial Policy and the Global Business Revolution
The case of the domestic appliance industry
Ling Liu

Managers and Mandarins in Contemporary China
The building of an international business alliance
Jie Tang

The Chinese Model of Modern Development
Edited by Tian Yu Cao

Chinese Citizenship
Views from the margins
Edited by Vanessa L. Fong and Rachel Murphy

Unemployment, Inequality and Poverty in Urban China
Edited by Shi Li and Hiroshi Sato

Globalization, Competition and Growth in China
Edited by Jian Chen and Shujie Yao

The Chinese Communist Party in Reform
Edited by Kjeld Erik Brodsgaard and Zheng Yongnian

Poverty and Inequality among Chinese Minorites
A.S. Bhalla and Shufang Qiu

The Chinese Banking Industry

Lessons from history for today's challenges

Yuanyuan Peng

Routledge
Taylor & Francis Group

LONDON AND NEW YORK

First published 2007
by Routledge
2 Park Square, Milton Park, Abingdon, Oxon OX14 4RN

Simultaneously published in the USA and Canada
by Routledge
270 Madison Ave, New York, NY 10016

Routledge is an imprint of the Taylor & Francis Group, an informa business

© 2007 Yuanyuan Peng

Typeset in Times by
RefineCatch Limited, Bungay, Suffolk
Printed and bound in Great Britain by
the MPG Books Group

British Library Cataloguing in Publication Data
A catalogue record for this book is available from the British Library

Library of Congress Cataloging in Publication Data
Peng, Yuanyuan, 1968–
   The Chinese banking industry: lessons from history for today's challenges /
Yuanyuan Peng.
      p. cm – (Routledge studies on the Chinese economy)
   Includes bibliographical references and index.
   1. Banks and banking—China.   2. Banks and banking—Government
policy—China.   I. Title.
   HG3334.P46 2007
   332.10951—dc22
   2006033960

ISBN10: 0–415–42347–3 (hbk)
ISBN10: 0–203–96223–0 (ebk)

ISBN13: 978–0–415–42347–2 (hbk)
ISBN13: 978–0–203–96223–7 (ebk)

To my husband and daughter Liu Ning and Liu Zixuan

History makes men wise.

Francis Bacon (1561–1626)

Contents

Illustrations

Figures

Tables

Acknowledgements

During the process of writing this book, I have received support from many people and institutions. I am most grateful to Professor Peter Nolan for his intellectual inspiration and encouragement during my PhD programme at Judge Business School, Cambridge. I am utterly indebted to Professor Ajit Singh of the University of Cambridge and Professor Christopher Howe of the School of Oriental and African Studies for their invaluable comments and advice.

I would also like to give sincere thanks to Dr Jin Zhang, Dr Fatima Wang, Dr Silas Brown, Dr Yuantao Guo, Dr Anne Bowlker and Dr Dawna Rhoades for offering me intellectual thoughts and assistance on specific issues.

The research involved extensive fieldwork in a number of banks in China. I am more than obliged to managers and staff at the Bank of China, the Industrial and Commercial Bank of China, the People's Bank of China and the various commercial banks of China, among others. I appreciate their sharing ideas on China's banking reform, and their willingness to be interviewed and provide research materials. Without their support, this book would not have come into being. For reasons of confidentiality, their names are not listed here.

From my former school, the Graduate School of the People's Bank of China, I received continuous help. I am particularly grateful to the materials supplied and the assistance rendered by Dr Tang Xu and Zhang Rui.

I am also enormously indebted to Standard Chartered Bank for giving me the chance to do an internship and fieldwork. Special gratitude goes to Susan Ho, Gareth Bullock and Kate James for their kind support.

Lucy Cavendish College has been my home in the UK for the last five years and I am greatly appreciative of all the people at Lucy, especially Dr Orsola R. Spivack, Susan Sang and Gaby Jones. Special thanks also go to Carmen Neagoe at Judge Business School for providing significant facilitation to my research.

I wish to thank the following institutions for funding my PhD research: the Cambridge Overseas Trust, the Lord Frederick Cavendish Fund and the George Bidder Fund. The financial assistance made my study and my work on this book possible.

This study is based on my PhD dissertation at the University of Cambridge. I am very grateful to the wonderful work done by the editorial staff of the book, particularly to Peter Sowden, editor at Routledge, for his valuable advice and suggestions.

Finally, I wish to thank my parents and my brother for their unfailing love and support. My special thanks also go to my father-in-law, Liu Yansun, who was an experienced banker and gave me lots of expert advice. And, most of all, I am deeply indebted to my husband Liu Ning and my daughter Liu Zixuan. It was, indeed, their love, enthusiasm and encouragement that sustained me to finish this book.

Nevertheless, I assume full responsibility for the content of this work.

Note on Chinese names and currency

Names

The Chinese phonetic alphabet (pinyin) is used throughout the book for the names of people and places, etc., with a few exceptions: Dr Sun Yatsen is known worldwide, and T.V. Soong instead of Song Ziwen is familiar to many English-speaking countries. For this reason, such names are maintained.

The traditional order of names for Chinese people is followed, where surnames precede their given names.

Currency

1 The silver tael (liang) was China's traditional unit of currency. There were many different kinds of taels depending on the region or type of trade. The Shanghai tael, about 33.9 gram (1.09 oz troy), was the most commonly used, and is adopted in this book.

2 C\$ = Chinese yuan, which, before 1935, was the silver dollar yuan, i.e. coins and redeemable banknotes. After 1935, the Chinese yuan was the legal tender yuan, i.e. unredeemable banknotes.

3 Until 1933, both the silver dollar and the tael were used as units of accounts.

   1 silver dollar (C\$1) = 0.72 taels, or,

   1 tael = 1.4 silver dollar yuan (C\$1.4).

Note on the English translation of some pre-1949 newspapers and magazines

Dagongbao	*L'Impartial*
Guowen Zhoubao	*National News Weekly*
Minguo Ribao	*Republic Daily*
Pinglunbao	*Critique*
Shehui Xinwen	*Society Mercury*
Shenbao	*Shanghai Daily*
Shiji Pinglun	*Century Critique*
Shishi Xinbao	*China Times*
Xingqiwu Huabao	*Friday Pictorial*
Xinwenbao	*News Report*
Yinhang Yuebao	*Bankers Monthly*
Yinhang Zhoubao	*Bankers Weekly*
Zhengyibao	*Justice*
Zhoubao	*Weekly Report*
Zhongyang Daobao	*Central Herald*
Zhongyang Ribao	*Central Daily*

Abbreviations

ABC	Agricultural Bank of China
ATM	automated teller machine
BBC	British Broadcasting Corporation
BBVA	Banco Bilbao Vizcaya Argentania
BNP	Banque National de Paris
BOC	Bank of China
BOCAR	*BOC Annual Reports*
BoCOM	Bank of Communications
BSCH	Banco Santander Central Hispano
CAB	Chongqing Archive Bureau
CBC	Central Bank of China (Taiwan)
CBRC	China Banking Regulatory Commission
CC	*China Critic*
CCB	China Construction Bank
CCD	*China Computer Daily*
CD	*China Daily*
CDFC	China Development Finance Corporation
CEO	chief executive officer
Chartered Bank	Chartered Bank of India, Australia and China (Standard Chartered Bank today)
City Bank	National City Bank of New York (Citibank today)
CNN	Cable News Network
CPC	Communist Party of China
CTC	China Textile Corporation
CWR	*China Weekly Review*
DBCO	Daqing Bank Clearing Office
DBS	Development Bank of Singapore
FBI	Federal Bureau of Investigation
FEER	*Far Eastern Economic Review*
FRI	Financial Research Institute (of the People's Bank of China)
FRO	Financial Research Office (of the Shanghai Branch, People's Bank of China)

FRUS	*Foreign Relations of the United States*
FSA	Financial Services Authority
FT	*Financial Times*
GITIC	Guangdong International Trust and Investment Company
HSBC	Hongkong and Shanghai Banking Corporation
ICBC	Industrial and Commercial Bank of China
IMF	International Monetary Fund
IPO	initial public offering
IT	information technology
KMT	Kuo Min Tang (China Nationalist Party)
M&A	merger and acquisition
MBO	management buyout
MOF	Ministry of Finance
NAO	National Audit Office
NCDN	*North China Daily News*
NCH	*North China Herald*
NPLs	non-performing loans
NRC	National Resource Commission
NYT	*New York Times*
OCC	Office of Currency Comptroller
OECD	Organization of Economic Cooperation and Development
PBC	People's Bank of China
PD	*People's Daily*
PLA	People's Liberation Army
POS	point of sale
PRC	People's Republic of China
R&D	research and development
RMB	renminbi (currency of People's Republic of China)
ROA	return on assets
ROE	return on equities
S&L	Savings and Loan Association
SBA	Shanghai Bankers Association
SHCS	Shanghai Commercial and Savings Bank
SOE	state-owned enterprises
WSJ	*Wall Street Journal*
WTO	World Trade Organization
ZJIB	Zhejiang Industrial Bank

1   Introduction

The 1997 Asian Financial Crisis had an adverse impact on countries like South Korea, Thailand and Indonesia, and especially exposed the serious problems in their banking systems. China was not engulfed in this crisis and maintained relatively sound economic performance. The frequently discussed contributing factors included the inconvertible Chinese currency under the capital account, a current account surplus throughout most of the 1990s, the dominance of foreign direct investment and long-term debt in total capital inflows, and the world's second largest foreign exchange reserves (Lardy 1998a).

However, China has many of the same banking problems as its neighbors, most notably, the bank-dominated financial system, highly-leveraged enterprises, excessive lending, and huge build-up of bad debts (Lardy 1998a). In recent years, the health of China's financial system has been deteriorating. In 1998, the central bank, the People's Bank of China (PBC), ordered the closure of the Hainan Development Bank, which collapsed under the weight of bad loans resulting from investments in Hainan's burst property bubble. It is thought to be the first time the government has decided to close a commercial bank (Zhou Jianping 2000: 49). In addition, the China New-Tech Pioneering Investment Company, the Guangdong International Trust and Investment Company (GITIC), and a number of urban and rural credit cooperatives were also shut down and declared insolvent (Xu Hongcai 2000). Among them, GITIC's collapse was truly historic. With the equivalent of about US$4.7 billion of debt, the bankruptcy was by far the largest in the history of the People's Republic of China (PRC) (Chang, G. 2001).

The sounding alarm of the Asian Financial Crisis and the deteriorating performance of China's domestic banks substantially increased the sense of urgency in the need for banking reform at the highest levels of China's leadership. In early 1998 the government announced ambitious reform programmes, particularly regarding state banks – Industrial and Commercial Bank of China (ICBC), China Construction Bank (CCB), Bank of China (BOC) and Agricultural Bank of China (ABC). The well-being of state banks is crucial for the safety and soundness of the entire banking sector and the financial industry at large (Liu Mingkang 2004b). Even at the end of

September 2005, the Big Four still constituted 53 per cent of the total assets, and 53 per cent of the total liabilities of China's banking system (China Banking Regulatory Commission (CBRC) website).

Several reform programmes have been undertaken in recent years:

1 In 1998, the sum of 270 billion renminbi (RMB) was injected into the Big Four to help them improve their capital base (Gao 2001).
2 Four asset management corporations were established in 1999 to take over RMB1.4 trillion, about 70 per cent of total non-performing loans (NPLs) from the four state banks (ibid.).
3 The commercialization of state banks has been pushed more aggressively, including: the lifting of the lending quotas by the PBC (the central bank); policy loans of the Big Four being taken over by three policy banks; more interest rate freedom for state banks in order to achieve the objective of the 'commercialization of banks and [the] marketization of [the] interest rate' (Lin 1998).
4 In early 2004, the government put US$45 billion into BOC and CCB, and further took away RMB278 billion NPLs from these two banks to strengthen their capital adequacy (Xie Ping and Lu Lei 2005).
5 The China Banking Regulatory Commission (CBRC) was formally established in 2003 to regulate and supervise all the banking institutions and their business activities.

Disappointingly, these measures have not brought about expected results. For one thing, with a 20 per cent non-performing loans (NPLs) ratio, the four banks had again accumulated RMB2,100 billion (US$254 billion)-worth of NPLs at the beginning of 2004 (*Caijing* 20 January 2004). Foreign experts estimated at US$500 billion, equivalent to around half of China's total GDP (Nolan 2004a; Zhang Allan 2004). This is alarming. The financial distress is 'likely to become systemic when NPLs share reaches 15%' (Sheng 1996: 10). Throughout the years 2004 and 2005, despite strict measures to cut down NPLs, the average NPL ratio of the four state banks still hovered above 10 per cent in 2005 compared with 5 per cent for other Chinese joint-stock banks and 1 per cent for foreign banks in China (CBRC website).

The accumulation of huge NPLs in the banking system is shaking public confidence and posing a danger to social security. In 1999 there was a run on the Bank of Communications in Henan province. Within just one day, the equivalent of US$108 million was taken out of the bank (Dow Jones Newswires 21 May 1999). In 2000 there was a run on CCB, which lasted for four days at six of its branches (*People's Daily* (*PD*) 3 November 2000). In 2001, people lost confidence in rural cooperatives and there were panic withdrawals (Li Yining 2001). When the BOC Kaiping scandal erupted, the alleged theft (US$500 million) was equivalent to around one-half of Kaiping's GDP and one-half of its total savings (Nolan 2004a: 53), and the authorities were forced to send in truckloads of cash to calm down the run on the bank.

Meanwhile, banking crimes are becoming rampant. Reports of the National Audit Office (NAO 2004) in China exposed fraud or misconduct with respect to four state banks. In 2004, CBRC found 2,202 financial institutions breaking regulations, a rise of 690 on the previous year, while 4,294 banking staff were punished, a rise of 1,974 (CBRC 2005b). 'The deep problems in Chinese financial institutions do not simply apply to the lower levels' (Nolan 2004a: 54). A series of high-profile scandals have astounded the nation. Wang Xuebing, former head of BOC, was jailed for 12 years for taking bribes. Besides Wang, Zhu Xiaohua, the former head of China Everbright Bank, Liang Xiaoting, the former deputy general manager of the BOC Hong Kong branch, Duan Xiaoxing, the former head of Huaxia Bank, and Liu Jinbao, the former chief executive of BOC Hong Kong Limited, just to name a few, have been netted for financial crimes (*Caijing* 5 March 2004). Recently, Zhang Enzhao, the CCB chairman, is under investigation after a civil lawsuit in the USA accused him of taking more than US$1 million in bribes (*Caijing* 21 March 2005). Ironically, Zhang was brought in to CCB as a breath of fresh air after his predecessor Wang Xuebing was dismissed (*The Times* 23 March 2005).

Accordingly, rating agencies have brought a stream of bad news too. In 2002, Moody's issued an evaluation of China's banking industry, reporting that banks are problematic in corporate governance, accounting standards, information transparency and operational risks (*Caijing* 30 May 2005). Standard and Poor's announced that none of the Chinese banks received Investment Grade Ratings of BBB (*Caijing* 5 December 2003). More embarrassingly, China's own central bank (PBC) in July 2004 issued 'The Competitiveness Report of Chinese and Foreign Banks in Beijing' after investigating 37 commercial banks in the capital city. The first 11 places were occupied by foreign banks. The China Merchant Bank was the most competitive Chinese bank at the twelfth position in that table. The Big Four banks were ranked the least competitive of the 37 (PBC website).

No doubt, China's banks are in trouble and, especially, the state banks have become one of the major destabilizing factors in China's economy. 'For many observers, the Chinese banking problem is one of the most serious in the world and perhaps the most serious' (Dornbuscha and Giavazzi 1999: 40). 'At some point "fire" will break out' (Nolan 2004a: 59). One senior official at the Bank of International Settlement said: 'This situation can't last for too long if the underlying problem is not dealt with' (*Far Eastern Economic Review* (*FEER*) 14 November 2002). Chinese banking insiders also realize the gravity. Guo Shuqing, the newly appointed chairman of CCB, acknowledged problems in almost every aspect of CCB's business, stating that 'Chinese banks would not find their way out if they do not engage in reforms' (*Caijing* 18 April 2005). Tang Shuangning, deputy head of the CBRC, commented: 'There are still quite a lot of problems to be resolved at Chinese commercial banks' (*The Times* 23 March 2005). Even Chinese Premier Wen Jiabao admitted that problems are numerous (Xinhuanet 14 March 2004).

What has gone wrong with China's state banks? How should these problems be sorted out? Given the intensity and extensiveness of the problems, just repackaging the bad loans, injecting capital, giving more interest rate freedom will not work (Lo 2004). The most important task is to find out and deal with the root problems of China's state banks. However, since banking problems in China are deep-seated and sensitive, involving important aspects of China's economy and politics, and even implicating top political authorities and government leaders, it is impossible to gather up all the necessary information and data, not to mention making them public. Hence, it is not feasible to organize this study solely around the contemporary banking industry. Alternatively, in order to shed light on these critical issues, this research will take a business history approach. Business history is the study of the operation and administration of business in the past. Its purpose is to apply the lessons learnt from the past to the current challenges faced by business (Jones 2002). Accordingly, this research attempts to make a detailed study about similar issues faced by a pre-1949 Chinese bank and then to use the past to mirror the present and guide the future.

In recent years, some research has been carried out on the history of China's banks, in works such as *A History of the Bank of China* (BOC 1995), *History of the Daqing Bank* (Kong 1991), *Historical Materials on Jincheng Bank* (FRO 1983), *Imperial Bank of China* (Chen Xulu *et al.* 2000), and *Farmers Bank of China* (FRI 1990). Nevertheless, many of these works are written in Chinese, and could not provide good secondary sources for western scholars. Furthermore, these literatures employ a traditional narrative approach. More often than not, they are collections of historical materials, rather than analytic works.

On the other hand, western and western-trained Chinese scholars have shown increasing interest in the history of Chinese banking. Some have delivered a survey about the evolution of China's banks, such as Hall (1917), Lee (1926), Tamagna (1942) and Ji (2003). Most significantly, some scholars have focused on defined aspects of banking history. In this regard, Coble's (1980) book, *The Shanghai Capitalists and the Nationalist Government, 1927–1937*, is a classic. Coble analysed the relationship between the Nationalist government and Shanghai's capitalists, especially how the government tried to control the capitalists, in particular, prominent Chinese bankers. But Coble mainly carried out his analyses from a political–economic perspective and also restricted his timeframe from 1927 to 1937. Professor Cheng's recent work, *Banking in Modern China* (2003), persuasively explained how and why major Chinese modern banks were able to grow into viable and self-sustaining institutions before the Japanese invasion in 1937. Nevertheless, this study didn't stress the internal and external challenges facing China's banks in those turbulent and dramatic times; also, with its focus on banking activities during the prewar period, it is difficult for readers to grasp a whole picture.

To fill in the gap, this study intends to use a historical perspective to explore the problems and challenges facing a big Chinese bank before 1949, the year of the Communist takeover. The Bank of China is chosen as the case study. The case study has an important place in social science research, for it offers the opportunity to study specific situations and changes in detail, allows new patterns to be discovered and presents multiple perspectives (Yin 1994). The main reason for choosing BOC is that BOC has the longest and most fascinating history among China's existing banks. Meanwhile, as one of the biggest four state banks in China today, BOC is representative of other state banks. Equally important, BOC itself keeps a good record of historical documents, and the China No. 2 Historical Museum in Nanjing maintains original archives of pre-1949 BOC. All these provide convenient facilities for the proposed research. For the purpose of this study, BOC's development phases and major characteristics are summarized as follows.

I BOC in the Qing Dynasty, 1905–11

After the Opium War (1840–2), China's door was forced open. Foreign banks began to establish a presence in China. In 1905, in order to solve the financial problems of the Qing Court and also to break the monopoly of foreign banks, the Qing government established the Bank of Revenue Board. In 1908, its name was changed to Daqing Bank, which was the predecessor of the Bank of China. Daqing Bank was a 50–50 joint state–private bank, and exercised both as a central bank and a commercial bank. By 1911, before the Qing Dynasty collapsed, Daqing Bank had established 35 branches in provincial capitals and treaty ports, and was the largest domestic bank at that time.

II BOC under the government of the Northern Warlords, 1912–28

In 1912, the Qing Dynasty was overthrown. China found itself under the rule of the Northern Warlords whose main characteristics were those of militarism and regionalism. Daqing Bank was reorganized as the central bank, and renamed as the Bank of China (BOC). BOC was authorized to handle treasury, underwrite public bonds and take charge of foreign borrowing and debt servicing. During this period, BOC gradually got rid of government control and became a de facto private bank. Its business grew by leaps and bounds.

III BOC under the Nationalist government, 1928–49

In 1928, after the Nationalist government was established by Chiang Kaishek in Nanjing, BOC was reorganized as a Government-Chartered International Exchange Bank. BOC specialized in foreign trade-related business, and also handled public bonds and issued banknotes on behalf of the government. During the early period of the Nationalist Kuo Min Tang (KMT) government, BOC modernized its corporate governance and undertook a series of reforms and innovations. As a result, BOC laid its foundation as an international commercial bank, and became a serious contender to foreign counterparts. After 1935, the government increased its monopoly of the banking system and took complete control of BOC. BOC became an instrument for the government to finance budget deficit, support money-losing state enterprises and amass personal fortunes. With the collapse of the KMT government, BOC was taken over by the Communists.

This book consists of seven chapters. Chapter 1 has presented a brief introduction to the background, objectives and significance of the proposed research. Chapter 2 identifies the challenges facing China's state banks today – corporate governance, government intervention, foreign competition and white-collar crimes. These issues not only threaten the health of the banking system, but also endanger the stability of the whole society, polity and economy. Chapter 3 to Chapter 6 employ a historical approach, with each of them analysing a key issue in BOC's early development: corporate governance, government intervention, foreign competition and white-collar crimes respectively. These topics are explored systematically and in-depth, and are related to wider academic debates. Among them, Chapter 3 focuses on the evolution of corporate governance of BOC and its arrangement and characteristics during different historical phases. Chapter 4 stresses the ways and extent of intervention in BOC by respective governments and how they affected BOC's business activities and performance. Chapter 5 concentrates on the competition between BOC and foreign banks in China, and addresses factors leading to BOC's rapid growth and successful catch-up. Chapter 6 compares and contrasts the forms and severity of white-collar crimes of BOC during different historical phases and examines the causations and impacts. The final chapter (Chapter 7) summarizes the major findings of this study and presents policy implications for today.

This study contributes to fulfilling the critical gap in the existing literature on the key challenges faced by a big Chinese bank and enhancing the understanding of China's banking industry prior to 1949. More importantly, the past can be used to serve the present and future. Through reconstructing historical reality, by offering a detailed and close-up picture of BOC, the research will help policy-makers and bank managers learn from the past, and objectively assess and formulate future policies. What's more, the study can serve other Chinese industries as well, which may share the same political and macroeconomic environment as banks. Finally, other developing countries, through comparison, may draw experience and lessons from China's story.

2 The challenges facing China's state banks today

Introduction

China's banking reform started in the 1980s. So far, despite many efforts at different levels and various reform packages, China's banking system is problematic. In particular, the state-owned banks are facing daunting challenges both internally and externally, including corporate governance, government intervention, foreign competition and white-collar crimes. Although these issues are interrelated, it is worth examining them one by one.

Corporate governance

According to OECD (2001), corporate governance is 'the system by which business corporations are directed and controlled'. It involves 'the set of relationships between a company's management, its board, its shareholders, and other stakeholders. Corporate governance also provides the structure through which the objectives of the company are set, and the means of attaining those objectives and monitoring performance are determined' (OECD 2004: 11). In essence, corporate governance deals with how effectively owners of companies supervise management to protect shareholders' interests and assure returns of investment (Kagawa 1999). Corporate governance is a crucial part of the modern enterprise system.

The importance of establishing an effective corporate governance structure was first recognized in 1995, when China initiated the 'modern enterprise system', which aimed at transforming the industrial state-owned enterprises (SOEs) into modern corporations. In recent years, the corporate governance issue has commanded great attention in the banking sector. The banking industry watchdog CBRC categorically pointed out that 'Improving corporate governance is the core of reforming state commercial banks' (CBRC 2005a).

Corporate governance in China's state banks

Unspecified property rights

The four state banks were born under a government-led banking system. They were wholly owned by the state. Theoretically, it was the Chinese people, from the standpoint of public ownership, who owned the property rights of the state banks. Since it was impossible for the Chinese people to exercise their rights in state banks' assets and monitor their management, the government, on behalf of the people, became the owner of the state banks (Kagawa 1999). But the government did not clarify which government department or agency should take full responsibility for bank performance. With the unclear assignment of property rights, there was an asymmetry in the allocation of rights and obligations (Broadman 2001). Multiple government departments and agencies exercised the roles of owner (Xu Meizheng 1998). 'Across agencies both horizontally and vertically there is fragmentation and partial exercise of the ownership function, with no single entity responsible for the enterprise's bottom line' (Broadman 2001). In China, the lack of clear identification of the owner(s) of state banks confused ownership and operational rights, and left open the issue of who should be monitoring the managers: state banks had multiple principals who may have neither the authority, nor capacity, nor motivation to monitor state banks (World Bank 1995). What's more, without an identified owner, it was also impossible to set up shareholders' meetings and a board of directors, which are indispensable to the modern corporate structure.

Multiple objectives

For a long time, state bank managers have remained an integral part of the governmental bureaucracy. Presidents of state banks are appointed by the government. As a matter of fact, the four presidents are government officials with the ranks of vice-ministers. Likewise, branch managers correspond with official ranks, such as director-generals or section chiefs. According to some rough statistics, by April 2004, BOC Head Office had about 100 'director-generals', more than 500 'deputy director-generals' and more than 1,000 'section chiefs' (*China Economic Weekly* 27 April 2004). If we add in the other three state banks, the number will be astonishingly high. Even the Central Bank Governor Zhou Xiaochuan commented that state banks are more like government agencies rather than commercial enterprises (*World Economic Report* 21 April 2004). As a government organization, its chief priority is to carry out government orders and directives. State banks are assigned multiple and often conflicting goals (e.g. ensure employment, bridge the regional gap, save the SOEs and maximize profits). Multiple objectives increase transaction costs, distort incentives facing bank managers, impair state banks' pursuit of profits and have an adverse impact on their balance sheets (World Bank

1995). Even worse, since state banks are expected to pursue commercial and non-commercial objectives, measuring state banks' performance is especially difficult (Ross 1973).

Party control

When new China was founded, China adopted Soviet-style central control, and there was no clear boundary between the CPC (Communist Party of China) and the government, nor between the government and business enterprises (Wu Jinglian 2000). The PRC administration is characterized by a dual hierarchy, 'with the administrative hierarchy paralleled by, and interwoven with, the party hierarchy' (Ma S.K. 1990: 1050). This kind of dual hierarchy has enormously strengthened the ruling party's control over the state bureaucracy. With 69 million members, the CPC is the world's largest political organization (*The Times* 2 July 2005). The party plays a vital and important role in state governance. 'It provides directions to state policies, supervises state operations, and more often than not, intervenes directly in everyday matters' (Kwong 1997: 8). At every level of the four state banks, the president is subject to the leadership of the secretary of the party committee. In most cases, the posts of bank president and party secretary are held by the same person. In this case, 'yiyuanhua lingdao (unified leadership)' is in its purest form (ibid.: 52). In China, not all bank staff are Communist Party members, but holders of important positions are required to be party members and are politically appointed. The characteristic problems with state banks are extensive party interventions in internal affairs, such as personnel appointment, wage setting, or deployment of demobilized soldiers. To ensure greater control, the CPC has inserted its cell – the party committee – into the only privately owned national bank in China, Minsheng Bank (*Asian Wall Street Journal* 29 July 1999). Besides, the Party often organizes many kinds of ideological education and campaigns. The president of the Bank of Communications spent his summer participating in more than 100 meetings as part of that Maoist-style campaign (*FEER* 19 August 1999). People wondered how he could have found the time to concentrate on banking business.

Principal–agent problem

The principal–agent problem arises due to the separation of ownership and management (Berle and Means 1932; Jensen and Meckling 1976). Without an effective restricting mechanism, managers tend to pursue private benefits at the expense of the firm (Shleifer and Vishny 1994). Managerial misbehaviour ranges from shirking duties and the misuse of company funds to flat-out expropriation (Zhu 2000). State banks in China have not established a governance structure which permits the manager (agent) the necessary degree of autonomy without endangering the interests of the owner (principal) (Kagawa 1999).

For example, in the 1990s reforms were undertaken at state banks and they were delegated more autonomy in operations (Xu Meizheng 1998). State banks expanded their business scope, carried out non-banking financial business, set up extensive networks, etc.; in particular, they were allowed to retain a portion of profits, which greatly motivated their enthusiasm. But more autonomous power without proper checks and balances is problematic and can lead to operational risks and opportunistic behaviour (Broadman 2001). In the second half of 1996, state banks and other financial institutions started pumping huge amounts of funding into the domestic securities market and even into the Hong Kong stock market (Lu 2000). The situation became so serious that, in early June 1997, the PBC ordered all state banks to close their securities trading accounts within ten days and stop lending to securities brokerages (ibid.). In other cases, bank managers made loans to get kickbacks, awarded contracts to relatives and friends and even embezzled and stole bank money (see later in this chapter).

The appearance of the agency problem is more dangerous in banks than in other manufacturing enterprises because of the nature of banking business.[1] First of all, one unique point which differentiates banks from other manufacturing enterprises is that banks accumulate huge sums of money, often from several generations of dispersed depositors over many decades; second, the business scale of banks is generally much larger than manufacturing firms – for example, at the end of 2003, the Chinese white goods giant Haier Group had about RMB7.3 billion of total assets (Haier website), whereas the figure was RMB5.3 trillion for ICBC (ICBC website). Moreover, unlike manufacturing firms which produce tangible products, banks need not actually produce physical goods in exchange for the cash flow for their customers. It is easier for agents/bank managers to divert bank funds without being detected. At the same time, 'globalisation, liberalisation and technological innovations have exposed all the banks to huge risks' (Liu Mingkang 2004a). Thus, the consequences of the agency problem in the banking sector could trigger a chain of events that might damage a country's economy or even an entire region. 'A crisis in the financial system would fan the flames amidst the "combustible material" in all other sectors of society, into which the long tentacles of the financial system extend' (Nolan 2004a: 177). No wonder one critical element of corporate governance is to establish an oversight mechanism and to control risk to ensure the safe operation of banks.

Recent reforms

The third plenary session of the sixteenth CPC Central Committee put forward the proposal to reform four state banks into joint-stock commercial banks (CPC 2003). In 2003, BOC and CCB were chosen to carry out the pilot programme. In order to clarify the owner of state banks, a new company, the Central Huijin Investment Company Ltd., was established. Central Huijin holds the state-owned equity interests in the key financial enterprises such as BOC and CCB on behalf of the Chinese government, to exercise its right and perform its responsibilities as the major shareholder. In March 2004, the CBRC issued 'Guidelines on Corporate Governance Reforms and Supervision of BOC and CCB' (CBRC 2004). The pilot banks are especially required to have in place a standard corporate governance structure comprising the general shareholders' meeting, a board of directors, a board of supervisors and an executive management, as well as other specific requirements and targets. By the end of 2004, both BOC and CCB had been restructured into joint-stock commercial banks and introduced overseas strategic investors. In October 2005, CCB took the lead in floating its shares on the Hong Kong stock market, and in the first half of 2006 BOC made its initial public offering (IPO) in Hong Kong and Shanghai.

Existing problems

Despite all the above efforts and seemingly successful incorporation and listing, problems still exist in the state banks' corporate governance.

First, the Central Huijin Company was established to represent the owners of the state banks, which seems a big step towards clarifying the property rights of the state banks. However, Li Shuguang, Professor of Politics and Law at China University, argued that Central Huijin was established overnight without careful discussion and deliberation, and has not received the legal authorization from the National People's Congress to manage the state assets (*Caijing* 27 July 2005). Furthermore, the status and essence of the Central Huijin Company is confusing. If it is a commercial enterprise, why are the top executives' roles assumed by government officials? If it is a government organization, why is it registered as an investment company (*China Economic Times* 20 October 2004)? Although Central Huijin holds the majority or whole shares of state banks, the right to appoint staff in state banks does not belong to Central Huijin (*Caijing* 4 October 2004); instead, the right still goes to the Central Organization Department of the Communist Party of China. This ambiguous status and insufficient power make it difficult for Central Huijin to fully realize its function, i.e. to effectively manage state assets.

Second, 'The two pilot banks shall have in place clear-cut development strategies with an aim at maximum profitability' (CBRC 2004). However, as mentioned above, the president and other top executives are appointed not by the board but by the Central Organizational Department of CPC. The bank president still maintains his deputy-minister official rank. Like before, the bank president may not concentrate on maximum profit, but will be interested in satisfying the government leaders who would determine his career success or failure. Xie Ping, the general manager of Central Huijin, admitted that under the incentives of official titles, it is highly possible that the bank president, especially the general manager of a provincial branch will use loans in exchange for a higher official rank regardless of the big risks (*Sanlian Shenghuo Weekly* 25 August 2005). In other words, the objectives of the state banks are 'more compatible with making policies rather than profits' (Chen Baizhu 2000: 5).

Third, 'The two pilot banks shall adopt market-oriented mechanisms for human resources management ...' (CBRC 2004). Since the later half of 2004, BOC and CCB have tried to establish a market-based recruitment system and a performance-based incentive mechanism. However, as long as party organs have a larger say in the selection of personnel, a modern and efficient human resource management is far from complete. In one of the reforming banks, it clearly stipulates that the first qualification for holding the position of a senior executive must be to 'comply with the basic principles of choosing cadres by the Central Committee of the Communist Party of China' (*Caijing* 7 February 2005). Bank employees are selected more for loyalty and for links to the government or the party than for professional skills (Xinhuanet 10 December 2004). In the Head Office of BOC, before the corporate restructuring, the party committee nominated and approved department chiefs; nowadays, the party committee nominates and the board approves.[2] There is no fundamental change. The principle of 'party manages cadres' is still being adopted (*Caijing* 1 November 2004)

Fourth, sound corporate governance requires the setting and enforcing of clear lines of responsibility and accountability throughout the organization (Basel Committee 1999). In BOC and CCB, three old committees (party committee, trade union and the congress of workers' representatives) co-exist with the new ones (the shareholders' meeting, the board of directors and the supervisory board). The lack of any clear definition of the responsibilities of these entities and the relationships among them cause internal conflicts and inefficiency in decision-making (Ma Jun 1998: 15). When Guo Shuqing was made the chairman of CCB after the former chairman was put under investigation, Guo was surprised to discover that the directors of the bank rarely met and the board played little role in overseeing the business. But the bank's Communist Party committee, headed by the former chairman, convened regularly, and even decided upon the granting of small loans (*FT* 20 June 2005).

Summarizing the above, the current corporate restructuring in state banks seems an unprecedented progress; however, it has not changed the fundamental and deep-seated problems. The unclarified status of the bank owner, multiple objectives, party control, unclear rights and obligations and agency problem are still in existence. Establishing efficient and effective corporate governance in state banks is far from complete.

Government intervention

After new China was founded in 1949, China had a simple mono-bank system which was typical of a centrally planned economy (Lardy 1998b). China had three banks – PBC, BOC, CCB and a network of rural credit cooperatives. PBC operated simultaneously as both the central bank and the sole commercial bank. The CCB was in fact the cashier of the Capital Construction Finance Department of the Ministry of Finance, and the BOC was the international business department of the PBC (ibid.: 61). Under a central planning system, 'the monetary system is to make sure that a pre-set plan for the output of the economy is fulfilled' (Howe 1978: 58). Credit was allocated administratively and the interest rate was treated neither as an allocative device nor as an incentive to savings.

Banking reform in China began in the early 1980s. During the next 20 years or so, the PBC was established only to exercise the central bank function; four state banks were formally set up: at first they were specialized banks, but later they were allowed to run a comprehensive business. With the transition toward a market economy, the importance of the credit plan gradually diminished until it was officially discontinued in 1998; three policy banks were established in order to take over the policy lending of the Big Four.

In particular, China's Commercial Bank Law, issued in 1995, set out the principles of profitability, security and liquidity for commercial banks, and required state banks to be responsible for their own operations and be freed from external interference. 'No government agencies or individuals should be allowed to interfere with banks' business.' Banking institutions are supposed to operate autonomously and commercially, subject only to general banking regulations and directives. However, it hasn't worked out that way. The interference from the government, both central and local, is still very strong. It is extremely difficult for state banks to maintain operational independence. The Chinese economy has commercialized, but financial intermediation has not (Steinfeld 2001). In other words, the system of government influence, although under attack, remains deeply embedded in China's political economy (Rawski 2002).

Intervention from the central government

First, during the reform period, the central government's fiscal capacity declined relatively. The share of budget revenue in GDP fell from 31.2 per cent in 1978 to 22.4 per cent in 1985 and 14 per cent in 2000 (Bottelier 2001). Due to the weak condition of the central government budget, the government frequently sought resources from the state banks to finance the projects and activities that otherwise would be covered by the state budget. This is often described in China as the implicit transfer of budget deficits (Huang Yiping 1998). The main categories of policy lending include: (1) loans for investment in fixed assets of basic industry and infrastructure; (2) loans for working capital for purchase of agricultural products and import/export activities; (3) loans for agricultural production, poverty alleviation, regional development and R&D activities (ibid.). Even after the creation of three policy banks in 1994, the state banks have continued to be burdened with policy loans. According to statistics, throughout the 1990s policy loans have accounted for about 35 per cent of the total loans made by state banks (Table 2.1).

Table 2.1 Policy loans in China's four state banks in selected years, 1990s (RMB billion)

Policy loans	1991	1992	1993	1994	1995	1996
Investments in fixed assets	191	196	274	390	538	663
Purchase of agricultural products	187	186	227	314	359	370
Purchase of products for exports	179	214	259	289	327	374
Agricultural loans	121	145	172	155	192	237
Policy loans total	678	741	932	1,148	1,416	1,644
Total loans by state banks	1,804	2,161	2,646	3,244	3,939	4,743
Proportion of policy loans (%)	37.6	34.3	35.2	35.4	35.9	34.7

Source: Huang Yiping 1998: 6; Lardy 1998b: 78.

Some policy loans, such as those for capital investment in agriculture and infrastructure development and those for circular fund needs in grain procurement, must be provided at preferential interest rates even lower than the standard deposit rates (Lu 2000: 207). The PBC only subsidizes a portion of the losses which arise from these services. The remaining losses must be absorbed by the local banks themselves (Lu 2000).

Second, Lardy (1998b) argues that at an even more general level, since interest on loans in the reform period has been held at below-market clearing levels, virtually all lending by banks is policy lending. Artificially low lending rates have stimulated excess demand for loans, particularly during inflation, when lending rates were adjusted upward only modestly, leading to sharply negative interest rates in real terms. For example, at the peaks of inflation in 1989 and 1993, inflation rates were 19 per cent and 24 per cent respectively, but the administrated highest loan rates for enterprises were only 11.34 per cent and 10.98 per cent (Lardy 1998b: 90). According to Shaw (1973), governments distort interest rates as taxes or subsidies. In China's case, bank credits were de facto subsidies in disguise to the borrowing firms (Lu 2000). On the other hand, these administrated interest rates have weakened the incentives of banks, and worsened their balance sheets. In both 1994 and 1995, state banks suffered losses of tens of billions of RMB due to slewed interest rates (Li Keping 1998).

Third, the Big Four are not only treated by the government as a 'secondary budget', a convenient source of funding for all sorts of social purposes, state banks are especially required to allocate capital to state-owned enterprises (SOEs), and other enterprises favoured by political leaders. To the State Council, the Central Bank, the Ministry of Finance (MOF), the State Planning Commission and the State Economic and Trade Commission, the Big Four is the last remaining powerful instrument through which they can directly influence resource allocation, thus they are reluctant to give up this power. More often than not, unwilling to bear the high level of unemployment and bankruptcy, the government forces state banks to lend to SOEs which are operating at a loss and cannot service their debt obligations. Foreign observers commented: '[I]t is through control of the financial system that Chinese leaders continue to bend the economy to their will' (Panitchpakdi and Clifford 2002: 167). From the mid- to late 1990s, SOEs were accounting for less than half of net asset growth in China's industry, yet they were consistently consuming 70–80 per cent of credits extended by state banks (Steinfeld 2001: 4). Even in 2003, the loans to SOEs from state banks still accounted for about 50 per cent of total state bank loans (*World Economic Report* 21 April 2004). A western banker who reportedly has worked closely with many Chinese banks stated, 'There's a lot of lip service to commercial concerns, but in the end they're not being paid to act commercially. When you ask why they made a loan they'll often say: "We know it's wrong, but we were told to do this" ' (Xinhuanet 10 December 2004).

Fourth, although state banks have built up huge NPLs, the loss reserves set aside by the four banks are not linked directly to the quality of loan portfolio, but rather are set at an arbitrarily low percentage. Adequate provisioning would directly reduce, if not entirely eliminate, the income taxes paid by banks to the MOF (Lardy 1998b). Thus the MOF limits banks' loss reserves. In retrospect, CCB had written off only RMB1 billion in bad debts in 1992. BOC reported write-offs of RMB3.6 billion, RMB1.7 billion and RMB1.6 billion in 1993, 1994 and 1995 respectively (Lardy 1998b: 118). That was an average of only 0.16 per cent of assets annually. In 1997, MOF allowed state banks to increase their reserves to 1 per cent of their loans outstanding. These extremely minuscule write-offs suggested that state banks had to continue to list some bad loans as assets on their balance sheets. In May 2002, banks could set aside loss reserves based on the operation status and loan risks. But writing off bad debts must still be submitted to MOF for approval. On the other hand, the government depends heavily on state banks for taxes. In the mid-1990s, about one sixth of central government revenues were derived from the taxes paid by the four banks (ibid.: 170). Even though state banks suffered losses in 1995, the banks still handed in taxes as planned (Li Keping 1998).

Intervention from local governments

State banks not only lack independence from central government, but are also subject to direct and indirect interference from local governments, including provincial, municipal and county governments. To provincial leaders, the province is often their centre of concern. At the county level, county interest is paramount. 'Although central authorities use the words "independent kingdom" (*duli wangguo*) as a term of reproach, it is the sacred objective of every unit and territorial jurisdiction to achieve precisely this freedom of action' (Lampton 1987: 15).

Local officials can exert tremendous power, both formal and informal, over the local branches of the four state banks – sometimes, more power than that exerted by the banks' headquarters in Beijing. Although local branch managers may have been, in theory, subordinate to their respective bank's headquarters, appointments and other personnel matters generally operate through the local party organization (Steinfeld 2001). In addition, 'some older general managers [in the provinces] will have closer ties to the government if they want to be elected to the [local] People's Congress' (*FT* 20 June 2005). For local bankers, the thinking runs along the following lines: if you defied a local official, you wouldn't be able to get your job done and you wouldn't be able to get another job once you failed. If you defied the headquarters and lost your banking job, your local contacts would find something else for you to do and generally take care of you (Steinfeld 2001). No wonder that state banks are 'dancing to the local tune' (Lu 2000: 205); furthermore, they even collude with local governments to abuse bank money.

Real estate is a typical example. In every part of China, local government leaders are zealous to build massive government office blocks, hotels, shopping malls, international conference halls, stadiums, etc. In 2003, local governments planned 122 exhibition halls, 45 of which aimed to be 'either the biggest in Asia or in the world' (*The Banker* 2 July 2004). One motive is to achieve something good to write on their curriculum vitae. In some cases, local officials contract these projects out to their relatives and friends, and grant land rights for these projects. Naturally, these multi-billion yuan projects are financed by medium- to long-term bank loans. Through opaque processes, money is diverted to pockets of local officials, property developers, project managers and bank managers. As a matter of fact, on the list of China's richest 100 released by *Forbes Magazine*, almost half are connected to real estate in one form or another (*AsiaTimes* 18 December 2003). For instance, Zhou Zhengyi, the Shanghai real estate tycoon, who once ranked No. 11 on the Forbes 100 Richest People in China list, colluded with Shanghai officials to obtain a 43,000-square-metre piece of prime land for free (*Caijing* 19 September 2005) and get at least RMB10 billion to RMB12 billion of bank money for his building projects, including from BOC and CCB (*Caijing* 20 June 2003). Zhou was later arrested for illicit property trading, granting illegitimate loans, and defaulting on statutory compensation for relocatees whose abodes were improperly demolished for redevelopment projects (*AsiaTimes* 18 December 2003). Although Zhou was sentenced to three years imprisonment in 2004, the repercussion of the Zhou Zhengyi case is far from over, since it involves quite a number of government officials and bank managers. Steinfeld (2001) also pointed out, in the industrial city of Chongqing, due to local political pressure, even the most progressive joint-stock banks still have to devote approximately 30 per cent of their loan portfolio to governmentally-funded infrastructure projects. 'In fact, realty and banking, which are closely linked, are the most corrupt industries in China' (*AsiaTimes* 18 December 2003). Property dealing orchestrated by local governments has escalated the banks' financial risk and weakened the debt-ridden banking system.

Besides supporting construction projects, local officials often instruct local banks to support their local firms or industries, mostly for the employment consideration. One example may vividly illustrate local officials' efforts to support small and grossly inefficient local producers (Lardy 2002: 107–8). In the mid- to late 1980s, more than 120 vehicle manufacturers were operating in China. Among them, the 13 largest manufacturers accounted for 92 per cent of the 1.6 million vehicles of all types produced, implying an average production of about 113,000 units. But the average production of the remaining companies was a mere 1,000 vehicles which was too small to gain any economies of scale and so they lost money. Since 1994, the central government has tried to consolidate the automobile industry. But dozens of local governments have fiercely resisted, each determined to maintain the pillar industry in the local area, and each has directed the local state banks to support them. Meanwhile, local governments imposed restrictions on the sale and licensing of producers from other areas. As a result, in 2003, China still had 123 auto firms in 23 provinces, autonomous regions and municipalities. Among them, about 60 per cent produced less than 1,000 vehicles a year (*PD* 18 Aug 2003). If loans from state banks had been based on commercial criteria instead of government instructions, small and inefficient vehicle producers could never have been established, let alone survived.

Irrational regulations and rules

There is a paradox: on the one hand, central and local governments are active in intervening in banks; on the other hand, they provide little of the regulatory infrastructure needed to support the commercialization of banks.

China's Bankruptcy Law, issued in 1986, discriminates against creditors. The most disputed point is that all properties will be first used to settle debts owed to the employees, instead of repaying external debts. Also, the collaterals are similarly used for the employees rather than being handed over to the creditor, which is in open conflict with 'Guarantee Law' (*Caijing* 5 June 2004). What's more, since the government appoints judges and allocates budgets for courts, Chinese courts are hardly independent of the government. They often rule in favour of labour groups over the owners of capital (Lo 2000). A saying is often used by banks trying to recover loans in this system: 'you sue, but the court won't accept your case; the court accepts your case, but won't begin the trial; the court begins the trial, but won't issue a judgment; the court issues a judgment, but then doesn't enforce it' (Zhou Xiaochuan 1999: 3). As a result, in many SOE bankruptcies, the rights of creditors are completely cancelled to allow for settlements to employees; other lucky creditors may recover their debt at a very low rate, around 10 to 15 per cent (Li Shuguang 2001; Clarke 1997). To make things worse, quite a number of enterprises abused the law to dodge their liabilities by dividing their businesses or changing licenses. Such practices are often supported by local protectionism. For instance, in the county of Chang Ling in the Jilin Province, the local government in 1998 arranged 200 government cadres to help 80 enterprises going through sudden and large-scale bankruptcy proceedings, to evade debts of RMB230 million, which accounted for 52 per cent of all ICBC Chang Ling branch loans (PBC 2001: 10).

China has long been in need of a modern bankruptcy law to deal with bankrupt companies and keep up with the pace of China's economic progress (PWC 2004). Since 1994 a new bankruptcy law has been under review and debate. A revised law, which would strengthen the position of creditors, was blocked by the National People's Congress, reportedly by provincial delegates who feared it would be unfavourable to their local business (Lardy 1998b). The latest draft is still waiting for the approval of the National People's Congress. However, Wang Xinxin, a legal expert, indicated that bankruptcy law was a highly technical law. The more detailed the better. Western bankruptcy laws usually cover 300 to 400 articles. But China's new bankruptcy draft only contains 160 rough articles (*Caijing* 5 June 2004). This situation may lead to confusing explanations and difficult enforcement. Professor Wang Weiguo commented that the long-awaited new law still left key issues of SOE's bankruptcy unresolved (*Caijing* 5 June 2004). For example, regarding the SOE employee allocation and other issues, no clear-cut article is formulated, only an appendix – 'subject to the State Council stipulations'. Legal mechanisms to guarantee creditors' rights are weak at best (Li Shuguang 2001).

Of course, this is not to say that all money-losing firms should go bankrupt and workers should be laid-off unsupported. The financial hardship of SOEs is a complicated issue and goes beyond the scope of this study. However, state banks are not gift-givers but should be autonomous commercial enterprises. An improved bankruptcy law should be adopted; meanwhile, a security network will be established by the government to cover laid-off workers.

Non-performing loans

One of the consequences of government intervention in state banks is the storing up of enormous NPLs, though the banks' own improper management was also responsible for this. Even in 1998, immediately after the Asian Financial Crisis, China's share of NPLs was much higher than those in Hong Kong and Singapore, and more or less the same as those in the crisis-hit countries of Thailand and South Korea (Table 2.2).

High NPLs directly endangered the security of China's banking system. In recent years, a series of strict measures have been adopted to deal with NPLs, such as massive government bailouts and stringent control targets for individual banks. Nevertheless, the NPL ratio in China's state banks is still disappointingly high. For the Agricultural Bank of China, the recent ratio is 25 per cent (*Caijing* 17 October 2005); for some branches of state banks in Northeast China, the ratio even reaches 36 per cent (*China Business Post* 12 March 2005). The general NPL ratio of the four state banks in 2005 is still above 10 per cent (CBRC website). Even this number is an understatement. In

Table 2.2 Ratio of NPLs in seven Asian countries and regions, 1998 (%)

Countries or regions	Ratio	All-time high ratio	All-time high NPLs to GDP
Singapore	2.0	>8	9
Hong Kong	2.1	>8	13
Malaysia	5.6	>20	28
China	20.0	>25	24
Indonesia	9.2	>40	25
South Korea	14.0	>25	34
Thailand	18.0	>25	40

Source: Hu Zuliu 1998: 4.

most instances, in order to show good performance, some banks intentionally grant new loans to insolvent debtors and get interest back, so that NPLs do not appear on balance sheets. For example, from the 2004 annual report of ABC, middle- and long-term loans doubled, and short-term loans reduced by RMB400 billion (*Caijing* 17 October 2005). The director of the statistics department of the CBRC spoke out frankly, 'The commercial banks use the loan reorganization, roll over old loans to delay the appearance of bad loans and reach the target of reduced NPLs for the current period . . .' (ibid.). Wu Jinglian (2004), a well-known Chinese economist, points out that, banks have greatly increased their total amount of loans, which increases the denominator of NPLs, so that the NPLs' ratio has declined without truly improving asset quality. He continues to caution that even for the newly issued loans, with the background of over-heated investment since 2003, it is hard to say how many of them will become NPLs in the future.

The massive build-up of NPLs in state banks is impairing the actual capital strength of banks, posing a threat not only to the banking system, but also to the stability of the national economy (*Xinhua* 19 May 2004). The *Wall Street Journal* (*WSJ*) (22 October 2004) warned that if NPLs were handled inappropriately, China might trigger the world's largest banking crisis. It is estimated that 80 pecent of the NPLs of state banks are due to direct or indirect intervention of the government (Chen Jianjun 2005: 39). As long as banks are still burdened with non-commercial tasks, as long as central and local governments continue intervening in lending practice, state banks will never become true commercial enterprises and the NPLs issue will in no way be solved.

Foreign competition

In the era of globalization, China can no longer be isolated from the outside world. Besides domestic problems, state banks are facing external challenges – increasing foreign competition.

WTO agreement

Since the late 1970s, China has begun to gradually open up its banking sector. Attracted by the fast growing economy, a huge potential market and a 40 per cent household savings rate, more and more foreign banks are tapping business in China. So far, almost all global big names have established a presence in the Middle Kingdom, like Citibank, HSBC, Deutsche Bank, Bank of America, Credit Suisse and Standard Chartered Bank. As of the end of October 2005, China's banking system consisted of 238 operational entities of foreign banks (138 can do RMB business) (CBRC 2005c). The total assets of foreign banks in China amounted to US$84.5 billion compared with US$53.6 billion in 2004 and US$29 billion in 1996. Foreign banks can offer around 100 types of products and services under 12 broad categories of business activity (ibid.).

In 2001, the China–US World Trade Organization (WTO) Agreement was a milestone in China's history. According to the commitment of WTO, all geographic and customer restrictions regarding foreign banks were to be removed within five years. To this end, China agreed to allow foreign banks to undertake local currency business with Chinese enterprises within two years of accession, and to allow local currency business with individuals from five years after accession. By the end of 2006, China's banking sector had been completely opened, and foreign banks are enjoying full national treatment (*Caijing* 29 November 2004).

American Trade Representative Charlene Barshefsky commented that the changes to be unleashed by China's WTO accession would be 'profoundly important' (Barshefsky 1999). In other words, accession will shake China to its foundations. The director-general of WTO remarked: 'Chinese banks will, for the first time, face real competition' (Panitchpakdi and Clifford 2002: 168). Again, renowned Chinese economist Li Yining alerted us that, 'This time the wolves really are coming' (*FT* 2 November 2002).

The ancient Chinese strategist Sun Tzu once stated that 'If ignorant both of your enemy and yourself, you are certain to be in peril'. How powerful and aggressive are these wolves? What is the balance of power between China's state banks and foreign counterparts? Before we go deep into the competition picture, it is extremely important to understand the changes of the global banking industry over the last two decades.

Globalization and financial business revolution

The period since the 1980s has seen a revolution in global business systems (Nolan 2001). The globalization has created a huge demand for world-wide financial services, and great opportunities for financial institutions to expand globally. Simultaneously, deregulation, particularly the abolishment of the Glass–Steagall Act in the US made it possible for aggressive financial institutions to take cross-sector transactions. Leading financial services firms, all from high-income economies, have been through a period of unprecedented merger and acquisition (M&A) (Nolan 2004a). 'A major motive is to provide a global service to customers who themselves increasingly operate on a global basis, as well as acquiring new customers in other countries through international M&A' (Wu Qing 2001: 816). A further driving force is to diversify the risk internationally. The rapid development of information technology (IT) has significantly increased the possibility of operating a bank on a global scale (ibid.).

Against this background, the mantra has become 'bigger is better' (Haddock 2000). From 1989 to 1999, it was estimated that there were 3,844 M&As in the global banking industry, with the acquiring institutions purchasing more than US$3 trillion in assets (Wu Qing 2001: 815). This latest merger wave has been characterized by it occurring amongst 'very large corporations' (Singh 1992: 4). In the late 1990s, the tie-up between Citicorp and Travelers has enabled the new Citigroup to move into new areas with new customers (Gao 2001). In 2000, a Wall Street powerhouse, JPMorgan Chase, was created by blending Chase's balance sheet muscle and JPMorgan's investment banking talent (*The Banker* 3 February 2004). After 2000, there were increasing mega-mergers. The year 2004 witnessed two giant steps in banking consolidation with the mergers of JPMorgan with Bank One, and Bank of America with Fleet Boston (*The Banker* 3 February 2004). In Europe, France's Crédit Agricole Group took over Crédit Lyonnais, and the Royal Bank of Scotland acquired Charter One of the US (*The Banker* 2004). At the beginning of 2006, the finalized merger between Japan's Mitsubishi Tokyo Financial Group and UFJ Holdings has upgraded it to the biggest bank in the world, boasting total assets of US$1,400 billion (*Caijing* 23 January 2006). Most significantly, Banco Santander Central Hispano (BSCH), Spain's largest banking group, took over Britain's Abbey National bank (BBC 26 July 2004), and UniCredit's (Italy) recently acquired Germany's Hypovereinsbank (*The Banker* 2005). These takeovers might trigger the start of the long-awaited surge in European cross-border mergers.

This trend for consolidation can be seen in the larger size of the banks in the top 1,000 (*The Banker* 2004). In 2003, aggregate total assets rose significantly, by 19.3 per cent to US$52,391 billion from the previous year, indicating the growth in banking assets in this new expansionary phase (ibid.). The top 25 giants are taking an increasingly large slice of the overall banking pie and they continue to expand and account for 37.06 per cent of the aggregate total assets of the top 1,000, a significant increase on the 31.08 per cent in the 1995 listing. Among them, six banks (Mizuho Financial Group, Citigroup, UBS, Crédit Agricole, HSBC and Deutsche) reported respective assets in excess of US$1,000 billion (*The Banker* 2004). Boston Consulting Group proclaimed a new era: the age of the banking titans.

We expect the banking titans, by their presence alone, to exert influence on the strategy of other global players. Focusing on operations that are subscale compared with the titans and following slow organic growth strategies are unlikely to guarantee independence anymore. A new challenge for top management is to survive successfully in the age of banking titans.

(Quoted in *The Banker* 2004)

In the latest top 1,000 listing, the top 25 banks provide 35.0 per cent of aggregate Tier 1 capital, 38.6 per cent of aggregate total assets and 39.3 per cent of aggregate profits (*The Banker* 2005). These banking titans are not only big, they are extremely powerful. They enjoy benefits of economies of scale and scope, global reputation, low cost, sophisticated IT systems, international branding, high quality human resources and a high level of technical expertise. They are 'clearly creating a separate strata of their own and look set to take over growing segments of the global banking market' (ibid.).

Indeed, foreign giants are taking every opportunity to penetrate into the developing countries. They not only establish their own branches and networks but, most notably, the foreign giants have taken into their hands the former national champions. According to an International Monetary Fund (IMF) survey in 2000, the extent of foreign ownership in the emerging market banking system has increased dramatically during the second half of the 1990s and market participants expect further increases (Gao 2001: 15).

In Poland, in Eastern Europe, along with the waves of privatization and permission for foreign participation, foreign capital poured into the domestic banking industry. Following Citigroup's acquisition of Bank Handlowy in 2000, the share of foreign ownership of bank assets in Poland reached about 79 per cent (Gao 2001: 2). The largest investments have been made by American, German and Dutch institutions. Bulgaria has a relatively similar situation: more than 83 per cent of Bulgaria's banking assets are under the control of foreign banks or financial institutions (*The Banker* 7 November 2005). In Romania, the consolidation process is accelerating towards putting more than 90 per cent of banking assets into foreign private hands (*The Banker* 5 December 2005).

In Latin America, the takeover phenomenon is more dramatic. With the initiative of the North America Free Trade Agreement, restrictions on foreign bank participation in Mexico were gradually eased. In particular, the 1994 peso devaluation forced an enormous bank bail-out. The wave of takeovers began in 2001. Citigroup took over Mexico's national champion, Banamex, with US$12 billion, in what is believed to be the biggest deal in Latin American banking history (BBC 4 August 2001). Next came Spain's BSCH acquisition of Serfin and then HSBC's buy-out of Bital. The latest move came when Banco Bilbas Vizcaya Argentania (BBVA) (Spain) paid US$4.1 billion for 40 per cent of Bancomer. So far, all but one of the country's six largest commercial banks has landed in foreign hands, and about 85 per cent of Mexican banking assets is controlled by foreigners, the highest such concentration in Latin America (*The Banker* 2 June 2004). These changes have astounded the world, since Mexico once strongly believed that domestic ownership of key industries was a crucial symbol of national independence: 'the one thing we want to preserve is Mexican ownership of Mexican banks. That is an essential element of our sovereignty, we must not give it up' (Hahnel 1999). In Brazil, Spain's BSCH bought Brazil's third largest state-owned Banespa Bank (*PD* 21 November 2000). In Argentina, there is only one privately owned bank of any size left that is not owned or substantially controlled by a large foreign bank (Gao 2001).

In recent years, the pace of consolidation in Asia has also picked up. For example, in South Korea, after the Asian Financial Crisis, the IMF agreement required the removal of all restrictions on foreign ownership of Korean firms and banks. Leading global banks are busy making targeted acquisitions in Korean markets, including Citigroup's US$2.7-billion take-over of KorAm Bank in 2004, the sixth-biggest lender in the country (*The Banker* 2 May 2004). In 2004, foreign investors already held 30 per cent of the domestic banking sector (*The Banker* 5 April 2004). 'It should soon become pointless to distinguish between foreign and locally-owned banks', said the head of Korea First Bank, which is owned by UK-based Standard Chartered Bank (*Yonhap News* 21 November 2005).

Challenges to China's state banks after WTO entry

Similar to that which happened in Eastern Europe, Latin America and South Korea, multinational banks are coming into China with unprecedented power, advantages and ambitions. The challenges posed by foreign giants to Chinese banks are daunting and severe.

Scale

There exists a big gap in scale between domestic and global financial institutions, in terms of assets and international networks. Take Citigroup as an example: its total assets reach over US$1.26 trillion, which almost equals the combination of the assets of the biggest four state banks in China (*The Banker* 2004). Citigroup alone has annual revenues of US$112 billion and profits of around US$14 billion, many times greater than the entire group of China's four big banks (Nolan 2004a: 57). As business is becoming global, so is the banking. Today, about one third of the world's largest financial institutions operate in three or more continents. Citigroup now has branches, subsidiaries or offices in more than 100 countries, with HSBC in 76 countries and Standard Chartered Bank in more than 50 countries. BOC, as the most internationally-oriented bank in China, only has operations in 27 countries (*BOCAR* 2004).

The relatively small scale of China's financial services sector means large competitive disadvantage against the global leaders in terms of unit costs, brand building, risk management, product development and application, and the ability to attract the best talent and to provide services for global clients (Wu Qing 2001).

Scope

Along with the liberalization of trade, increasing multinational production, active cross-border capital movements and rapid development of technology, the needs of bank customers are growing and diversifying. George S. Moore, the former president of Citibank, passionately claimed: 'if it is financial, we do it' (Cleveland *et al.* 1985: 4). Foreign conglomerates have integrated commercial banking, investment banking and insurance business and are increasingly enjoying economies of scope, and wining top clients around the globe. On the other hand, China's Commercial Bank Law in 1995 separated commercial banking from investment banking and insurance. The policy of separation is to serve the purpose of risk prevention rather than international competition and nurturing internationally competitive players (Wu Qing 2001). The narrow business scope is becoming an increasingly significant shortcoming for China's banks. Without providing one-stop-shopping services, Chinese banks are unable to contract quality global clients. Meanwhile, because the Chinese banks are not presently engaged in profitable activities such as investment banking, securities and insurance, the average rate of return in 2004 for banking institutions internationally was 1.2 per cent, three times higher than the 0.4 per cent in China (Chan 2005).

Innovation capability

In order to maintain the competitive advantage, big global giants make huge investment in IT to create and deliver new products, improve services and reduce costs. IT is becoming a powerful instrument for creating competitive advantage and expanding market share. 'It is the easiest, most cost-effective and rapid way to become a global operator' (Wu Qing 2001: 818). In the 1990s, 35 global banks led by Citigroup made an IT investment of US$175 billion (Jiao 2001: 138). The trend is escalating. At present, the annual IT input of Deutsche Bank is US$4.8 billion, for Citigroup, the annual input is as high as US$5 billion (*China Computer Daily* (*CCD*) 21 September 2004).

Huge investment in IT is crucial for innovation and development. Through automated teller machines (ATMs), point of sale (POS), bank cards, the internet, satellite and so on, foreign giants have not only changed the operation methods and environment of banks, but also re-engineered and restructured the business flows and management streams. One of the important consequences of rapid IT development is the financial innovations and easier deliverance of products and services. Foreign banks, from the 1980s, have created a wide range of new products, reaching 1,200 types

(Liu Mingkang 2002: 11), including financial futures, options, swaps, bill facilities, e-business, all kinds of derivates and securitized financial assets.

> [T]here will no longer be clear dividing lines between raising money for corporations through commercial paper or through share issues, through long-term or through short-term instruments, depending on regulation and requirement. Instead, debt will become interchangeable, an endless stream flowing one currency to another and from one type of paper to another without difficulty.
>
> (Hamilton 1986: 17)

On the other hand, the IT input of China's state banks is quite small, compared with foreign giants. For BOC, during the 1990s, the annual input was about US$0.24 billion. IT staff account for 2.6 per cent of all BOC staff, compared with the average level of 7 per cent in global giants.[3]

An industry expert commented, 'The competition of banks focuses on IT strength' (*China Computer Daily* (*CCD*) 21 September 2004). In order to maintain and further sharpen competitive advantage in China, Citigroup has applied for 19 patents relating to e-banking, two of which have been approved in China. At least eight other foreign banks have submitted patent applications to the State Intellectual Property Office of China. Domestic banks will have to pay a patent fee for some types of businesses, otherwise, they face huge fines. One result of lagging behind in innovation capability is that Chinese banks are gradually marginalized in the global value chain. That is they have to cling to their traditional banking products, especially the lending business, which brings about 90 per cent of their profits (Chen Jianjun 2005: 34), whereas the high-growth and lucrative products such as syndicate loans, asset management and internet-banking will be lost to their foreign competitors.

Productivity and quality

Table 2.3 indicates that not only the scale of assets of domestic state banks was much smaller than that of leading global firms, but, critically, their asset quality was much lower. For example, the NPL ratio for Banque Nationale de Paris (BNP) Paribas, which was 6.45 per cent, the highest among the foreign banks on this list, was much lower than the 20 per cent for the Chinese state banks. Chinese banks have a chronic problem with issuing improper loans. This is related not only to the state banks' loan management and business operations, but also to government intervention.

Besides asset quality, the productivity of China's state banks is disappointing (again, see Table 2.3). In 2002, the net profit of Citigroup was almost ten times that of BOC, which was the most profitable bank among the Big Four. If the factor of employees was considered, the profits per capita in China's state banks was negligible compared with the global giants. In 2002, ICBC and CCB's profits per capita were about US$1,842 and US$1,694

Table 2.3 Efficiency comparison, domestic versus international banks, 2002 (US$ million)

	Total assets	Net profit	Profit per capita	ROA	ROE	NPL ratio (%)
BNP Paribas	710,319	3,295	37,571	0.52	16.74	6.45
Citigroup	1,097,190	15,276	61,104	1.48	20.01	2.34
Bank of America	66,458	9,249	n/a	1.23	16.40	1.47
HSBC	795,246	6,239	33,833	0.90	13.69	2.90
ICBC	571,768	746	1,841	0.14	3.35	25.69
BOC	350,931	1,141	5,927	0.34	4.31	22.50
CCB	372,367	520	1,694	0.15	4.01	15.17

Source: Xu Xiaonian 2004: 3.

respectively; in sharp contrast, Citigroup and HSBC had profits per employees of US$61,104 and US$33,833 respectively. Everybody knows that Chinese state banks maintain a huge number of employees. Even recently, after corporate restructuring, BOC discovered 70,000–80,000 surplus employees. But due to the consideration of social impact, the staff will not be fired, but will receive training or be transferred to other banking posts (*Jinghua Daily* 15 April 2004). The return on equity (ROE) and return on assets (ROA) noted on this table also strongly suggest that foreign banks are much more profitable and efficient than their Chinese counterparts.

In addition, there are some other advantages enjoyed by foreign banks. For example, they have established sound and effective corporate governance, and in particular, are very experienced in strategic planning and risk control. They have more freedom than Chinese banks in their personnel policies, such as recruiting the best talent and professionals from the market and laying off surplus employees (Gao 2001). Meanwhile, because of their stringent internal control and monitoring mechanisms, foreign giants suffer far fewer banking crimes than their Chinese counterparts, and they enjoy a higher reputation and operation stability. Foreign institutions are also able to operate without the Chinese government intervention faced by domestic competitors. All these have intensified their competitive advantages in China's financial markets.

The aggressive efforts of foreign banks in China

Wolves are very strong, but also extremely aggressive. Foreign banks have, at high speed, acquired dominant positions in the financial markets of most of Latin America and Eastern Europe (Nolan 2004a; Gao 2001). When Citigroup acquired Banamex, Mexico's national champion, the *Financial Times* commented: 'The acquisition of Banamex underscored the rapacious appetite of Citigroup for assets in the developing world' (Nolan 2004a: 57). Citigroup itself said: 'China is top of our radar screen' (ibid.).

It is no surprise that foreign banks have accelerated their pace of development in China, with their influences extending day by day. So far, with a small asset share of 1.6 per cent of total banking assets in China, they have already grabbed 40 per cent of international settlement and 23 per cent of foreign currency lending (Liu Mingkang 2004b). The annual growth of their assets, deposits and loans all exceeds 30 per cent (CBRC 2005c). During this intensified competition, foreign banks have gradually proved their advantages in providing services in such areas as loan syndications, trade financing, retail banking, asset management and derivative business (CBRC 2005c). China's top think tank, the Chinese Academy of Social Sciences, warned that WTO accession would result in state banks losing their best customers to their foreign competitors. The warning was realized in 2002 when the telecommunication joint venture Ericsson in Nanjing dumped ICBC and shifted its business to Citibank, Shanghai branch (E-Market (EMKT) 2002). The so-called 'Ericsson incident' shocked China's banking community and became a big issue in the newspapers. Soon afterwards, Tianjin Motorola followed suit and suddenly repaid its loans of RMB1 billion to BOC ahead of schedule and transferred its accounts to Chase Bank Tianjin branch (Huang Jinlao 2003). In May 2003, a joint venture in Qin Huangdao complained about the coarse and informal statements provided by state banks and became the client of a foreign competitor who could provide better services (*China Business* 28 May 2003).

Besides making heavy green-field investment in China, foreign financial institutions speed up their stake investments. By the end of 2005, 18 foreign financial institutions participated in 16 Chinese banks, with the total investment reaching US$12.6 billion (Tang 2005). The Royal Bank of Scotland, Merrill Lynch and other investors bought 10 per cent of BOC. The Bank of America spent $3 billion for 9 per cent of CCB. Only recently, a team of Goldman Sachs, Allianz of Germany and American Express paid US$3.78 billion for a 10 per cent stake of ICBC, China's largest state-owned bank (*Caijing* 27 January 2006). Foreign capital also participated in joint-stock banks like the Bank of Communications (BoCOM), Shanghai Pudong Development Bank, Shenzhen Development Bank and other city commercial banks (Tang 2005). It is estimated that, by 2007, foreign financial groups might control one sixth of China's banking system (Chan 2005), although as of the end of October 2005, the share was only 2 per cent (CBRC 2005c).

It is true that foreign stake investment may bring local players advanced management expertise, scientific risk control mechanisms and more transparent corporate governance, amongst other advantages. On the other hand, as strategic partners, foreign banks can benefit from local bank networks and gain a rapid foothold in China's market. For example, for the time being, no foreign banks can issue their own credit cards within the mainland independently due to regulatory restraints (*China Daily* (*CD*) 5 November 2004). As strategic investors, foreign banks can sidestep this restraint. Citigroup issued a dual-currency credit card with the Pudong Development Bank in Shanghai. HSBC also launched a jointly-operated credit card unit with BoCOM (ibid.). More importantly, by acquiring an existing bank in China, the acquirer gains a more rapid development than would be possible with an organic growth strategy. By becoming a partner with CCB, for example, which has 136 million deposit accounts and 14,500 branches across the country, the Bank of America will be able to engage in corporate lending as well as consumer banking activities such as mortgages and wealth management (Chan 2005). In other words, the Bank of America can instantly get access to the huge customer base that it would otherwise take years to build.

The explicit objective of the global giants is to penetrate and dominate the financial market of China. A concern is that foreign banks might 'cherry pick' the most lucrative domestic markets or customers, leaving less competitive domestic players to serve other (more risky) customers and thus increase the risk borne by domestic institutions (Gao 2001: 19). Another worry for China's policy-makers is that the international banks are able to make more rapid progress than predicted within the Chinese market, provoking a run on state banks to transfer deposits to the international banks (Nolan 2004a). Worse, if China's indigenous large banks fail to achieve their own self-reform, global giants will find strong arguments to allow them to 'take command of the boat' as experienced sailors, who can run the country's financial institutions well (Nolan 2004a: 57). Furthermore, a much deeper worry is that, with the rapidly diminishing ground of China's domestic players, foreign-owned institutions will in fact decrease the stability of aggregate domestic bank credit, by providing additional avenues for capital flight, or by more rapidly withdrawing from local markets in the face of crisis (either in the host or home country), and as a result paralyse the host economy (Gao 2001). With the WTO entry, not only will the competitiveness of China's state banks be challenged, but the very safety of the banking system will be threatened (Wu Qing 2001).

In short, since the 1980s, globalization and the financial business revolution have completely changed the landscape of the global banking industry. The removal of trade and regulatory barriers, the advancement of information technologies and the fierce competition for market share are leading inevitably to a situation where banking services are dominated by a handful of powerful companies. After accession to the WTO, China's state banks, which evolved from the old planned economy, will encounter unprecedented challenges. Time is not on China's side. A major issue for Chinese policy-makers and bankers is how to survive in this increasingly competitive environment.

White-collar crimes

White-collar crime is 'an illegal act or series of illegal acts committed by nonphysical means and by concealment of guile, to obtain money or property, or to obtain business or personal advantage' (Edelhertz 1970). White-collar crime in this study is interchangeably used with banking crimes and financial crimes. Laurence Brahm, a political economist, described China's financial institutions as 'rotten, spread with cancerous problems of illegal lending and embezzlement of state and depositor funds' (*The Times* 23 March 2005). In particular, state banks have been deeply and frequently beleaguered by white-collar crimes. 'The management of the state-owned banks are generally unpopular and disliked by the general Chinese population, where they are often compared to leeches who steal and abuse public money' (Reuters 16 March 2004). The following BOC cases expose deep-rooted problems in banks' internal management and controls.

Loan management: the case of BOC Shanghai branch

The asset quality in a bank is a key factor for its liquidity, safety and profitability, and loans are an important asset business of commercial banks. According to Commercial Bank Law, when extending loans, banks shall adopt a comprehensive system of loan management in order to identify, prevent and minimize risks (Fang 1999). However, in practice, many state bank branches don't follow this procedure. As the BOC Shanghai case demonstrates, the loan business has become the biggest black hole in Chinese banks.

In 2004, Liu Jinbao, the chief executive of BOC Hong Kong Ltd and the chairman of the Hong Kong Association of Banks, was sentenced to the death penalty with two years' suspension. Although a 20-page document charged Liu with embezzlement, accepting bribes and being in possession of large amounts of assets of unverifiable origin (*Caijing* 29 November 2004), a major factor contributing to his fall was that of loans the Shanghai branch of BOC extended to the Wantai Group, a real estate development company in Shanghai. Zhou Lu, the general manager of BOC Shanghai after Liu, was also implicated in the Wantai case. At least another four top and mid-level managers of the Shanghai branch were also placed under investigation (*Caijing* 5 March 2004).

Liu was the general manager of BOC Shanghai before 1997. Qian Yongwei, chairman of Wantai, was Liu's close friend. From 1996, Liu extended loans to Wantai worth nearly RMB800 million (US$96 million) (*Caijing* 5 March 2004). When Zhou Lu succeeded Liu to the post of general manager of the Shanghai branch, he continued to offer ten batches of loans involving RMB700 million to Wantai. Altogether, Wantai had obtained 28 loans totalling RMB1.48 billion (US$178 million) from BOC Shanghai through 20 of its related companies over a period of four years. The total value of the loans plus interest was nearly RMB1.6 billion (US$193 million). Loans were granted with only RMB300 million-worth of collateral. Worse yet, most of the loans were transferred to the Hong Kong stock market for speculation. Only two projects were built according to the loan agreements. At the end of 2000, apart from two loans that were not yet mature, 95 per cent of the loans had become NPLs. As a result, BOC Shanghai, one of BOC's most important and profitable branches, was pushed into a risky and vulnerable situation.

On close examination, loans made by BOC to Wantai blatantly violated the basic loan principles of commercial banks (*Caijing* 5 March 2004).

1 Making loans against the set procedure

The normal procedure of making loans in BOC should be as follows: the corporate banking department makes the duty investigation – the risk control department evaluates and double-checks – the branch general manager examines and approves – loans are made. However, in the Wantai case, the loans were granted first and after that the various departments were instructed to make up the paperwork. Especially after 1998, at least four tranches of loans, with a total value of RMB350 million, were disbursed first, examined and evaluated afterwards.

2 Exceeding lending limits

The Shanghai branch had its lending limits set by the Head Office. Nevertheless, in the Wantai case, the branch either directly made loans exceeding the lending limit, or sidestepped regulations by dividing what was essentially one big loan into smaller ones. In 1997, one loan of US$29 million was split into six tranches.

3 Ignoring the mutual guarantee of affiliated companies

Wantai used more than 20 affiliated companies to get loans from BOC. These affiliated companies provided guarantees for each other, which involved RMB800 million. The clients' interrelationship and credit standings were completely ignored by the Shanghai branch.

4 Overlooking post-loan management

The most shocking part of the Wantai case is that after loans were illegally obtained from the Shanghai branch, loans were transferred to Hong Kong in an open way. Among the RMB1.6 billion loans, only two projects were carried out according to loan agreements. BOC Shanghai turned a blind eye to what was going on. Very possibly, like gamblers, bank managers hoped to reap abnormally high returns through stock market manipulation and they did not care about banking capital being diverted away.

5 Rolling over old loans

In order to delay the exposure of problems and create a good profit picture, the Shanghai branch chose to provide new loans to recover interests. In June 1999, RMB40 million was loaned, with a one year term and purpose of project; in fact, it helped Wantai to repay the interest.

Why did BOC Shanghai permit such things to happen? Why did BOC make such reckless loans to the Wantai Group? The answer is simple. Among many things, Liu Jinbao received a bribe of RMB1.12 million (US$135,266) from the Wantai Group (*Caijing* 20 November 2004). There is another reason unknown to many: Qian Yongwei once presented to Liu a generous 'gift' (*Caijing* 5 March 2004). In 1993 Shanghai Jinli Property Investment Ltd, for the purpose of developing Dianshanhu Villa, got a loan of US$22.35 million (RMB180 million) from BOC Shanghai. Only RMB70 million had been used on the property, whereas over RMB100 million was used for other purposes. By 1995, the project had been abandoned and the loan became bad. At the critical time of this huge black hole being exposed, Wantai took over the Dianshanhu Villa project with the tacit agreement of BOC Shanghai. In 1997, the equities of Jinli were formally transferred to Wantai, and Jinli became known as the Taidu Property Co. As a result, the debts of the former Jinli company were carried over by the new company. Liu Jinbao got a clean balance sheet, which later helped his promotion to the position of deputy director of BOC Hong Kong and Macao Managing Office, and finally, chief executive of BOC Hong Kong Ltd. Due to the Dianshanhu Villa deal, Qian Yongwei gained the full trust and favour of Liu. Under Liu's arrangement, BOC Shanghai continuously injected capital into Wantai. For merely resuming the Dianshanhu Villa project, another RMB100 million was granted in loans, none of which had any collateral. Qian Yongwei did not use one cent on the Dianshanhu project. For the time being, the Dianshanhu Villa project remains a notorious episode. In short, Liu Jinbao and his associates granted irregular loans to Wantai, while bank managers accepted bribes, kickbacks and other intangible benefits from the borrower.

Supervision of branches: the case of the BOC Kaiping sub-branch

All Chinese state banks have a similar organizational set-up: a head office and various levels of branches. According to Commercial Bank Law, the head office is the legal entity that assumes all responsibilities for operations. It is logical that important decision-making powers must be concentrated in the head office. However, China's state banks have too many hierarchical layers (Liu Mingkang 2004a), and branches have excessive operational and decision-making powers. This causes an agency problem and poses danger to internal risk control. On numerous occasions, high-profile incidents have emerged at grassroots level.

In 2002, a banking scandal shocked China and the foreign banking community. From the early 1990s, for a period of nine years, three bank officials of the BOC branch in Kaiping City, Guangdong province – Xu Chaofan, Yu Zhendong and Xu Guojun, serving successively as branch managers of Kaiping sub-branch of BOC – had stolen US$483 million of bank funds (*Caijing* 5 May 2002). A small portion of the money was used for local loans, some were lost in the crash of the Hong Kong real estate and stock markets after 1997, but the major portion was transferred to personal accounts in foreign countries. Only about US$75 million has been accounted for so far (ibid.). This is the biggest embezzlement case since the founding of the PRC (*FT* 16 March 2002).

In hindsight, the theft had taken various forms. According to BOC (HK)'s listing prospectus, they included 'foreign exchange trading activity in violation of regulations, off-balance sheet loans, and the diversion of bank funds to third parties'. The three men had 'established a pipeline into the BOC's foreign currency reserves in Beijing' (*FEER* 30 May 2002). One method used by Xu Chaofan to shift money offshore was through issuing bogus loans to local town and village enterprises, which then transferred the funds as payment for orders of raw materials to companies controlled by Xu in Hong Kong (ibid.).

In its report on the Kaiping scandal, *Caijing* (5 May 2002) said, it illuminated the 'terrifying complexity and scale of the challenge facing China'. Xinhuanet (10 December 2003) called it an 'elaborate international financial scam'. So far, only Yu Zhendong has been transferred by the American Federal Bureau of Investigation (FBI) to China's judicial department (*Caijing* 11 July 2005). Other major suspects and their families are still in North America. The Kaiping scam allows us to see the obvious weakness in supervision of branches in China's state banks.

First, the binding and controlling power of the distributed management framework is too weak (*Caijing* 5 May 2002). Nowadays most major banks in the world have adopted the matrix administrative framework (Jiao 2001). Namely, the business divisions of the headquarters are responsible for assessing the relevant business staff in the branches and controlling the business operations with an effective motivation and binding mechanism. However, the major state banks in China have taken the opposite approach and released the power from the higher levels to lower ones. This has reflected the impact of the reform thinking of 'administrative division of power' during the early period in order to stimulate the enthusiasm of grassroots banks (*Caijing* 5 May 2002). As a result, the branch institutions have become fairly independent economic entities. The head offices have had little idea of what has been going on in far-flung branches and even less power to control them (*FT* 20 June 2005).

The distributed framework, plus interference by local interests, has resulted in the extreme power of the branch managers of each level. Take Xu Chaofan as an example: when he was the Kaiping sub-branch manager, he was in charge of accounting, business authorization, personnel and general affairs. Checks and balances among these powers became empty words. As a result, Xu could transfer a huge amount of money across the border without being detected. He could also choose his successors, and made perfect arrangements to continue stealing money after he was transferred to a higher position.

Second, the internal and external auditing of the state banks is seriously inadequate. The supervision system in Chinese banks is still at its early development stage. Banks, which manage large amounts of other people's money, should have a very powerful and effective auditing system. However, auditing is just about the most fragile aspect of Chinese banking. The auditing staff usually account for 5 per cent of all bank staff in international banks, but in

China, the number is less than 1 per cent (*Caijing* 5 May 2002). What's more, there is a big gap in auditing techniques. International banks adopt computer real-time monitoring, quantitative analysis and on-site inspection (ibid.). But domestic auditing mainly depends on experience. Banks have not established centralized computer databases, which also seriously affects the effectiveness of auditing. What's more, auditing staff lack professional training. Most audits are merely arithmetic checks of the books or comparisons of vouchers with recorded payments. Auditors seldom go behind the books to make sure that paper assets have any real existence. In some cases, auditors even become accomplices of law-breaking business managers. It is only recently that state banks have begun to use external auditing. It is not surprising that incidents like the Kaiping case occur. It is not surprising that this organized crime group had embezzled, stolen and laundered at least $500 million through accounts in Hong Kong, Macau, Canada and the US (FBI website).

Rotten to the top: the case of Wang Xuebing

If the Kaiping crime involved the largest amount of money in the banking sector, Wang Xuebing's case goes right to the top. At the age of 42, Wang Xuebing already held the position of president of the Bank of China, which was China's most profitable and most internationalized bank. Later, Wang was transferred to be the president of CCB and remained in that position until 2002 (*Caijing* 20 December 2003). Wang had been a rapidly rising super-star in China's banking sector. Wang was said to be an 'absolutely smart man' (ibid.). He also attracted international attention thanks to his fluent English, sharp mind and rich professional experience. Western media commented that Wang was a 'reform-minded banker, famed among Western businessmen' (*Washington Post* 15 February 2002). *Business Week* (28 January 2002) regarded Wang as 'one of the brightest stars in the often dark sky of the Chinese financial world'.

However, in 2002, Wang was dismissed. Later, Wang was sentenced to 12 years imprisonment for taking bribes amounting to RMB1.15 million. The court ruled that Wang had taken 400,000 yuan (US$48,192) in cash and five expensive watches with an average price above 100,000 yuan (US$12,048) (*Caijing* 20 December 2003). Obviously, Wang exchanged his position and power for money; meanwhile, in return, bribers received financial benefits at the expense of the Bank of China. Among the bribers, Brilliance China was offered a loan of US$29.5 million. The Beijing Re-orient Advertising Company, in which Wang's wife Zong Lulu was a major shareholder, was also awarded handsome advertising deals from BOC (ibid.).

The court did not mention Wang's legal responsibility for the BOC New York branch's misconducts, nevertheless, both banking insiders and outsiders know that the New York case actually triggered the fall of Wang. The American Office of Currency Comptroller (OCC) is in charge of on-site reviews of 2,200 American banks and 52 foreign bank branches operating in the US (*Caijing* 20 December 2003). After an 18-month-long investigation, the OCC discovered several instances of misconduct occurring between 1991 and 1999 at BOC New York when Wang Xuebing was the general manager. The scandal forced the BOC to pay Chinese and US authorities a US$20 million fine, the single largest civil penalty ever imposed by the American Department of the Treasury (BusinessWeek Online 4 February 2002).

What happened at BOC New York is a long and complicated story. In brief, some managers 'provided favourable loans to connected clients' and led to 'huge losses of New York branch' (*Caijing* 20 March 2003). According to the OCC report, the New York branch provided US$1 million to a metal trade company – NBM, founded by an American Chinese, Zhou Qiang. Soon the credit facility increased to US$7 million. This was a small recently established company without a powerful asset background or proven performance record (ibid.). Zhou Qiang, however, had a 'personal and direct relationship' with important managers of BOC New York, especially Wang Xuebing (*Caijing* 5 August 2002). Zhou often invited managers to parties and barbecues in his luxurious house and often used his car to take managers out for sightseeing and amusement and even took them shopping. It was an open secret that Wang Xuebing loved French wine, golf and beautiful women (University of International Business and Economics (UIBE) 2004; Xinhuanet 10 December 2003). Disregarding the opposition of the risk control department of the New York branch, Wang gave instructions to grant loans to Zhou Qiang's company. Even when the company suffered consecutive losses, loans by the end had increased to US$18 million, all of which became bad (*Caijing* 20 December 2003). Furthermore, BOC provided a US$50 million low-interest loan to the company and permitted the money to be deposited in another BOC branch to gain interest benefit. To make things worse, BOC also granted US$12 million in loans to a company held by Liu Ping, the wife of Zhou Qiang. From the OCC report, the above dealings included 'large exposures to a single borrower, the facilitation of a fraudulent letter of credit scheme, the facilitation of a loan fraud scheme, the unauthorized release of collateral and the concealment of that action, and other suspicious activity and potential fraud' (ibid.). These are typical swindles manipulated by insiders and outsiders. All in all, BOC New York lost US$34 million between 1992 and 2000 (ibid.).

Like Zhu Xiaohua and several other scandal-hit bankers, Wang Xuebing was a protégé of Premier Zhu Rongji (*New York Times* (*NYT*) 16 August 2002), and was part of Premier Zhu's team of 'can-do-commanders' (Nolan 2004a: 55). Wang's case must be embarrassing to the top levels of the government. Wang was soon removed from his position and expelled from the party, being accused of taking bribes, leading a debauched life and breaking financial rules (*Caijing* 20 December 2003). The Wang Xuebing case is, however, even more embarrassing and devastating for the Bank of China. BOC has 100 years of history and has always been regarded as the forerunner in

China's banking reforms, and also the most influential Chinese bank abroad. If the monetary value of the American penalty is taken into account, the heavy losses on the Bank's reputation and future development are immeasurable. For one thing, BOC Hong Kong's planned listing in New York had to be aborted.

Implications

Nowadays, state banks have become one of the most corrupted areas in China. Hardly a week goes by without a report of a banker in China being arrested for corruption. 'Sometimes, suspects jump from tall buildings before the noose is tightened. At other times, they flee abroad' (*FEER* 31 January 2002). The stakes of crimes have also grown. In the early 1980s, bribes and embezzlement typically yielded a few hundred to several thousand yuan. Nowadays, criminals tend to haul in millions, even billions of yuan in illegal gains (*Caijing* 7 March 2005). Despite the tightened supervision and discipline from the PBC, the CBRC and other state authorities (Xie Ping and Lu Lei 2005), and despite incessant exposure and punishment, why is white-collar crime spreading like a fast-moving 'fire' in China's banks?

The reasons are manifold. Besides ineffective corporate governance, especially weak internal controls, during recent years, along with the exploding international banking business and advanced technology, the nature of white-collar crime is becoming more complicated. 'More than 400 billion US$ is exchanged every day on the foreign exchange markets, while the flow of commercial transactions is only about 12 billion US$' (Calavita *et al.* 1997: 64). The electronic transfer of money has made detection more difficult, thus making it easier for dishonest banking officials to divert money away. Plus, white-collar criminals often have the financial means to flee abroad. It is very tough for Chinese authorities to track them down. For example, Xu Chaofan and Gao Shan, who are major suspects in the BOC Kaiping case and the Hesongjie case respectively, are still at large in North America. According to the statistics of the Ministry of Commerce published in August 2004, about 4,000 officials and executives have fled abroad, taking with them US$50 billion. Among them, the biggest fish were from the banking sector (*China Economic Times* 5 April 2005). Since there are so many bank managers who have successfully fled abroad, even with the party's tough words and discipline, and occasional high-profile sentencing and even executions, to many bank chiefs the potential gains from crime still far outweigh the risks, and they choose to follow suit (*The Economist* 15 February 2002).

White-collar crimes are not confined to banks, but are prevalent in many sectors and even central government leaders are being exposed as being involved in financial crimes and corruption. For example, a 1985 central directive explicitly forbade children of senior officials to engage in business, but the 1989 high-profile case concerning the Kanghua Development

Corporation and four other companies revealed that children of politburo members were involved in business, tax evasion and speculation (Kwong 1997: 131). Even recently, according to *Eastweek* (Europe version 8 October 2005), children of the highest central government leaders are holding key positions in big business; they are called the 'party of princes'. People suspect that they take advantage of family positions and privilege to make big fortunes. 'So pervasive is corruption in China that it would be hard to find any leader whose associates and family members are beyond suspicion' (*The Economist* 15 February 2002). Corruption is not new to China. In China's modern history, the Northern Warlord government of the early 1920s was weakened both politically and militarily by corruption. Corruption was rampant under the Kuomindang rule and contributed to its collapse in 1949 (Johnston 1995). The new China has always experienced the same problems, but in pre-reform days party–state domination kept corruption within limits (ibid.). In recent years, corruption became so widespread as to elicit popular protest culminating in the 4 June Tian'anmen incident of 1989 (Kwong 1997). Corruption, like a cancer, erodes society from the inside (Narvaez 1978), angers Chinese people more than anything else and poses the greatest threat to China's economic reforms and the rule of the Communist Party.

Conclusion

Since the late 1970s, China has been one of the world's fastest growing economies. However, as China enters the twenty-first century, it is at a crossroads (Nolan 2004a). In particular, state banks are facing challenges in connection with corporate governance, government intervention, foreign competition and banking crimes. These challenges not only have an adverse impact on the health of the banking system, but also endanger the entire social, economic and political system.

Banking reform is a prerequisite for continued high economic growth and is the most crucial part of overall economic reforms. A banking crisis will not only lower the living standard of the general public, but will also eliminate the many achievements of economic reform overnight. In the words of Nicholas R. Lardy, the reform of the banking sector will determine China's development in the coming two decades (*PD* 7 March 2004).

It is encouraging that the Chinese government has increasingly realized the urgency of banking reform. '[The] Chinese government is not stupid enough to allow the state-owned banking system to collapse' (Brahm 2000: 12). The fact that so many deep problems in China's state banks have come to light is precisely because the government has tried to clean up the sector from the highest to the lowest levels (Nolan 2004a). Meanwhile, the 'progress of reform has meant scandals are unable to hide anywhere' (*FT* 20 June 2005). In 2003, the CBRC was officially launched to regulate and supervise financial institutions. The CBRC chairman indicated:

Clearly, the promotion of the reform of the state-owned banks has been a priority on our agenda. Specifically, we are striving to transform these banks, in the next three years, into well-capitalized shareholding banks, operating on a safe and sound basis and offering quality services in a competitive international banking market.

(Liu Mingkang 2004b)

Since assuming office, the new Chinese leadership led by President Hu Jintao and Premier Wen Jiabao has stepped up its efforts on SOE restructuring, especially on state banks:

We will carry forward the reform of the financial system. We need to accelerate the reform of the wholly state-owned commercial banks, focusing on a pilot project to transform the Bank of China and China Construction Bank into stock enterprises. Other commercial and policy banks must also deepen their reform.

(Wen 2004)

More importantly, a consensus has been reached that this current round of bank reforms are so crucial that social progress and stability depend on their success. 'This reform is a last-ditch attempt. We can only succeed, we cannot fail', according to Premier Wen (Xinhuanet 14 March 2004).

In the search for a way forward amidst the immense challenges that China's state banks confront, China's leaders can, in line with Confucian wisdom, 'gain new insights through reviewing old materials'. That is, turn to the country's own past for a source of inspiration (Nolan 2004a). Jiang Zemin, the former Party General Secretary, emphasized that:

We must inherit and develop the fine cultural traditions of the Chinese nation . . . with regard to the rich cultural legacies left over from China's history of several thousand years, we should discard the dross, keep the essence and carry forward and develop it in the spirit of the times in order to make the past serve the present.

(Jiang 2001)

'History repeats itself, first as tragedy, second as farce' (Marx 1869). Neither tragedy nor farce is desirable for China. What matters is to learn lessons and gain experience from the past and to use the past to serve the present and the future. To this end, the following chapters will use a historical perspective to examine the Bank of China from 1905 up to 1949. In relating to the current challenges faced by China's state banks, the research attempts to answer the following questions:

- How did the corporate governance structure of BOC evolve? How was it arranged and what were its characteristics during different historical phases?

- In what ways and to what extent did the respective governments intervene in BOC? How did they affect BOC's business activities and performance?
- What competitive advantages did foreign banks possess? How did BOC meet the challenge?
- What kinds of white-collar crimes did BOC incur under different governments? How did they happen and with what impacts?

Through reconstructing history, by offering an illuminating picture about previous events, history, like a mirror, can shed light on our journey forward.

3 Corporate governance

Introduction

Corporate governance is concerned with the processes by which corporate entities, particularly limited liability companies, are governed (Tricker 1984: 8). In the early days of capitalism, companies were owned and managed by their owners. As the size of companies grew with the progress of industrialization, owners of companies found it difficult to deal with the heavy demands for capital and the increasing risks incumbent upon running businesses by themselves (Kagawa 1999). What's more, the possession of wealth may not always meet in one person with the possession of managerial talents. In order to accumulate capital, control risks and utilize professionals, shares of a company were enlarged and dispersed, and company ownership was gradually separated from management. 'The joint-stock company, with limited liability for its shareholders was an elegantly simple and eminently successful development of the mid-19th century' (Tricker 1984: 2).

With the separation of owners and managers, it is necessary to establish a governance structure which controls managers and assures the achievement of efficiency, maintaining transaction costs at as low a level as possible (Kagawa 1999). Since shareholders are numerous, scattered and disengaged, they employ a board of directors to oversee the company. The directors in turn employ professional managers to run the firm. Corporate governance therefore 'is the relationship among various participants in determining the direction and performance of corporations' (Monks and Minnow 2001: 1). A corporation depends on shareholders for capital, but leaves the day-to-day running of the enterprise to management. This might create efficiency far beyond that which any one owner/manager, or even a group of owners/managers, could accomplish. It also creates opportunities for abuse (ibid.: 164). No wonder Adam Smith raised this issue: 'The directors of companies, being the managers of other people's money rather than of their own, it cannot well be expected that they should watch over it with the same anxious vigilance with which the partners in a private co-partnery frequently watch over their own' (Smith 1776 Vol. II: 330). Undeniably, the single biggest challenge addressed by corporate governance is how to grant managers the necessary enormous discretionary powers over the conduct of the business whilst holding them accountable for the use of that power (Monks and Minnow 2001: 165). In other words, 'how the owners – the principal – can achieve efficiency, profitability and accountability while also permitting the managers – the agents – the necessary degree of autonomy to operate the corporation in a competitive market environment' (Muir and Saba 1995: 3).

Corporate governance is a crucial part of a modern enterprise system. The arrangement and characteristics of corporate governance are different from country to country, depending on each country's history, culture, laws and economy. This chapter discusses the evolution of the corporate governance of BOC, its arrangement and characteristics during different historical phases, and how it affected BOC's business activities and performance.

The background of the Daqing Bank

Presence and expansion of foreign banks in China

After the Opium War (1840–2), China's door was forced open. The expansion of foreign trade in the wake of the treaties of 1842, 1858 and 1860 created fresh demands for credit and transfer facilities which encouraged the creation of foreign banking outlets in the treaty ports (Rawski 1989). A British–Indian joint venture, the Bank of Western India (later renamed the Oriental Bank), led the way into China in 1845. Other British banks followed suit one after another, such as the Commercial Bank of India, Chartered Bank of India, Australia and China, and the Hong Kong and Shanghai Banking Corporation (HSBC) (Wang Jingyu 1983).

The boom in China's international trade in the late nineteenth century continued to attract banks from France, Germany, Japan and Russia (Wang Jingyu 1983). With the British banks playing the major role, they formed a network which not only completely controlled China's international remittance and foreign trade financing, but also exercised the freedom of running other banking business, such as investing in the railways and mines, taking deposits from Chinese customers and consequently made short-term loans to Chinese Qianzhuang (Chesneaux *et al.* 1977a).

By virtue of extraterritorial rights, foreign banks enjoyed immunity from Chinese laws and taxes, and they had the freedom to circulate their own banknotes in Chinese territory (Hong 2001). With the support of their respective governments, they managed China's Maritime Customs Revenue and other Chinese government transfers. Their financial power was further enhanced since they played critically important roles in representing their home governments in granting loans to the Qing Court (Ji 2003).

Before the end of the nineteenth century, altogether a total of 21 foreign banks with 101 branches had operated in China (Wang Jingyu 1999: 299). Their activities and expansion gave Chinese officials and merchants a good understanding of the functions and profitability of commercial banks, and motivated their desire to set up their own modern banks in China (Chesneaux *et al.* 1977a).

Demands of modern industrial enterprises

After 1840, China had decades of commercial contacts with the outside world and the painful experiences of military defeats at the hands of western powers. In particular, China's defeat by Japan in 1894 and the terms of the Treaty of Shimonoseki alerted many Chinese people to China's weakness (King 1968). More and more Chinese people realized the superiority of industrialization and modern industrial enterprises. Starting in the 1860s, Zeng Guofan, Li Hongzhang and other high-level officials in the Qing Court launched a self-improvement initiative (Bergère 1986). These officials adopted western military and technological devices and created various munitions works and modern factories for manufacturing production. Attracted by the high profits that foreign factories in China earned, private industrialists also developed and flourished in the early 1870s. A partial census shows that 52 new factories opened in China between 1885 and 1894 (Chesneaux *et al.* 1977a: 283).

Different from native handicraft workshops, modern industry (using power-driven machinery) needed large amounts of capital for much longer periods of time. For example, the total product value of all of China's more than two million handicraft workshops was only a little more than C\$4 billion, or C\$2,000 each in 1912 (Cheng 2003: 21). Clearly, their average capital was much less. On the other hand, the average capital of 104 modern factories established in China between 1872 and 1896 was C\$282,663, with their total capital reaching more than C\$29 million (Yan Zhongping *et al.* 1955: 93). The much larger modern enterprises had greater demands for working capital from financial institutions. The financing demand for railway construction was ever more considerable. The Jin-Hu railroad (Tianjin to Dahu, 87.5 kilometres long) cost C\$1.82 million in 1888 (Mi 1963: 145–6). The Jinghan railway (Beijing to Hankou), completed in 1905, was 1,311 kilometres in length and involved more than C\$68 million (Yang Yonggang 1997: 32). The growth of modern enterprises in China called for new financial institutions which could provide much bigger loans with a longer maturity term.

China's existing domestic financial institutions

Prior to the coming of foreign banks, China's indigenous financial system 'paralleled that of pre-industrial Europe in its complexity and sophistication' (Rawski 1989: 126). There were numerous intermediaries, ranging from local money changers and pawnshops to large institutions with widespread networks of branches or correspondents (ibid.). They provided a broad variety of services (Tamagna 1942). The most powerful and influential institutions fell into two categories: Qianzhuang, or native banks, and Shanxi Piaohao, or Shanxi banks.

Qianzhuang were owned by individuals, partnerships, or small groups of stockholders who bore unlimited liability (Rawski 1989). Qianzhuang usually had no nationwide branches and were linked mainly by correspondent relationships with counterparts in other commercial centres. Most Qianzhuang conducted local money exchanges, issued cash notes, made loans to merchants and discounted notes and bonds before their maturity. Qianzhuang maintained a very close relationship with local merchants. 'Their methods and services were well suited to the needs of Chinese business concerns' (Cheng 2003: 15). Before China's opening to foreign trade, Qiangzhang dominated local financial businesses in various aspects (ibid.).

The Shanxi Piaohao, named for their province of origin, usually had nationwide branches (Huang Jianhui 1992). At the end of the nineteenth century, 32 Piaohao with 475 branches were in operation covering all of China's eighteen provinces, plus Manchuria, Mongolia, Xinjiang and other frontier areas (Cheng 2003: 12). Remittance was the major focus of Piaohao, including remittances by drafts, by letters and by cheques, and they could be cashed at any of Piaohao branches or by their correspondents throughout the country (ibid.: 13). Piaohao monopolized China's domestic remittances before the introduction of China's modern banking systems.

Piaohao and Qianzhuang complemented each other. Geographically, while the Piaohao's power centred in the Yellow River Valley and radiated out from there, the Qianzhuang concentrated in the south Yangtze Delta area (Cheng 2003). From a business perspective, Piaohao often deposited their idle cash in local Qianzhuang that acted as intermediaries between Piaohao and merchants in many treaty ports (*Shenbao* 12 January 1884).

Qianzhuang and Piaohao seemed to have served China well so far as her internal trade was concerned, but neither Qianzhuang nor Piaohao were equipped to finance China's foreign trade (Allen and Donnithorne 1954). Meanwhile, Qianzhuang found it difficult to finance modern industry. Most of Shanghai's Qianzhuang, even the largest, had only 20,000 taels of silver (C$28,000) in capital before the end of the nineteenth century (FRO 1978: 5). Even though they got chop loans from foreign banks, chop loans were made on a daily basis, and foreign banks could call them back anytime without notice, especially when the market liquidity was tight (Cheng 2003). Therefore, most Qianzhuang made only short-term loans to merchants, rather than long-term loans to modern enterprises.

Piaohao were also unable to exercise modern banking functions. Their branch system scattered their relatively larger capital base (Cheng 2003). What's more, while enjoying their absolute advantage in the domestic arena, Piaohao did not realize the potential profitability of new business opportunities. As a result, Piaohao failed to switch from clients with whom they were familiar or comfortable to taking on new ones. Thus, until the end of the nineteenth century, Piaoaho were rarely involved in China's modern industry (ibid.).

Unfortunately, both Qianzhuang and Piaohao had more fatal, inherent problems. Piaohao became deeply involved with government funds. With the decline of the Qing Dynasty, the Piaohao gradually lost momentum and faded into obscurity (Rawski 1989). As far as Qianzhuang were concerned, they retained traditional features which distinguished them from western banking institutions. Personal reputation and credit, rather than tangible collateral or securities, served as the cornerstone of Qianzhuang operations (Coble 1980). As a result, Qianzhuang were vulnerable to financial risks. For example, the sudden bankruptcy of a silk shop, 'Jinjiaji', triggered the 1883 Shanghai financial crisis when 87 per cent of Qianzhuang were forced to close their doors. The number of Qianzhuang in Shanghai fell from 78 at the beginning of year to only ten at the end of the year (Consular Reports 1883: 232). In a word, the capital strength, the organizational structure and operational methods made it increasingly difficult for Qianzhuang and Piaohao to serve modern capitalism.

Inspiration of nationalism

The late Qing Court was troubled with internal conflicts, political turmoil and several wars with foreign powers, and the Qing government was financially weak. Foreign debt made up a significant part of the government's budget. Since contracting its first foreign debt in 1853, the Qing government had borrowed from foreign banks and banking consortiums 43 times before 1894, amounting to around 45.7 million silver taels (about C$64 million) (Xu Yisheng 1962: 4–13). The 1894 Sino-Japanese war and the ensuing indemnity payment further exhausted government coffers. During the three years between 1894 and 1896 alone, the Qing government borrowed more than C$350 million from foreign banks (ibid.: 92). It was often stipulated in loan agreements that the Chinese government had to assign special taxes or revenues earmarked as guarantees for loans (Cheng 2003). Besides, 'The foreign loans were often related to privileges of railways, mines, treaty ports and spheres of influences of foreign powers' (Wang Jingyu 1999: 195). Many Chinese officials and scholars worried that the situation might lead to China's downfall. Therefore, the establishment of Chinese modern banks was seen as key to protecting China from economic exploitation and invasion by foreign powers (Cheng 2003).

The example of foreign banks, the demands of modern industry, unsatisfactory domestic financial institutions and growing nationalism stimulated the emergence of China's banks modelled on western practices (corporations of limited liability, relatively impersonal relationships with customers and secured loans). The first modern bank, the Imperial Bank of China, was established in 1897 by Sheng Xuanhuai, an entrepreneur and Qing high-ranking official (Hong 2001). The founding of the Imperial Bank realized only in part the desire to form a modern-style national bank. It did not, however, create a central bank under the direct control of the government (Ji 2003).

Establishment of rudimentary corporate governance

During the first decade of the twentieth century, the idea of establishing banking institutions to control government revenues and to support a unified currency, led directly to the establishment of the Bank of the Board of Revenue in 1905 in Beijing (Rawski 1989). The Board of Revenue was renamed the Ministry of Finance later, and thus the Bank of the Board of Revenue became the Daqing Bank (meaning 'Great Qing Bank') in 1908 (BOC 1999).

Corporate governance of the Daqing Bank

The Daqing Bank was guided by '24 Items of Ordinance' (Kong 1991). The Bank was a limited liability company. The capital of 10 million taels of silver was divided into 100 thousand shares, one half of which was to be subscribed to by the Ministry of Finance and the other half by Chinese citizens (ibid.). It was the largest amount of capital a Chinese financial institution had ever possessed. The top management of Daqing Bank included the superintendent, the deputy superintendent, four directors and three supervisors. Superintendents were appointed by the Ministry of Finance. Directors and supervisors were elected by private shareholders. Managers, deputy managers, accountants and other professionals were chosen and contracted by the top management (ibid.).

The limited liability company was one of the most important features that distinguished Daqing Bank from the old-style Chinese financial institutions. Most Piaohao and Qinahuang were organized on the basis of individual proprietorships or partnerships. Chinese businessmen had little enthusiasm for adopting a corporate structure until the success of western corporate companies in China demonstrated the superiority of this new style (Cheng 2003). The greater ability of corporate companies to accumulate large amounts of capital, disperse risks and implement professional management was increasingly recognized and appreciated in China. The reformers in the late Qing Court advocated that only by imitating corporate structures could Chinese enterprises hope to compete with their western and Japanese counterparts (ibid.). As a result, in 1904, China's first company law (Gongsi Lu), based on Japanese and English models, was issued to encourage entrepreneurs to establish limited liability joint-stock companies (Goetzmann and Koll 2004).

The second special feature of Daqing Bank was that, since the corporate form was new and unfamiliar to most Chinese people in the late nineteenth and early twentieth centuries, it was difficult for entrepreneurs to start a new corporation. To dispel public doubts, the founders of these companies used a special method to guarantee investors' investments – the 'official interest' (guanli) system (Cheng 2003: 181). In addition to getting dividends, which varied according to a company's operations and profits, a shareholder could expect a certain fixed interest for his stock share. The guanli of Daqing Bank was set at 6 per cent annually (DBCO) (Daqing Bank Clearing Office 1915: 83). Almost all Chinese corporate companies adopted this system. Company laws issued by the Northern Warlord government in 1914 and by the Nationalist government in 1929 legalized this traditional practice (Cheng 2003).

The third striking feature of Daqing Bank was its Guandu Shangban system (government supervision with merchant management). Historically, this system was a 'very important political instrument', and deserves special mention (Ji 2003: xxvii). This policy emerged initially in the 1870s, when the Qing government attempted to construct an early Chinese industrial base (Feuerwerker 1958). Behind this concept was the fact that the government lacked sufficient funds and professional managers to operate modern industrial state enterprises (Ji 2003). Also, Li Hongzhang, the superintendent of foreign affairs and advocate of the Foreign Affairs Movement, proposed that the most efficacious means of withstanding foreign economic pressure would be to have Chinese merchants organize companies which would be supervised by officials and granted concessions or monopoly rights in order to guarantee their success. This was quite explicit in his famous memorial of 1872 in defence of building steamships (Feuerwerker 1958: 28). Based upon the original political economic policy, Sheng Xuanhuai extended this concept to create China's modern banks. In the memorandum sent to the Zongli Yamen, the chief executive office of the Qing Court, Sheng suggested:

> Banking is a matter for merchants; if merchants do not trust the government, the financial power of the country cannot be concentrated; and if this power cannot be concentrated, a bank will not be successful. If we wish to begin carefully in order to get good results, we must accumulate small sums [from investors] to make a big fund. I venture to request that a high official be appointed to select honest and reliable gentry and merchants from all the provinces and recommend them for service as directors [of the bank]. . . . Following western business practice, this bank should be managed by merchants.
>
> (Quoted from Feuerwerker 1958: 227)

The Guandu Shangban system directly promoted the expansion of Daqing Bank. From its inception, Daqing Bank functioned as both the central bank and a commercial bank. The Daqing Bank's banknote was granted exclusive privilege to be used in all public and private fund transfers, including tax payments and debt settlements (Cheng 2003). The Qing government warned that anybody who blocked the circulation of its banknotes would be punished harshly (ibid.: 31). With the government's special protection, the bank's note issuance increased considerably.

Another exclusive privilege of Daqing Bank was that of running the state treasury. As the biggest shareholder of the Bank, the Ministry of Finance, which controlled most of the central government's revenue, became its largest client (Cheng 2003). The Ministry often kept more than one million taels of silver in the Daqing Bank as a deposit bearing low interest or no interest at all; in some occasions it reached as much as 10 million taels (Kong 1991: 187). Most of the Ministry's tax remittance was also transferred through the Daqing Bank and its nationwide networks. Indeed, Daqing Bank successfully took away most of the lucrative official remittance business from the Piaohao (Huang Jianhui 1992).

Supported by the central government, the Bank also handled many other official transactions. The Bank transferred the Salt Surplus Tax, Customs Tax and the government's diplomatic expenditures, managed foreign loans, foreign indemnity and donations, and even handled the repository on behalf of the Yunnan provincial government (Kong 1991: 189–97).

Last but not least, Daqing Bank received preferential treatment regarding business fees. For example, the fees to the Daqing Bank for sending inward and outward telegrams were reduced by half, which was later reduced to 40 per cent of the official rate, and there was no surcharge on the cipher code (Kong 1991: 200). When the Daqing Bank used government railways or steamships to transport silver stocks, the fee was also reduced by half by the government (ibid.).

The government protection and supervision was only one side of the Guandu Shangban system; professional management was the other. 'The superintendents appointed by the Qing government assumed the supervision duty but did not intrude into the management rights of professional merchants' (Kong 1991: 91). A group of business-conscious merchants were chosen as managers and played an important role in the Bank's growth. Among them, some later became famous bankers, such as Wu Dingchang, the general manager of Yien Yieh Commercial Bank; Ye Kuichu, the chairman of the National Commercial Bank; Song Hanzhang, the general manager of the Bank of China (Hong 1990).

Benefiting from government protection and merchant management, the Daqing Bank expanded its business by leaps and bounds. By 1911, Daqing Bank had established 35 branches in provincial capitals and trade ports, and was the largest bank in China (BOC 1999). Its tael banknotes were the only paper accepted by foreign banks (Tamagna 1942). The business prosperity brought huge profits to its shareholders. On top of the 6 per cent fixed guanli, the Bank gave out 2,944,537 taels in dividends in five years and rewarded stockholders a total return of 13 to 34 per cent annually (DBCO 1915: 86). When Daqing Bank stock was initially offered, it attracted few investors. Two years later in 1907, however, the price of the Bank's stock went up from its issuing price of 100 taels to 206 taels (Kong 1991: 85). The public gradually approved and trusted modern-style banks.

Chesneaux *et al.* (1977a: 232) commented on the historical role of the Guandu Shangban system: 'Government supervision that was part of the Guandu Shangban system furnished protection for infant industries.'

Certainly, the privileges granted to the Guandu Shangban enterprises were intended to put them in a stronger position in response to foreign and domestic competition. Without protection, Daqing Bank could not have survived long enough to train Chinese managers and provide experience in modern management. And it was state support that eventually led the public to accept the modern banking system and develop new social attitudes towards modern capitalism (Chesneaux *et al.* 1977a). This is consistent with the infant industry argument proposed by Alexander Hamilton (1791) and Friedrich List (1885). They both claimed that protection was warranted for small new firms especially in less developed countries, since new firms had little chance of competing head-to-head with the established firms from the developed countries. Similarly, the late Qing reformer Zheng Guanying (1893) concluded that direct government's aid and support of Chinese commerce and industry was a vital necessity. He defined his position as advocating 'the use of official authority to compensate for the weakness of the merchants'.

Nevertheless, the corporate governance of Daqing Bank was not problem-free. To some extent, Daqing Bank only established a rudimentary form of the western corporate system. The shareholders' meeting was formed, but in some years no meetings were convened. No formal board of directors was set up (Kong 1991: 87). Compared to old-style Qianzhuang or Piaohao, Daqing Bank was supposed to adopt modern business rules and ordinance, but in reality, comprehensive and sound management and accountancy were not established, internal monitoring was weak, and old habits of extending credit loans were prevalent. No wonder that there erupted several banking scandals (see Chapter 6).

Advancement of corporate governance

Change of the Daqing Bank to the Bank of China

The 1911 revolution wiped out China's last dynasty as well as the more than two thousand years-long monarchical rule. The Republic of China was founded in 1912. However, from 1912 to 1928, Warlords, bureaucrats and politicians from various factions took over the rule of the country in turn. Most of them belonged to different cliques of the Warlords of the North (BOC 1999). China suffered from militarism and regionalism.

Soon after the Republic of China was founded, the private shareholders of the Daqing Bank, in order to protect their interests, sent a proposal to the provisional government headed by Dr Sun Yatsen, suggesting that the Daqing Bank should be renamed the Bank of China (hereafter BOC) and be made the central bank of the new government. The original 5 million taels of private shares would be recognized as capital stock of the same nature of the BOC (BOC 1999: 4). Sun approved this proposal. The succeeding Yuan Shikai administration, however, revoked this plan and decided to establish a new central bank under the same name (Cheng 2003). The new bank set its capital at C\$60 million, to be equally subscribed to by the government and private investors. The government allocated C\$2,662,622 as BOC's initial capital (BOC 1991a: 74–111). Private shares of 5 million taels in the Daqing Bank were paid back by deposit slips payable in four years with 5 per cent annual interest (BOC 1995: 21). Even so, BOC developed on the basis of Daqing Bank, since BOC took over the debts and credits, premises and equipment of Daqing Bank; the liquidation office of Daqing Bank was under the administration of BOC; most private shareholders of Daqing Bank later became shareholders of BOC; many staff at Daqing Bank were transferred to work at BOC; BOC used Daqing Bank banknotes, only adding a seal 'Bank of China banknote' for circulation (BOC 1995: 25–7).

Privatization of the Bank of China and its new corporate governance

Although the ordinance stated that BOC was a limited stockholding company, half of the total capital was subject to public subscription; however, before 1915, BOC didn't recruit private shares and the government-appointed president and vice president managed the Bank. The official nature of BOC worked as a two-edged sword. While it did help BOC compete with other financial institutions, it also put BOC under the total grip of the government and drew it to the brink of bankruptcy (Cheng 2003). The Yuan Shikai government was constantly short of funds after coming to power in 1912. To meet financial needs, the government forced BOC and BoCOM (Bank of Communications, set up by Ministry of Posts and Transportations in 1907, the predecessor of today's Bank of Communications) to advance huge amounts of money without providing sufficient security. By the end of 1915, the Ministry of Finance owed BOC C\$12 million (Cheng 2003: 54).

Yuan Shikai's failed efforts to restore the monarchical system further deteriorated the financial health of the central government. In 1916, BOC was ordered to cease the encashment of banknotes, so as to collect silver for the government (BOC 1999). At that time, the paper notes issued by banks were convertible, and note holders could at any time cash silver at issuing banks. The order to stop encashment immediately led to public panic. In order to maintain the credibility of the Bank of China, the BOC Shanghai branch firmly rejected the government order. The Shanghai branch was the largest branch of the BOC. Its manager and assistant manager were then Song Hangzhang and Zhang Jia'ao (or Chang Kia-ngau, courtesy name Zhang Gongquan). With the support of Shanghai's various banks and social groups, the Shanghai branch continued carrying out the encashment of banknotes, and finally survived the bank-run. The example of the Shanghai branch was followed up by other BOC branches along the Yangtze River Valley.

This victory in defiance of the government order greatly enhanced the confidence of BOC managers. More importantly, after Zhang Jia'ao was promoted to the vice presidency of BOC in 1917, he was determined to change the bank–government relationship and reorganize the corporate governance of the Bank (BOC 1999). With the support of Liang Qichao, the new Minister of Finance, Zhang successfully revised the BOC Ordinance. The merits of these amendments were quite obvious.

First of all, the new regulations restricted the government's power in choosing the Bank's chief executives. According to the previous BOC Ordinance, the Bank's president and vice president were appointed by the Minister of Finance. The complex political struggle of the early Warlord period led to the constant reshuffle of the cabinet. The president and vice president of BOC, in line with the ups and downs of various political cliques, changed twelve times between 1912 and 1916 (BOC 1995: 112). Seven of them served for less than half a year and nobody kept the position for more than one year, and even the title of its chief executive was changed five times (Cheng 2003: 59). The frequent change of top management in BOC made it impossible to formulate strategy and carry out long-term policies. The new regulations stipulated that there was no distinction between private and official directors and supervisors. Directors and supervisors were elected by shareholders, and the government could only choose and appoint the president and vice president from the board of directors (Yao Songling 1982: 1633). The term for presidents and directors was four years, and the term for supervisors was three years. Both terms could be prolonged, thus freeing the Bank's leadership from continuous political unrest (BOC 1995).

Second, the new regulations made it easier for the Bank to get rid of official control of its business. Previously, BOC was under the direct control of the Ministry of Finance. The creation or closedown of any branch and the contracting of agency agreements with counterparts had to be approved first by the Ministry of Finance, which also appointed all BOC managers, from its chief executives to its branch managers and assistant managers (BOC 1995). As a subordinate organization, BOC obviously had no way of rejecting orders from the Ministry, including orders to continuously finance government expenditures. The new regulations thus gave the Bank more independence to run its business, for example, it stated that issuance of banknotes must be approved by the board of directors (Yao Songling 1982: 38).

Third, the new regulations expanded the power of private shareholders. The fixed ratio between the Bank's official and private shares were abolished. Private shareholders were allowed to buy as much of the Bank's stock as they liked (Cheng 2003). After the new regulations were passed, Zhang Jia'ao made a trip to Shanghai to persuade commercial banks and private institutions and enterprises there to purchase BOC stock (BOC 1991a: 93). As a result, Shanghai Commercial and Savings Bank (SHCS), National Commercial Bank, Zhejiang Industrial Bank (ZJIB), Shanghai Securities Exchange, Shenxin Cotton Mill (under Rong Zongjing), Baocheng Cotton Mill, and others, actively answered the call (ibid.). The purpose was to 'form a core of private shareholders, so that BOC can follow the normal trail to do business' (ZJIB 1921).

Finally, according to the new regulations, government stocks could be sold to the public at any time. Since the government's financial situation was tight, after 1917, it began to sell its BOC stocks to the public and private financial institutions. By 1924, government shares shrank to the symbolic level of C\$50,000, accounting for only 0.25 per cent of the Bank's capital (BOC 1991a: 87). BOC finally got rid of government control and became a de facto private bank.

The change of BOC Ordinance in 1917 was of vital importance to the survival and development of the Bank, since establishing an effective corporate governance structure is a key task for operating modern corporations in which ownership and management are separated. The general assembly of the shareholders of BOC held the first meeting in 1918 and the first boards of directors and supervisors were elected. Feng Gengguang was appointed the president and Zhang Jia'ao the vice president (BOC 1999). The new corporate governance gave great leverage to a group of professional managers in BOC, people like Feng Gengguang, Zhang Jia'ao and Song Hanzhang. Theoretically speaking, they were elected by the board of directors, who had final authority on all important issues in BOC. In practice, however, the president and vice president of BOC exercised a great deal of power in running the Bank's business and enjoyed a high degree of operational autonomy (Cheng 2003).

Different from the Anglo-Saxon one-tier board model, BOC adopted the German-style two-tier board system. That is, the function of supervision and monitoring was taken by a board of supervisors instead of a board of directors. The Articles of Association of BOC clearly stated that the board of supervisors should examine whether the president, vice president and other directors complied with company rules and resolutions of shareholders' meeting; they should inspect and confirm the BOC annual reports; they should investigate the business situation and property of BOC; and they should monitor banking operations and examine all accounts, securities and vaults (BOC 1991a: 145). The checks and balances were built into the BOC governance structure, so that no single person had unfettered power.

Very creatively, BOC established a joint committee of directors and supervisors (BOC 1991a: 145). The duties of this joint committee were as follows: determining the distribution of shareholder dividends and staff bonuses; handling issues which could not be settled by the board of directors; reviewing BOC Articles of Association and other regulations (ibid.: 146). It was up to the joint committee to take final decisions regarding important and unexpected issues.

If the BOC corporate structure in the Qing period laid a basic foundation and framework for modern banking, during the Warlord period, BOC further developed its corporate governance, which set and enforced clear lines of rights and obligations throughout the organization. With the new corporate governance in place, BOC improved efficiency and enjoyed rapid business growth. The predominance of private stocks enabled the Bank to keep a distance from government domination and politician interests and to concentrate on business development. BOC improved efficiency, enjoyed rapid business growth and maintained the largest, strongest and the most distinguished Chinese bank at that time.

The Jiang-Zhe Bankers and their relationship with the Bank of China

The tremendous results of Yuan Shikai's order to suspend redemption were not merely limited to the banking business and change of BOC Ordinance. Of more far-reaching significance was that it helped the Jiang-Zhe Bankers (Jiangsu–Zhejiang bankers) establish a close relationship of mutual support and interdependence with the Bank of China over the following 20 years, and, in a gradual way, 'to bring the Bank under control' (BOC 1999: 26).

Characteristics of the Jiang-Zhe Bankers

Many scholars have shown interest in the Jiang-Zhe Bankers, who are also known as the Jiang-Zhe Caifa (financial magnates from Jiangsu and Zhejing provinces) (Cheng 2003); Jiangsu–Zhejiang bourgeoisie (BOC 1999); new bourgeoisie (Bergère 1986); Shanghai finance capitalists (Ji 2003); Zhejiang Jiangsu financiers (Coble 1980); and Jiangsu Zhejiang Bankers' Clique (Hong 2004).

No matter what they are called, the Jiang-Zhe Bankers were a group of leading Chinese bankers, in particular, the chief executives of the BOC, the BoCOM, the Southern Three Banks (which were located south of the Yangtze River: including Shanghai Commercial and Savings Bank, Zhejiang Industrial Bank and National Commercial Bank), and the Northern Four Banks (which were located north of the Yangtze River, including Jincheng Bank, Continental Bank, China and South Sea Bank, and Yien Yieh Commercial Bank). Table 3.1 gives a basic background summary of these bankers, and Cheng (2003: 226–9) has helpfully summarized several common characteristics.

NATIVE-PLACE CONNECTIONS

The first common feature of these bankers was their shared native place of birth (or ancestral home). The chief executives of the nine banks were all exclusively natives of Jiangsu and Zhejiang provinces (see Table 3.1).

The dominance of Jiangsu–Zhejiang people in the Chinese financial field was not an occasional accident but something with long historical roots (Cheng 2003). Jiang-Zhe merchants appeared in Shanghai as early as the Ming Dynasty (1368–1644). Chinese merchants in an unfamiliar environment tended to gather into two kinds of groups called 'bang'. One was on the basis of the native place, and the other on the ground of common occupation

Table 3.1 The representative Jiang-Zhe Bankers, 1930s

Name	Bank	Place of birth	Education
Zhang Jia'ao	Vice president, Bank of China	Jiangsu	Japan
Qian Yongming	Chairman, Bank of Communications	Zhejiang	Japan
Hu Zutong	GM,* Bank of Communications	Zhejiang	Britain
Chen Guangfu	GM, Shanghai Commercial and Savings Bank, Managing Director, BOC	Jiangsu	USA
Li Ming	GM, Zhejiang Industrial Bank, Chairman, BOC	Zhejiang	Japan
Ye Kuichu	Chairman, National Commercial Bank	Zhejiang	China
Xu Xinliu	GM, National Commercial Bank	Zhejiang	Britain
Zhou Zuomin	GM, Jincheng Bank	Jiangsu	Japan
Tan Lisun	GM, Continental Bank	Jiangsu	Japan
Hu Bijiang	GM, China and South Sea Bank, Chairman, Bank of Communications	Jiangsu	China
Wu Dingchang	GM, Yien Yieh Bank	Zhejiang	Japan
Nine banks' ratios out of 146 Chinese banks in 1934	Paid-up capital	21.10%	
	Total assets	52.07%	
	Total deposits	60%	

Note: *General Manager.

Source: Cheng 2003: 225; Hong 2004: 82–3.

(Cheng 2003: 226). Among China's ten great merchant bang appearing during the Ming and Qing Dynasties, Ningbo merchants from Zhejiang province and Dongting merchants from Jiangsu province became the most powerful and capable groups (Zhang Haipeng 1993). Jiang-Zhe merchants were, for a long time, well-known for their business shrewdness and enterprising spirit (Jin and Sun 2001). Sun Yatsen praised Ningbo merchants for being 'excellent at commerce. No one can compare to them in terms of their capability and influence in China's treaty ports' (*Minguo Ribao* 25 August 1916). Though Jiang-Zhe merchants dealt in diversified businesses in Shanghai, the greatest concentration of their resources was in Qianzhuang, and Shanghai finance lay primarily in their hands (Mann 1974: 73). At the turn of the twentieth century, nine powerful families controlled Shanghai's Qianzhuang. Five of them came from Zhejiang and four from Jiangsu province (Cheng 2003: 226). Along with the development of modern capitalism, Jiang-Zhe merchants expanded into comprador activities, modern industry and later banking (Coble 1980). Susan Mann (1974) observed that the Ningbo bang moved from leadership positions of traditional organizations into eminent roles in modern institutions, such as banking, shipping, insurance and utilities. Jiangsu and Zhejiang people held key positions not only in China's major banks but in many other middle-sized banks as well (Cheng 2003). The same native place easily fostered social networking, personal loyalty and business cooperation. An interlocking directorate became common, with many bankers assuming positions in one another's banks, such as bank director or supervisor. Coble (1980: 25) noted that in 1931, six Shanghai bankers were on the board of directors of five or more of the major Shanghai banks, and fifteen bankers served on three or more.

WESTERN-STYLE EDUCATIONAL BACKGROUND

The second common feature was their educational background. Most of the bankers had been educated abroad. Table 3.1 shows that nine out of eleven bankers studied banking or economics at western universities. Though Ye Kuichu and Hu Bijiang didn't study aboard, both of them spent several years learning western culture in Chinese schools (Cheng 2003: 228). The western education broadened their minds and acquainted them with modern banking practices. 'They were updated with the realities of the contemporary world and less bound by traditional constraints' (Bergère 1981: 125). These Shanghai bankers had often become thoroughly international in outlook, 'capable of surveying equally attentively the Stock Exchanges of London or New York and the Szechuanese [China's Sichuan] market' (Bergère 1981: 33). What is even more important is that the combination of western and Chinese educational background provided vital leadership qualities for these people. Zhang Jia'ao pointed out in his autobiography, that 'All of those who later achieved prominence as key banking personnel were graduates of Chinese and foreign universities' (quoted from Cheng 2003: 239). Without exception, they all applied their knowledge and experience to their banking reforms, and played a key role in building and promoting China's modern banks.

Jiang-Zhe Bankers' controlling power in BOC

The nine major banks controlled more than half of the banking business and made up 51 per cent of the circa 140 Chinese banks during the 1920s and 1930s (Table 3.1.) Their actual strength was far greater, because they also cooperated with and controlled many other industrial and commercial concerns through their loans and investments (Cheng 2003). The controlling power within the General Chamber of Commerce, the Bankers Association and the Native Bankers Association in Shanghai was almost totally in their hands (BOC 1999). The most active and financially strongest among the shareholders of BOC were the Jiang-Zhe Bankers. Therefore, it can be said, that BOC's successful rejection in 1916 of the Yuan Shikai's order received the backing of the Jiang-Zhe Bankers. After the new BOC Ordinance was passed, the general managers of SHCS Savings, ZJIB, National Commercial Bank, Jincheng Bank, and others responded enthusiastically to buy BOC stocks (Cheng 2003). From 1918 the first BOC boards of directors and supervisors were elected, and up to 1935, Jiang-Zhe Bankers always held a distinct predominance in BOC. That is to say, they were in control of BOC for as long as 17 years (BOC 1999).

Modernization of corporate governance

The reorganization of the Bank of China in 1928

In 1926, the Nationalist Party (Kuo Min Tang or KMT) launched the northern expedition and ended the Warlord era. In 1927, Chiang Kaishek established the Nationalist government in Nanjing.

When T.V. Soong (the brother-in-law of Chiang Kaishek) became Minister of Finance of the new government, he suggested that the Bank resume its function as the central bank of China, with the government retaining a controlling interest. Zhang Jia'ao preferred to maintain the independence of BOC, and tactfully declined the proposal (Coble 1980; BOC 1999). In fact, BOC had a strong anti-Warlord tradition that would make it very difficult for the new government to take over the Bank immediately. Meanwhile, the new government did not have the power to compete with the large numbers of private shares in the Bank (Ji 2003). Therefore, the government decided to create a new central bank.

Soon, the government announced a new BOC Ordinance and changed BOC into a 'Government-Chartered International Exchange Bank'. By issuing treasury bonds, the government held C\$5 million of shares, which accounted for 20 per cent of the total capital of BOC (BOC 1999: 48). Accordingly, the Bank amended its Articles of Association and held re-elections for the boards of directors and supervisors. The newly elected boards comprised twelve directors and four supervisors elected by the private shareholders, and the remaining three directors and one supervisor were appointed by the government. The directors also elected from among themselves five managing directors, and then, from the managing directors, Zhang Jia'ao was recommended by general acclaim to be the general manager, with real power in his hands. Li Ming, general manager of Zhejiang Industrial Bank, was appointed chairman of the board by the Ministry of Finance. The Head Office of BOC was moved from Beijing to Shanghai (BOC 1999: 48–9).

Although the reorganization gave the government a larger role in the BOC, it had a small impact upon BOC business. Private shareholders retained de facto control of BOC. Among the 12 directors elected in 1928, more than half were from Jiangsu and Zhejiang. Again, of the five managing directors, four were Jiang-Zhe Bankers (BOC 1999: 28). BOC was semi-government only in form and it was free to operate as a commercial bank (*Shenbao* 24 April 1929).

The modern and sound corporate governance of the Bank of China

Figure 3.1 shows the organizational structure of BOC in the 1930s. In reference to the western corporate model, BOC had established an integrated framework of the shareholder's meeting, the board of directors, board of supervisors and a joint committee of directors and supervisors. Rights and obligations were clearly defined, as in Figure 3.1.

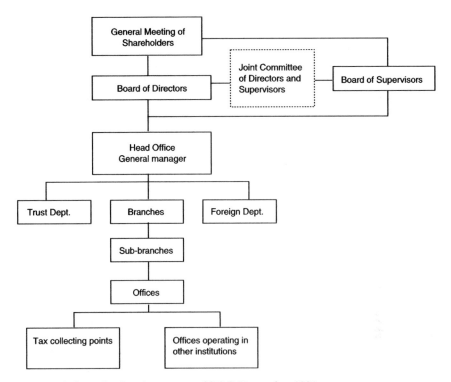

Figure 3.1 Organizational structure of BOC, December 1931.

Source: BOC 1995: 166.

The shareholders were the members of the BOC and their liability was limited to the sums they had agreed to risk when investing in the company. Shareholders had all the rights related to property rights. These rights included decision-making, electing directors and supervisors and investment beneficiaries. The shareholders expressed their interests through the shareholders' meeting, which exercised supreme control over the company (BOC 1991a: 166). The shareholders' meeting was set once a year, but an extraordinary meeting could be convened in the case of emergency or on important issues (ibid.: 126).

The board of directors, representing shareholder interests, was the top decision-making organ within BOC. Its main responsibilities included the formulation of policy and objectives, the selection of strategies, the evaluation of corporate performance and the appointment and dismissal of executives (BOC 1991a: 164). For the first time in BOC history, the post of chairman was set up, therefore ending the concentration of the roles of chairman and chief executive in one person, something which BOC experienced during the Warlord era. The board met once a month (ibid.: 194). The regularly and frequently-held board meetings facilitated information exchanges and allowed prompt decision-making.

The board of supervisors was the corporate organ designed to hold managers accountable to capital providers for the use of firm assets. The board of supervisors was composed of five people, among them, one 'standing supervisor' was elected and resided in the Bank to exercise daily duties (BOC 1991a: 165). The board of supervisors monitored and controlled executive action. The purpose was to ensure that managers' interests were in line with those of shareholders and to avoid principal–agent conflict. The mechanism of checks and balances was stressed. There were detailed rules regulating the manager's behaviour, defining what managers of different levels could do and what they could not do. For example, the general manager was forbidden to borrow money or take mortgage loans from the Bank (BOC 1991a: 210). 'If the branch manager needs to sign a contract with the third party, he must get the examination and approval of the Head Office' (BOC 1991c: 2578).

The joint committee of directors and supervisors mainly handled shareholder dividends and BOC staff compensation packages, the opening and closing of branches, and so on (BOC 1991a: 165). This arrangement strengthened the communication and coordination among directors and supervisors regarding important issues.

Managers conducted the daily management of the Bank, and took full responsibility for the Bank's business dealings. The responsibilities included planning, execution and control of banking business. The management was accountable to the board of directors. BOC insisted that the appointment of a commercially-oriented general manager was vital in ensuring banking profits (BOC 1991a: 137). The general manager Zhang Jia'ao was one of the most prominent professional bankers in China's modern history. He studied at Beijing High Industrial School, and got an economics degree from Japan's Keio University (BOC 1995: 897). Bergère (1986: 185) commented that Zhang Jia'ao had the exceptional gift of 'rejecting old, worn-out ideas and welcoming new ones', and made a contribution to the process of 'bringing Chinese society up to date'. Zhang began his long and distinguished service with the BOC in 1913. He focused on BOC's business development and modernization and led BOC into financial success and a great reputation.

Meanwhile, after 1928, BOC set high standards in selecting directors and supervisors (BOC 1991a: 381). It sought:

1   Chinese and overseas Chinese bankers with a good reputation, modern thought and foresight: accordingly, Li Ming – chairman of Zhejiang Industrial Bank; Chen Huide – the general manager of SHCS; Zhou Zuomin – the general manager of Jincheng Bank; and Li Qingquan – the general manager of Philippines Zhongxing Bank, were elected;
2   influential persons in industrial and commercial circles: accordingly, Wu Lingsu – a large shareholder of Shanghai Cotton Yarn Exchange; Zhou Liang – a tycoon of the dye industry; Chen Jiageng – the overseas Chinese

rubber leader; and Rong Zongjing – China's largest industrialist, were
elected;

3   outstanding BOC staff: accordingly, Song Hanzhang – the former
Shanghai BOC manager; and Bei Zuyi – the incumbent Shanghai BOC
manager, were elected.

Finally, important private shareholders of BOC, such as Feng Gengguang,
were elected (BOC 1991a: 382). The directors and supervisors at BOC were
made up of a combination of internal staff from within the company and
external members who had no financial interest in the company but were
specialists with influence and authority, thus increasing the element of
independence and objectivity in board decision-making.

As mentioned above, BOC exercised effective monitoring and supervision
of management; meanwhile, in order to attract and retain the most talented
managers, and make managers maximize their efforts, BOC provided appropriate remuneration packages (BOC 1991c). For example, in 1923, in the
Head Office, the highest monthly salary of the Bank's staff (general manager)
was C$700; the deputy general managers and managers: C$300–700; auditors:
C$220–420; clerk: C$40–300; assistant: C$14–35 (BOC 1991c: 2608). The
monthly bonus was set at one fourth of the salary (BOC 1991c: 2617). As a
result, the monthly salary plus bonus for a general manager could reach
C$875, whereas for the lowest clerk it was C$17.5; the former was 50 times
that of the latter. In addition, managers received social expenditures. The
general manager Zhang Jia'ao's social expenditure every month was C$500;
after 1928, it was raised to C$1,000 (Cheng 2003: 207). Also, on top of the
fixed income, managers received a performance-based reward (Chung 2003).
For example, Zhang Jia'ao was awarded a big bonus – C$160,000 for his
24 years of service at BOC (Yao Songling 1982: 61). Song Hanzhang, as the
manager of the Shanghai branch, was offered a western-style house as a
bonus (Cheng 1993). Other outstanding managers also got rewards thanks to
good performance. High income, prestige and non-monetary benefits promoted professional managers to take the Bank's long-term growth as their
goal, rather than short-term personal gains. These managers clearly realized
that their incomes, careers and fame relied on the success of BOC.

When Zhang Jia'ao was later asked about his most satisfying achievements
during his leadership at BOC, he first listed 'the pioneer of China's large
corporate system, i.e. first large stockholding company with capital of
C$20 million and several thousand stockholders in which all business activ-
ities followed the law' (Zhang Jia'ao 1977: 49). Indeed, at the end of 1934,
BOC became the biggest enterprise in China with its C$25 million of paid-up
capital (Cheng 2003: 216). BOC and other modern banks were regarded as
'the framework of China's new venture' (Ma Yinchu 1933). In particular,
public opinion acclaimed that BOC was one of the three best-governed
institutions in China. The other two were China Customs and the Postal
Bureau (BOC 1991a: 105), both of which were headed by foreigners.

Table 3.2 Comparison of Central Bank, Bank of China and Bank of Communications, end of 1934 (C$ million)

	Central Bank	BOC	BoCom	Ratio of BOC in three banks (%)	Ratio of BOC in all Chinese banks (%)
Paid-up capital	100	25	8.7	18.70	7.50
Total assets	478	976	425	51.94	22.70
Banknotes issued	86	205	112	50.87	32.90
Deposits	273	547	293	49.15	18.35
Loans	167	535	263	55.44	20.52

Source: BOC 1995: 370.

Modern corporate governance helped BOC achieve an efficient system of management, and deal with the principal (owners)–agent (managers) problem. Accordingly, BOC had built up impressive financial strength and laid the foundations for a strong and modern international commercial bank. Its banknotes issuance, deposits and loans accounted for approximately half of the total of the Central Bank, BOC and BoCOM put together (Table 3.2). Total assets of BOC alone amounted to C$976 million, more than twice the assets of either the Central Bank of China or the Bank of Communications, and accounted for 22.7 per cent of the combined assets of all Chinese banks. Tamagna (1942: 9) accurately praised BOC as 'the leading public institution in the domestic market, the trusted financial agent of China abroad'. Meanwhile, in the Shanghai financial market, BOC became a serious contender to foreign banks.

According to Alfred Chandler (1977), when modern enterprises, owned by many shareholders and managed by a hierarchy of salaried managers, replace traditional types of business firms, it represents a fundamental institutional transformation in the business world. This institutional innovation greatly promotes professional management and organizational capability, stimulates productivity and accelerates the expansion of the capitalist economy. Therefore, Chandler called it a 'managerial revolution'. With no doubt, BOC was at the forefront of this managerial revolution in China.

Decline of corporate governance

Banking coup of 1935

From the establishment of the Nationalist government until 1934, only the Central Bank and Farmers Bank were completely controlled by the government. Nanjing owned 20 per cent of the shares of BOC, but BOC exercised considerable business independence. In order to strengthen the government's monopoly of finance, Chiang Kaishek had long cherished the hope of 'setting up an apparatus to hold the reins' of the Central Bank of China,

BOC, BoCOM, etc. (BOC 1999: 179). The BOC, in particular, was the leader of China's banking community by virtue of its size, history and prestige (Coble 1980). Through its quality publications, the *Bank of China Monthly*, *Financial Statistics Monthly*, *Yearbook of Banks in China*, it exercised a major voice in China's banking circles (ibid.).

From the beginning of the Nationalist government, there were tensions between the government and BOC. As early as 1930, when the BOC had already been reorganized into an international exchange bank, Chiang Kaishek invited T.V. Soong – Minister of Finance at that time – and Zhang Jia'ao to discuss an additional issuance of treasury bills. Zhang suggested that this matter should be handled by the Central Bank, and BOC should keep a distance from the government and concentrate on nurturing its reputation as a bank of international standing (BOC 1999: 54). In 1934, Zhang openly opposed Nanjing's policy of heavy deficit financing, arguing that 'The government should eliminate all unnecessary and wasteful expenditure, and apply savings so effectuated to a constructive policy for the increase of the country's productivity' (*BOCAR* 1932: 42). Moreover, what Zhang said or did had heavy influence on the Jiang-Zhe Bankers. By late 1934, the entire Jiang-Zhe Bankers' group began to back Zhang Jia'ao in a refusal to accept further government bonds (Coble 1980). Hence, Kaishek concluded that Zhang had no respect for the central leadership and sought to go his own way, and must be removed (ibid.).

In March 1935, H.H. Kung (also a brother-in-law of Chiang Kaishek), on behalf the government, suddenly announced that the government was taking control of BOC and BoCOM. Both institutions were ordered to increase their stocks and sell the majority control to the government. Before that time, the government held only 20 per cent of BOC stocks. The government now earmarked C$25 million of the new bond issue for purchasing new stocks in BOC, so that government shares could reach 60 per cent of BOC (BOC 1999). Meanwhile, a wide-ranging personnel change was announced even before the stockholders met (Coble 1980). Zhang Jia'ao, the general manager, and Li Ming, the chairman, were both dismissed. T.V. Soong would fill both posts.

BOC was shocked by the announcement, which was completely unexpected. Thereafter, Coble (1980: 172) called this reshuffle the 'banking coup'. The board of directors of the BOC voiced strong objections. But political pressure was so intense that they could not turn the tables. Zhang Jia'ao later wrote, 'Since the shareholders were perfectly satisfied with progress achieved under private management they would not have yielded to the government except under extreme duress' (Zhang Jia'ao 1958: 181).

The government later made some compromises to ease opposition. Instead of taking 60 per cent of BOC total capital stocks, the government now created an equal balance between private and government holdings (Table 3.3). This move, however, by no means restricted Nanjing's control. The government shares voted as a block, and the government promulgated new

Table 3.3 Change of capital and control in BOC, 1928–43

Year	Total capital (C$ million)	Government			Private			Chief executive
		Shares	Directors	Supervisors	Shares	Directors	Supervisors	
1928	25	20%	3	1	80%	12	4	Zhang Jia'ao
1935	40	50%	9	3	50%	12	4	T.V. Soong
1943	60	67%	13	5	33%	12	4	H.H. Kung

Source: BOC 1995: 384, 584, 838–42.

voting rules which limited the power of private shareholders (Coble 1980: 185). Those people holding less than ten shares, for instance, could not attend stockholder meetings. Consequently, many of the private shareholders were effectively disenfranchised (*Xinwenbao* 30 March 1935).

The government also compromised on the new position of Soong within the Bank. Soong would only become chairman of the board. The government appointed Song Hanzhang, one of the Jiang-Zhe Bankers, to be the new general manager (Coble 1980). Nonetheless, the responsibility of governing the Bank was shifted from the general manager to the chairman of the board, and the post of the general manager was changed from being elected by board members to be appointed by the chairman (BOC 1999). It was T.V. Soong who had real control of the Bank.

The shareholders' association elected a new board of directors, which were expanded from 15 to 21 members to include additional government appointees (BOC 1999). The board of supervisors was also expanded (see Table 3.3). With this reorganization, the Jiang-Zhe Bankers who had controlled the BOC for 17 years yielded their power to the Nationalist government. Meanwhile, BoCOM, the Shanghai Chamber of Commerce and the Shanghai Bankers Association (SBA) all fell into the hands of the government. Coble (1980: 3) commented, 'The capitalists were stymied as a political force, and by 1937, had become an adjunct of the government'.

In 1943, the Ministry of Finance once again increased government shares in BOC from C$20 million to C$40 million, and thus controlled 67 per cent of total BOC stock (BOC 1995: 584). Accordingly, the government directors and supervisors outnumbered their private counterparts (Table 3.3). The mandatory increase in government shares further weakened the power of the private shareholders, and demonstrated a continuation and deepening of Chiang Kaishek's monopolistic financial policy. H.H. Kung was appointed chairman under written orders from Chiang Kaishek (BOC 1999: 186), since T.V. Soong had already been appointed Minister of Foreign Affairs in the Nationalist government.

Decline of modern corporate governance

'The takeover of BOC was a death blow to the Jiang-Zhe Bankers. With a single stroke of brute political force, the government deprived the Jiang-Zhe Bankers of their largest bank' (Coble 1980: 182). The banking coup drastically changed the relationship between business and government. As Y.C. Wang (1966: 449) observed, 'Managers of the large Chinese banks had been the only business group that had important political influence, and their eclipse therefore signified not only complete government domination over the Chinese financial world, but also the end of the entrepreneurs as an independent pressure group'. Likewise, Chen Boda (1947: 5) commented, 'They [the Four Great Families] caused the original so-called "Zhejiang–Jiangsu financial clique" to dissolve and change into satellites of the four big families'.

Consequently, the modern and sound corporate governance established since the 1920s could no longer be exercised. One of the core issues was the growing party control of BOC. Zhang Jia'ao (1958) lamented that the leader of the party encouraged KMT members to occupy leading positions in the banking industry, and especially after 1948, the frequent reshuffles at the top of BOC showed that personnel appointments and dismissals were heavily controlled by party politics. As a result, BOC operated more like a political entity than a commercial one. The professionalism and operational independence emphasized by the Jiang-Zhe Bankers died out, and BOC became a tool in financing government deficits (*Guowen Zhoubao* 1 April 1935). As Zhang Jia'ao (1977: 49) pointed out, 'The government opinion contradicted my belief. The authorities snatched the Bank and used it as a national treasury. I, however, took the Bank as a bank.' Indeed, the controls of BOC 'provide an unlimited convenience to the national treasury in operating according to its needs' (Wu Chengxi 1936: 82).

Besides strong party control and the official nature of its business, the boards of directors and supervisors were now dominated by powerful extended family members. For example, among the government representatives in 1935's board of directors were T.V. Soong, T.L. Soong (the brother of T.V. Soong), Xi Demao (the father-in-law of T.L. Soong) (BOC 1995: 696) and Du Yuesheng, the leader of the underworld Green Gang, and a close friend of Chiang Kaishek (Pan 1984). Since authority was concentrated in a few closely related family members, the supervisory board's primary role of monitoring management on behalf of the shareholders became futile. No effective checks were exercised against frauds and self-seeking behaviour, and abuse of power was inevitable. As a result, BOC was subject to the personal desires of a small number of people. BOC rules and regulations were openly violated, the agency problem became serious and white-collar crimes became rampant (see Chapter 6). BOC was in decline day by day until it was finally taken over by the Communists.

Table 3.4 Summary of BOC's corporate governance and banking performance, 1905–49

Timeframe	Government	Characteristics of corporate governance	Banking performance
1905–11	Qing Dynasty	Rudimentary western corporate governance; Joint-stock limited liability company; Guandu Shangban system	Business grew; Largest bank in China with 35 branches
1912–27	Northern Warlord	Further development of corporate governance; Clear lines of responsibility and accountability	Improved efficiency and rapid business growth
1927–35	Nationalist government	Modern and sound corporate governance; Control by Jiang-Zhe Bankers	Strong and modern international bank; Serious contender to foreign rivals
1935–49	Nationalist government	Decline of modern corporate governance; Tool of deficit financing; No checks and balances; Abuse of power by top leaders	Declining business; Rampant financial crimes; Damaged reputation

Conclusion

Motivated by the presence and expansion of foreign banks, called upon by Chinese modern industrial enterprises, and inspired by nationalism, at the beginning of the twentieth century BOC came forth as the most important representative of modern banking in China. The evolution of BOC's corporate governance structure and its banking performance from 1905 until 1949 is summarized in Table 3.4.

From the outset, in reference to the western model, Daqing Bank was set up as a limited liability company, which distinguished it from the traditional financial institutions such as Qianzhuang and Piaohao, and laid a fundamental basis for a modern corporate structure. Here, the special Guandu Shangban system ensured the protection necessary for the development of a new industry, and helped make the Bank profitable and competitive.

The development of BOC during the early Warlord period showed one significant feature: the increasing power of private interests in the Bank. The turning point was BOC's successful rejection in 1916 of Yuan Shikai's order, which paved the way for the privatization of China's largest modern bank (Cheng 2003). Afterwards, BOC further developed its corporate governance structure, which set and enforced clear lines of responsibilities and accountability throughout the organization. BOC greatly improved its efficiency and enjoyed rapid business growth.

Under early Nationalist rulership, BOC had constructed a modern and effective corporate governance structure, the board of directors and supervisors, in particular, enjoyed a high reputation both at home and abroad. Professional and salaried managers took the chief responsibilities in the Bank, while a group of Jiang-Zhe Bankers had real control. Although compradors might have been pioneers on the path of China's modernization during the nineteenth century, BOC was, no doubt, the leader in the first half of the twentieth century in introducing and improving modern enterprise and corporate structure (Cheng 2003: 246). In parallel to this, the Bank's reputation and its financial strength continued to improve. BOC was 'capable of confronting the foreign banks in China', and began to 'represent China in taking up a decent position in the international financial arena' (BOC 1999: 129). Indeed, starting in 1930, BOC began to construct a 15-storey building on the Bund of Shanghai. It changed the pattern of the 'Foreigners' World' on the Bund, and demonstrated the status and strength of the Bank of China (BOC 1999: 60).

Under later Nationalist rule, the twice-forced reorganization, in 1935 and 1943, allowed the leadership of BOC to fall under the control of the government ruling clique. Basically, the government intended to eliminate the private bankers, seeing them as an obstacle to deficit spending and to the controlling of China's financial system. Sound corporate governance no longer existed. BOC was troubled with party control, conflicting objectives and the principal–agent problem. BOC degenerated into a tool of government deficit financing and the amassing of personal fortunes. Along with the decline of private entrepreneurship and modern corporate governance, BOC lost its previous vigour and momentum, and was finally taken over and reorganized by the Communists in 1949.

4 Government intervention

Introduction

Since Adam Smith, an invisible hand has been esteemed as a kernel of economic activity by mainstream economists, who believe that a market can adjust the supply and demand through the price mechanism and allocate resources in an optimal way; therefore, 'getting the price right' is essential. Mainstream economists blame past and present state interventions for most economic problems, and their solutions mainly centre on deregulation, free market-oriented reforms and minimizing the economic role of the state to that of a 'night-watchman' (Hayek 1941; Niskanen 1973; Krueger 1974; Posner 1975; Peacock 1979; Bhagwati 1982; Lal 1997).

However, as early as the 1930s, seeing the Great Depression as a market failure, Keynes (1936) began to challenge laissez-faire economics. By showing that the free market economy may not be able to achieve an optimal resource allocation at the full employment level of output, the Keynesian 'revolution' justified the new practice of active government fiscal policy to fight unemployment and business cycles. In fact, even the forefather of laissez-faire economics acknowledged the frequency with which market failure necessitated state intervention. In the well-known *Wealth of Nations*, Adam Smith pointed out the importance of state intervention on behalf of the interests of society where markets failed. In particular, in the last sentence of the following quotation, Smith emphasized that, as time changes, the degree of state intervention should change accordingly:

> The third and last duty of the government [apart from establishing peace and maintaining law and order] is that of erecting and maintaining those public institutions and those public works which, though they may be in the highest degree advantageous to a great society are, however, of such a nature, that the profit could never repay the expense to any individual or small number of individuals, and which it therefore cannot be expected that any individual or small number of individuals should erect or maintain. The performance of this duty requires too very different degrees of expense in the different periods of society.
>
> (Smith 1776 Vol. II: 310)

Indeed, due to the existence of an incomplete and imperfect market, asymmetrical information, public goods, production externalities, uncertainly and so on, market failure arises. Thus, it is necessary for the government to intervene to correct the failure. Also, the role of the state in economic life can be viewed from different perspectives. The famous infant industry argument (List 1885; Hamilton 1791) indicated that in the presence of more developed countries, backward countries cannot develop new industries without state intervention, especially the use of tariffs and subsidies. The 'Big Push' theory of industrialization accorded a crucial role to the state as the coordinator of complementary investment decisions (Rosenstein-Rodan 1943). Alexander Gerschenkron's (1962) late development thesis provided further justification of state intervention: as a country embarks on a developmental process later and later, it needs to raise relatively bigger and bigger amounts of savings, and therefore needs a powerful institution for industrial financing, the state being the most powerful such institution. According to H.-J. Chang (1999), the central functions of the developmental state go far beyond correcting for market failures in the conventional sense. The state has to play a number of important roles, namely, coordination of large-scale changes, provision of entrepreneurship vision, institutional building and conflict management.

Empirically, the success stories of East Asia after the the Second World War vividly demonstrated that state intervention actually worked well. In Japan, South Korea and Taiwan, the state played a vital role, in a wide variety of ways, in realizing rapid industrialization (Singh 1995). It pursued in each of these nations a vigorous and aggressive industrial policy to carry out the required structural transformation of the economy. The government 'guided' the market, instead of following a hands-off approach (Singh 1998; Wade 1990; Amsden 1989; Johnson, C. 1982). In fact, 'there is no industrial country in which government has failed to play an influential role in promoting and supporting economic change' (Panić 1995: 51). For example, in the nineteenth century, it was precisely with the 'special encouragement' and 'active help' of home governments that western banks built up their financial strength, expanded their influence, gained the privileges from Chinese government and developed a forceful momentum to enter, grow and expand in China (see Chapter 5). Even nowadays, quite a number of European governments regard the banking industry as being strategically important, and protect their domestic banks. Article 16 of the European banking directive was originally designed to safeguard the stability of national financial systems in M&A with banks from other EU member states (*The Banker* 5 December 2005). As a result, it gives national supervisors lots of room to veto a foreign takeover. Besides, some credit institutions' legal structures are very protective. For example, in Germany and Spain, savings banks are protected by law and cannot be acquired by banks (ibid.).

It is fair to say that, before 1949, the late Qing, the Northern Warlord and the Nationalist governments, to some extent, all devised an institutional framework favourable to the growth of BOC. Indeed, the governments directly promoted the business activities of BOC. For example, BOC was entrusted to handle treasury, to issue banknotes and was encouraged to explore the foreign trade business. The Nationalist government recovered a series of 'rights', with the result that western banks lost their former privileges and had their power weakened in China (see Chapter 5). Without government support and protection, it was impossible for BOC to achieve considerable financial success before 1935, or gain a favourable position to compete with foreign banks.

This is not to suggest, however, that the respective governments in China did a satisfactory job. '[T]he legitimacy of corporate business enterprise is the efficient provision of goods and services needed by the society, fuelled by the creation of surpluses to reward the investor and provide for reinvestment and growth' (Tricker 1984: 104). As a shareholding company, and as a bank with commercial business, during the process of providing the necessary services to the public and channeling the social savings to investment, safety, liquidity and profitability should be the major concerns of BOC managers. However, the chronic deficit of the Chinese government, the mounting military expenses, and bureaucratic self-seeking activities led to inappropriate governmental intrusion into BOC. This chapter mainly discusses the government intervention in BOC's major banking businesses at different historical phases. In particular, the KMT's excessive intervention finally led to economic disaster and speeded up regime collapse. However, since the same KMT exercised heavy intervention in Taiwan after 1949 with successful results, a comparison will be made at the end of the chapter to help understand the different interventions and divergent outcomes.

Government bond business

Except for the late Qing Court, both the Northern Warlord and KMT governments issued, for whatever reason, a huge number of bonds during their governance. As the biggest bank in China, BOC was deeply involved in government bonds. It was particularly in bond business that government intervention was heaviest.

Government bonds and BOC in the late Qing period

Although the Qing Court had been deeply troubled by its financial situation after the Taiping rebellion, it never made government bonds a major source of its revenue (Cheng 2003). The main reason was that China's financial market was not ready for public debts. More important, there was a long-held ideology: both officials and common people were used to the thought that 'there is nothing under heaven which does not belong to the emperor' (Cheng 2003: 106). It was hard to imagine that the Qing Court would borrow money from the public.

Government bonds and BOC during the Warlord era

However, with the ending of the Qing Dynasty and the establishment of the Republic (1912–1949), the situation was totally reversed. Only one week after its inauguration in Nanjing, Sun Yatsen's provisional government issued the first batch of bonds of C\$100 million (Qian 1984: 33–6). Soon, the Temporary Constitution of Republican China categorically stipulated that one of the Senate's powers was to take charge of the issuance of government bonds (Xu Cangshui 1923).

After Sun Yatsen, the financial situation of the Yuan Shikai government became more embarrassing. In the four months from September to December 1912 alone, the government's total expenditure was C\$70 million, while the total revenue was only C\$27 million, with the deficit reaching C\$43 million (BOC 1995: 73). Yuan Shikai's short-lived monarchy in 1916 resulted in political turbulence and endless civil wars. The central government's treasury was exhausted and had to rely on foreign and domestic debts. 'Almost every single item of the government expenditure depends on borrowings' (Cheng 2003: 108). The *Millard's Review of the Far East* once commented that 'China's minister of finance is merely a minister of borrowing' (Zhang Yulan 1957: 46).

From 1912 to 1925, the Warlord government issued bonds totalling C\$872 million (Table 4.1). The bonds were used largely for interregional war expenditures and maintaining the government treasury. The issue and repayment of bonds were originally the responsibilities of the Ministry of Finance, but after the establishment of the Bank of China, these functions were handed over to the latter.

At first, handling government bonds seemed an attractive business. Most government bonds had been sold through BOC and BoCOM. In general, the BOC could get 6 per cent commission for its services (Cheng 2003: 129). Before the bonds were sold to the public, BOC usually provided the government with cash advances at around 50 per cent of the bonds' face value. The BOC then listed the bonds on the stock exchange and offered them to investors, making the difference up to the government. Newly issued bonds were generally sold to investors at a discount of 50–70 per cent of face value, plus 6–7 per cent annual interest (Qian 1984: 26). Meanwhile, the government bonds could be used as reserves to note issue (BOC 1995: 42). Due to these reasons, besides handling bonds on behalf of the government, the BOC also kept a large amount of government bonds as investments, as most other banks did.

However, as time went on, China's chaotic political and economic situation backfired. Holding government bonds became a precarious business. While low credibility and a desperate demand for money forced the government to sell bonds at high discounts, these same reasons also led to delay and even cancellation of bonds payment (Cheng 2003). For example, the Beijing government sold part of the '6 per cent Bond (1912)' at prices as low as

Table 4.1 Domestic bonds issued by the Northern Warlord government, 1912–25 (C$ million)

Year	Bond name	Issuing amount	Purpose
1912	Patriotic Bond	30	Supplement to treasury
1912	8 per cent Military Bond	100	Military expenditure
1912	6 per cent Bond	200	Bank of China fund and others
1914	Domestic Bond	24	Adjustment of finance
1915	Domestic Bond	24	Land loans and others
1915	Savings Bond	10	Supplement to government expenditure
1916	Domestic Bond	20	Payment of government budget deficit
1918	Long-term Bond	45	Clearing BOC and BoCOM debts
1918	Short-term Bond	48	Clearing BOC and BoCOM debts
1919	7 per cent Bond	56	Supplement to budget
1919	Short-term Bond	40	Supplement to revenues
1920	Consolidated Finance	60	Consolidate finance
1920	Consolidated Bond	54	Consolidate domestic bonds and interest
1921	Relief Bond	4	Relief funds for North China
1921	8 per cent Bond	30	Clearing short-term bonds
1921	Vehicle Bond	6	Supplement to vehicles
1922	8 per cent short-term	10	Government emergency administrative funds
1922	8 per cent Treasury Bill	96	Payment of short-term bonds
1925	8 per cent Bond	15	Government emergency administrative funds
Total		**872**	

Source: Ji 2003: 106; Zhang Yulan 1957: 62.

40 per cent of its face value. If the principal and 6 per cent annul interest were to be paid on time, the bond could have yielded more than 60 per cent annually (Cheng 2003: 122). However, contrary to this great expectation, after payments of interest for several terms, the bond fell into arrears. Its market value sank to as low as 15 per cent of its face value. This was not an isolated case. The payment of the principal of the 'Domestic Bond (1916)' was delayed for five years (BOC 1995: 43).

In 1921, the government was compelled to reorganize the bonds, which was the first restructuring in China's Republican era. This reorganization designated bond payments at 30 per cent of their face value, and reduced the Beijing government's bond payments from C$39 million to C$24 million each year (Xu Cangshui 1923: 146). However, in order to pay back the former bonds at maturity, the government repeatedly issued new bonds, but continued to fall into arrears and plunged into a vicious cycle. Of the more than C$229 million in 13 bonds and treasury bills issued from 1918 to 1926, more than two-thirds, or C$153 million, were still outstanding by

1935 when most of these debts were long-term overdue (*Yinhang Zhoubao* 8 October 1935).

Although the Charter of BOC had been changed several times since its establishment, one article had always remained unchanged throughout its history, i.e. 'raising or collecting bonds for government' (BOC 1991a: 110–32). Restricted by this special requirement, although disappointed and upset with government's continuous default, BOC had little leeway to resist government bonds; even after 1917, BOC was almost entirely owned and run by private bankers. Statistics show that at the beginning of Warlord era, in 1913, the Bank held slightly more than C$36,000 worth of security holdings; at the end of the Warlord government, in 1927, its security holdings reached around C$20,000,000, about a 550 times increase over its 1913 figure (Cheng 2003: 130). It was assumed that two-thirds of the Bank's security holdings were government bonds (ibid.). Calculated from the data of Cheng (2003: 113–30), BOC bond holdings accounted for about 30 per cent of bond holdings of the 24 principal Chinese banks in 1927. Obviously, BOC was a major underwriter and distributor of government bonds.

Government bonds and BOC under the Nationalist government

During the Nationalist period, the government still could not balance its budget. To make things worse, the war against Japan (1937–45, hereafter the War) and the relentless wars with Communists further deteriorated the financial situation. The Nationalist government's annual deficits ran from C$73 million in 1927 to C$600 million in 1936 (Cheng 2003: 115), then to C$1,106,698 million in 1945, soaring to an alarming C$434,565,612 million in 1948 (Zhang Jia'ao 1958: 374).

In order to finance this expanding deficit, from 1927 to 1935 alone the Nationalist government issued altogether C$1,636 million-worth of bonds (Cheng 2003: 116), that is, C$182 million every year on average: much more than the amount issued by the Warlord government (C$872 million in total, or C$55 million annually on average) (Ji 2003: 106)

In the beginning, few Shanghai bankers regarded government bonds as a secure investment because they had little confidence about the new government. Coercion and strong-arm measures were employed by the government to force Shanghai banks to purchase bonds (Coble 1980). According to Seagrave (1985: 235), the government used soldiers and Green Gang thugs to force everyone from small shopkeepers to bank presidents to buy bonds. When one millionaire refused, his son was kidnapped. Journalist Sokolsky commented, 'Every form of persecution was resorted to on the pretext of hunting Communists. Men were kidnapped and forced to make heavy contributions to military funds . . . this anti-Communist terrorism has frightened the people of Shanghai and Jiangsu as nothing else in recent times' (*North China Daily News* (*NCDN*) 9 August 1927). Later, following Chiang Kaishek's direct orders, the Jiangsu Financial Commission apportioned quotas to various banks before the bonds were absorbed by the market (*Shenbao* 18 May 1927). BOC, controlling one-fourth of all Chinese banking resources and being the biggest bank in China, was often ordered to take the largest share, about 30 per cent amongst the major banks (BOC 1995: 249). In 1928, BOC held C\$21,000 of securities, accounting for 2.5 per cent of BOC's total assets; three years later, in 1931, the holdings leapt to C\$48,000, 5.7 per cent of BOC's total assets (Cheng 2003: 130).

For a long time, a commonly accepted view among both Chinese and western scholars claimed that Chinese banks' expansion 'resulted from the close relationship between banks and the government', because modern Chinese banks earned a 'high interest by issuing government loans and purchasing government bonds at considerable discounts' (Wang Yeh-chien 1981: 76–7). Zhang Yulan (1957) declared that modern Chinese banks developed simply by speculating in government bonds. Tamagna (1942: 45) pointed out that 'the rapid growth of Chinese modern banks was connected with government financing'. Contrary to the above claims, Cheng (2003) argued that Chinese modern banks actually suffered considerable losses from bond business. Take BOC as an example: between 1921 and 1930, BOC's returns of its security holdings and other sources were listed separately and always recorded in red ink, except for the year 1930 (Cheng 2003: 130). Surprisingly, the Bank's total loss on securities was twice as much as its net profit during the same period. 'In 1927, the loss on securities reached C\$4.6 million, which was more than general expenses and gave the Bank a net loss for the first time in its history' (Cheng 2003: 131). On the whole, the Bank lost more than C\$10 million on its security investment during this decade (ibid.).

Worse yet, in 1932, due to the Japanese invasion of Manchuria and the attack on Shanghai, the prices of major government bonds in Shanghai dramatically dropped 50 per cent in only five months (Cheng 2003: 122). Shanghai's exchange market was forced to close for more than three months. The banks had held government bonds both for investment and as a reserve to cover their banknotes, and had made loans to individuals secured on government bonds. The 50 per cent decline of bond prices was a grave blow to the Shanghai banks. Nevertheless, faced with the prospect of default, the banks were forced to accept a reorganization of the debt in February 1932. This was the second restructuring in the Republic of China, and first under the Nationalist government. This consolidation reduced interest payments to a fixed 6 per cent and extended amortization periods to roughly double their former length (Feuerwerker 1995: 165). Although the plan entailed heavy losses for the bankers, they had little alternative but to accept the proposal. The bond reorganization also contained a pledge that the new conditions were unalterable and that no further reduction would ever be made (Soong 1932). It was widely reported that Soong, in addition to the public pledges, had made a verbal promise that no new bonds would be issued for the coming four years (Coble 1980: 107).

However, from 1930 to 1933, Nanjing carried out five large-scale extermination campaigns against the Communist Red Army in Jiangxi and the military expenditures skyrocketed. The budget deficit of the government in 1933 reached C$12 million per month (Chen Tingyi 2004a: 218). Nanjing devised new methods to pressure bankers to purchase government bonds (Coble 1980). In July 1934, for example, the government promulgated the Savings Bank Law, which required all savings banks to purchase government bonds or approved securities equivalent to one-fourth of their total deposits (BOC 1937). Since savings departments of commercial banks were regulated by the Savings Bank Law (Tamagna 1942), this regulation would have inordinately interfered with the banks' internal business. Shanghai bankers strongly opposed this law. However, the government continued to exert pressure and ordered all banks to reveal the names, addresses and balances of depositors with accounts in excess of C$2,000 (Coble 1980: 171). Neither of these two laws was fully implemented. Nonetheless, their possible promulgation was another potent weapon at the government's disposal to pressure bankers into become obedient. As a result, bankers had to absorb bonds to please the government.

However, there was an exception. BOC became increasingly upset with government bonds. The general manager, Zhang Jia'ao, who always advocated the operational independence of banks, argued that BOC resources were being drained away by the government bonds. He further suggested that 'The government should eliminate all unnecessary and wasteful expenditure, and apply savings so effectuated to a constructive policy for the increase of the country's productivity' (*BOCAR* 1932: 42). In the words of Seagrave, 'This maverick banker was now saying: Japan was the real enemy, too much money was being squandered on the army's Communist suppression campaigns, and Nanjing bonds were worthless' (Seagrave 1985: 324).

In a final attempt to save BOC's independence, Zhang Jia'ao fought back by dumping BOC's holdings of government bonds. BOC's holdings of securities declined from C$72 million in 1931 to C$25 million in 1934, a drop of over 60 per cent (Table 4.2).

This divestment of government bonds appeared a conscious move to gain operational independence from Nanjing and was an open challenge to the government's bond policy. In the latter half of 1934, the entire cadre of the Jiang-Zhe Bankers began to back BOC in its resistance to accepting further government bonds (Coble 1980). This apparently enraged Nanjing and directly triggered the Banking Coup of 1935, as discussed in Chapter 3. This was a very significant event in China's banking history. The government deprived the Jiang-Zhe Bankers of their largest bank. Zhang Jia'ao was expelled once and for all.

Afterwards, the government had complete domination over China's financial world, and there were no more barriers to deficit-financing policy. The government continued issuing bonds, and BOC's security holdings increased rapidly after 1935 (also Table 4.2). However, the government had the second

Table 4.2 Security holdings of the Bank of China, 1927–37 (C$ million)

Year	Total amount	Ratio in principal Chinese banks (%)	Ratio in BOC assets (%)
1927	29.97	28.37	5.68
1928	32.60	25.83	5.48
1929	33.21	23.41	4.96
1930	65.09	29.28	8.42
1931	72.02	30.10	8.51
1932	64.54	27.10	8.02
1933	32.02	30.98	8.99
1934	25.36	18.99	8.80
1935	33.83	17.38	7.70
1936	31.18	32.30	9.40
1937	50.09	n/a	13.00

Source: BOC 1995: 249.

bond reorganization in 1936, which was the third in the Republican era. This time, the government consolidated more than thirty bonds into five and once again extended amortization schedules. This not only overthrew the promise of 1932, but also the government did not consult the banking community beforehand (Hong 2004: 39). The bankers were furious at the government's plan. But, the government apparently had the Green Gang leaders Du Yuesheng and Zhang Xiaolin impose pressure on bankers (Coble 1980). At a meeting of the Shanghai Bankers Association attended by both Du and Zhang, the bankers quietly accepted the government's proposal (Qian 1984). 'It was Chiang's alliance with the Green Gang that gave him this unprecedented control over Shanghai' (Coble 1980: 36).

In the following years, the government didn't slow down bond issuing. The various bonds floated by the government from 1937 to 1945 are shown in Table 4.3.

The year 1938 marked the beginning of the banks' paying advances to the government before the banks released government bonds to the public, regardless of their marketability, a practice that was to be repeated year after year (Zhang Jia'ao 1958). Arthur Young, American Financial Adviser to China from 1929 to 1947, summarized that of the total issues, which amounted to about US$280 million at the exchange rates of 1945, only the equivalent of about US$20 million, or about 7 per cent, was sold to the public (Young 1965: 80). The rest was compulsory allocated to the government banks. Accordingly, during the same period, BOC's security holdings jumped from C$50 million in 1937 to C$2,893 million in 1945 (BOC 1995: 913). On the other hand, the Nationalist government consistently had difficulty in paying off the bonds. Starting in February 1939, the government stopped paying principals and interest, citing the war with Japan as the excuse. After the War, the government, in 1946, agreed to liquidate bonds, but based on

Table 4.3 Wartime government bond issues, 1937–45

Year	Loan	Total issue (million)		Public subscriptions (million)	
1937	National Liberty Bonds	C$	500		
	Guangxi currency adjustment loan	C$	17	C$	256
1938	National Defence Loan	C$	500		
	Gold loan	C.G.U.	100*		
	Relief Loan	£	10		
		US$	50		
		C$	30	C$	18
1939	Military Supply Loan	C$	600		
	Reconstruction Loan	C$	600	C$	24
1940	Military Supply Loan	C$	1,200		
	Reconstruction gold loan	£	10		
		US$	50	C$	7
1941	Military Supply Loan	C$	1,200		
	Reconstruction Loan	C$	1,200	C$	127
1942	Allied Victory American gold loan	US$	100		
	Allied victory loan	C$	1,000		
				C$	362
1943	Allied Victory Loan	C$	3,000	C$	3,886
	Readjustment Loan	C$	175		
1944	Allied Victory Loan	C$	5,000	C$	1,988
1945				C$	62,823
		C$	15,022	C$	69,495
Total		£	20		
		US$	200		
		C.G.U.	100		

Note: *C.G.U. Customs Gold Unit; one C.G.U. equals C$20.

Source: Zhang Jia'ao 1958: 149.

the prewar book value (Hong 1990). With the escalating inflation – the price index of August 1945 in Shanghai was 86,400 times that of January 1937 (Hong 2001: 344) – this kind of clearing of debts was, de facto, a repudiation.

In a nutshell, respective Chinese governments heavily intervened in BOC bond business and, in most cases, BOC was pressured to buy bonds to finance government budget deficit. This is by no means to suggest that BOC did not benefit at all from government bonds (Cheng 2003: 135). A consideration of all the facts, however, indicates that because of the unstable political and economic environment, and due to the government's several bond reorganizations and defaults, bond business did not bring about the assumed profits, but imposed a burden on the Bank. It was mainly due to the BOC's disobedience in bond policy that the general manager Zhang Jia'ao was expelled and the Bank seized by the government.

Note issue

From its birth in 1905 until 1943, BOC held the privilege of issuing banknotes. 'Bank notes were a profitable source of funds if they could be kept in
circulation' (Cleveland 1985: 13). However, to maintain a bank's liquidity and
security, note issue must be kept moderate and be backed by sufficient
reserves, no matter whether the note is convertible or not. Before 1949 various
governments tended to intervene in BOC's note issue, which led to inflation,
bank-runs and even some economic and political disasters.

Note issue of BOC in the late Qing period

Following its establishment in 1905, Daqing Bank was given an authority to
issue banknotes. At that time the paper notes issued by banks were convertible notes. The note holders could at any time cash silver at issuing banks.
Therefore, without sufficient silver reserves, banks could get into trouble
(Li Xuewen 1998). Daqing Bank exercised cautious note issues. Until the end
of the Qing Dynasty, the Bank had twelve banknote issues, totalling 68
million taels (Kong 1991: 182). In general, the Bank's silver reserves were
much higher than 50 per cent of its note issue, the minimum required by
the government, and the Bank was in a good position to cash notes without
the danger of currency depreciation and bank-runs. As a result, the Bank's
notes enjoyed increasing popularity. In particular, its tael notes were the only
paper money accepted by foreign banks (Tamagna 1942).

Even though Daqing Bank had sensible note issues, in China's modern
history, 'the leaders of the government, whether politicians or Warlords,
conservative or revolutionary, seldom gave up the belief that the government
could spend more than its income simply by increasing the note issue' (Zhang
Jia'ao 1958: 3). In fact, the petition sent by the Board of Revenue to the
Emperor in March 1905 suggested that the Bank of the Board of Revenue
(subsequently to become Daqing Bank) was founded with this belief in mind:

> The Bank is the key to finance and the note issue the key to the Bank.
> In western countries, notes are issued in normal time to collect and
> accumulate gold and silver. In times of emergency the government can
> obtain money from the Bank, which the public will accept because of its
> confidence in the notes.
>
> (Zhang Jia'ao 1958: 3)

Note issue of BOC during the Warlord era

The philosophy contained in the above statement became widely accepted by
policy-makers throughout the Republican period (Zhang Jia'ao 1958). Due
to financial difficulties, from the very beginning fiscal advances became an
obvious problem. Every month, before the Ministry of Finance received tax

revenues, it required BOC to make advances. At the end of month, more often than not, government expenditure was bigger than income, so advances became short-term borrowings, which later became long-term borrowings. At the end of 1915, advances made by BOC totalled C$12.04 million (BOC 1995: 74), almost equal to the paid-in capital of the Bank. Since Yuan Shikai was determined to become an emperor, the government compelled BOC to advance more money to fund this monarchial movement. BOC had no choice but to issue banknotes without cash reserves. According to government regulations, issuing banks had to retain at least 50 per cent silver reserve against the banknotes they issued (BOC 1995: 55). By May 1916, the total note issue of BOC nationwide was about C$40 million, but total silver reserves were only C$9.78 million (BOC 1995: 77). That is to say, the ratio of silver reserve was only 24 per cent. BOC was in a highly vulnerable position.

When the public got the news of BOC's reserves drying up, the market quickly responded. BOC banknotes depreciated to 80 per cent of their face value in Beijing (BOC 1995: 79). In Shanghai, the whole city was filled with panic and disturbance. Some people were worried that BOC banknotes might become waste paper, while some feared that banknotes issued by other smaller banks were riskier. In many money shops, a premium of 10 cents, 20 cents or even more had to be paid to exchange C$1 paper money for 1 silver coin (ibid.: 76). The whole market became chaotic and lots of transactions and dealings were suspended.

In a desperate attempt to collect silver stocks for the government, BOC was ordered to cease the encashment of banknotes in 1916 (BOC 1995). The BOC Shanghai branch, which was the biggest and most important BOC branch, rebelled courageously against the government order and decided to continue redeeming the banknotes in order to maintain the credibility of the Bank. But it was easier said than done. May 12 was the most panic-struck day in Shanghai's financial history, and a big bank-run erupted. At 8 o'clock in the morning, more than 2,000 people packed into the three main roads in front of the BOC Shanghai branch. According to the accounts written by then deputy manager Zhang Jia'ao (BOC 1991a: 296), 'People pushed against each other, broke into doors and climbed up windows, disregarding their safety. The situation was chaotic and crazy. Some people only held several banknotes with denomination of C$1 or C$5, some with one deposit certificate of C$200 or C$300'. The shop apprentices came to queue for their bosses, some rich men carrying money from Zhejiang, even Anhui, Jiangxi and Hubei provinces, desperately exchanged banknotes for silver (Li Tiangang 2005). The following two days were Saturday and Sunday, and the bank-run persisted. BOC Shanghai asked for an overdraft from the foreign banks, using BOC premises and the Suzhou River warehouse and other title deeds as collateral. On 14 May, the Shanghai Foreign Banks Association decided to allow BOC to overdraw its credit of C$2 million (BOC 1995: 78). HSBC, Chartered Bank, and a total of ten foreign banks participated in the scheme. This news gave the market confidence, and the panic withdrawal calmed

Table 4.4 Note issue of BOC during the Northern Warlord government, 1912–27 (C$ million)

Year	Note issue	Remarks
1912	1.06	
1913	5.02	
1914	16.39	
1915	38.45	
1916	46.43	
1917	72.98	
1918	52.17	Irredeemable notes: 24.94
1919	61.68	21.98
1920	66.88	10.91
1921	62.49	6.57
1922	77.77	6.19
1923	80.99	5.97
1924	89.98	5.89
1925	127.00	5.83
1926	137.00	4.19
1927	159.00	16.78
Total	**1095.29**	**109.25**

Source: BOC 1995: 58.

down before BOC actually had to use this overdrawing facility. Due to the bank-run, 1.6 million of silver dollar reserves were taken out within a few days (BOC 1995: 78; Hong 2004: 138). The bank-run had a seriously adverse impact on the reputation of BOC. The market price of BOC shares fell from C$100 per share to C$70 and the preparation for opening the Singapore branch was suspended (BOC 1995: 102).

In the following years, the government continued to press BOC to make advances. By the end of 1925, the total accumulated advances of BOC to the government reached C$23 million, accounting for 78 per cent of the total advances of all banks (BOC 1995: 57). Consequently, the note issue had continued to grow at a rapid rate. As shown in Table 4.4, in 1912, banknotes with a total face value of C$1.06 million were issued. The note issue of 1927 was C$159 million, almost 150 times of that in 1912. Worse yet, because of the political turmoil and Warlord extortions, from time to time some BOC branches ran out of reserves, and banknotes became irredeemable (also see Table 4.4). Not surprisingly, in Beijing and other areas, the market value of BOC banknotes often declined to 60–70 per cent of their face value (Yao Songling 1982: 35). This not only adversely affected the credibility of BOC, but also led to market chaos and widespread public complaints.

Note issue of BOC under the Nationalist government

Under the Nationalist government, with the creation of the Central Bank in 1928, BOC expressed its willingness to give up the right of issue and to withdraw its notes from circulation as soon as the government had paid back the outstanding balance of its advances, along with that owed to BoCOM, amounting to C$100 million, or no less than 42 per cent of their combined note circulation (Zhang Jia'ao 1958: 176). The government, however, could not clear its debts with the two banks; furthermore, it was unwilling to lose two sources of money supply. Thus, no change was made in the situation and BOC continued to issue notes as before.

Theoretically, issuing banknotes is like taking zero-interest deposits, hence it is profitable to the bank. However, BOC understood that 'The water can carry a boat; meanwhile, it can overturn a boat' (BOC 1995: 229). Before 1935, BOC private shareholders gained a controlling power and exercised a prudent policy on note issue. The government law stipulated that issuing banks had to provide a 100 per cent reserve against the banknotes they issued, with 60 per cent held in metals and 40 per cent in guaranteed securities (BOC 1995: 227). BOC opened up its reserves once a month to the authorities and the public for examination (BOC 1995). From 1927 to 1934, the annual note issue was around C$200 million, the annual increase was 4 per cent and the notes had sufficient reserves (ibid.: 229). At the same time, among the total note issues of government banks, the ratio of BOC declined year by year, from 71 per cent in 1927 to 50.76 per cent in 1934 (ibid.). This is explained by BOC's practical move to focus on commercial business and hand over the right of issue to the Central Bank.

In 1935, the government unexpectedly increased the shares in BOC and made BOC a government-controlled bank. At the same time, because of the wild swings in the price of silver, Nanjing planned to abandon the silver standard and carry out currency reform throughout the country. From November 1935, notes issued by the Central Bank of China, BOC and BoCOM, as well as, later, the Farmers Bank, became legal tender (fabi). Unlike previous banknotes, legal tender notes were inconvertible (*Shishi Xinbao* 4 November 1935).

Rawski (1989: 168) commented that 'In the wake of the 1935 reform, China's monetary system was well along the path toward a managed currency of the sort familiar in the industrial world'. For the first time in China's history, there was a uniform monetary accounting unit; without doubt, this was a significant progress. But, on the other hand, there appeared potential dangers. Without effective measures of financial constraint, it was impossible to prevent the government from depreciating the value of the currency through excessive borrowing and uncontrolled note issue (Zhang Jia'ao 1958).

The apprehension became real. Japan's invasion of China in 1937 forced the Nanjing to retreat to the interior, depriving the government of its rich coastal revenue base while simultaneously generating increased demands for higher wartime expenditure. The proportion of military spending in total government expenditure increased from 36 per cent before the War to 66 per cent during 1937 8, and shot up to 78 per cent in 1940 (BOC 1995: 445). The tax revenues could only finance 6 per cent of the total government expenditure (ibid.: 446). Except for the relatively negligible revenue from the sales of bonds to the public, the government deficit was financed from government bank advances, which caused a persistent rise in the issuing of notes (Zhang Jia'ao 1958). From time to time, government banks were threatened with the revocation of their charters or the withdrawal of government support in the event of a bank-run if they refused to comply with government demands for credit (ibid.). In fact, the increase in currency issues by BOC was closely correlated to its advances to the government. Advances to the government by the Bank between 1937 and the first half of 1942 aggregated C$6,815 million (about 60 per cent of which were advances for military expenditure), as can be seen in Table 4.5. During the same period, the increase in note issue totalled C$6,338 million, about 93 per cent of the advances in aggregate. The remaining 7 per cent of advances to government was financed by increasing customer deposits in BOC.

The excessive note issue was problematic. Alfred Marshall (1923: 38) wrote that the total value of an inconvertible paper currency could not be increased by increasing its quantity; and increase in its quantity, if being repeated, would lower the value of each unit 'more than in proportion to the increase already made'. American financial advisor Arthur Young criticized the KMT government on this matter. In a memorandum in 1941 to Chiang Kaishek, Young stated that:

> [B]y far the greatest cause of the price difficulty is the heavy issue of fabi as the result of financing the war mainly by borrowing from the four government banks. The remedies therefore have to be sought chiefly in

Table 4.5 BOC note issues and advances to the government, 1937–42 (C$ million)

Year	Note issue	Increased note issue compared to previous year	BOC advances to government		
			BOC advances (1)	Among (1), military advances	BOC advances as a percentage of total bank advances (%)
1937	617	107[a]	128	77	10.67
1938	711	94	440	264	51.77
1939	1,227	516	754	452	32.64
1940	1,947	720	1,267	760	33.08
1941	4,349	2,402	2,937	1,762	31.11
1942[b]	6,848	2,499	1,289	773	n/a
Total	**15,699**	**6,338**	**6,815**	**4,088**	

Notes:
a: compared with the note issue at the end of June 1937. The aggregate note issue from January to June 1937 was C$10 million.
b: end of July, 1942.

Source: BOC 1995: 446 and 453.

the strictest possible measures to control the further growth of fabi
issues.

(Young 1965: 56)

However, the government could not control the note issues. Basically, as
Chiang Kaishek said, 'The military expenses must be guaranteed' (Cheng
Tingyi 2004a: 196). It was not wrong to incur military expenditure, since the
government needed to put down ambitious Warlords and the Communists, as
well as arm against Japanese aggression. But the point was that the money
was not well spent. China supported too many troops with little fighting
value. With the increase in size went a decrease in efficiency (Young 1965;
Zhang Jia'ao 1958). Furthermore, military expenditure was never brought
under proper fiscal control. High-level officials purchased military supplies
from abroad with big kick-backs (Qiu 2004). Commanders of units withheld
pay from their troops, sold military equipment provided for them, and
collected the wages of nonexistent men (Pei and Wei 1997). With escalating
military expenses, the Nationalist Army seriously lacked training, leadership,
weapons and morale.

On the other hand, the printing-press approach to government spending
yielded the worst inflation of China's modern history. In 1942, the note issues
of four government banks were 24 times those of prewar 1937, but the price
index in Shanghai increased by 50 times (Hong 2004: 238–9). After July 1942,
the right of issue was concentrated on the Central Bank. In late 1948, the fabi
was replaced by a new gold yuan at an exchange rate of 3,000,000 fabi to 1
gold yuan. However, the issuance of gold yuan once again went out of control and soon the notes became waste paper. According to authoritative
statistics, the note issue in May 1949 was 140 billion times that of June 1937,
and the price index in Shanghai approached 36 trillion times during the
corresponding period (Hong 2004: 236).

The galloping inflation severely affected BOC business. Although the
account ledgers for deposits, loans and remittances registered unusual growth
as a result of runaway inflation, the Bank's business operations were under
constraint in many ways. For example, in those years, demand deposits
accounted for over 97 per cent of the Bank's total deposits (BOC 1999: 205).
Deposits and withdrawals were made at such frequency that it was impossible
to apply the funds to lending. Also, huge amounts of overseas Chinese remittances flowed into the black market or else fled to Hong Kong. As a result,
overseas Chinese remittances handled by the Bank dropped yearly. Taking
the remittances received in 1945 of 30.84 million US dollars as 100 per cent,
the figures were respectively 76.50 per cent in 1946, 26.50 per cent in 1947 and
23.20 per cent in 1948 (BOC 1999: 208). After the gold yuan became widely
refused, silver coins, foreign currency, or even barter trade became popular.
The Bank's business in deposits, loans and remittances could in no way be
carried on. Hyperinflation, along with the rampant black market and the
flight of capital, paralysed BOC business.

Worse yet, hyperinflation lost the government its public support. Students went on strike. Workers organized a union to join with the students. Even the middle-class citizens (who, as members of the capitalist class, presumably had most to fear from the Communists) had likewise abandoned hope in the KMT (Eastman 1984: 3). In 1947, about 6,000 bank employees (including most of the middle-level managers, who were regarded as holding 'golden rice bowls') declared a hunger strike (BOC 1995: 730–1). Shen Yunlong (1979: 42), one of Taiwan's leading scholars wrote: 'After only forty days, the value of the gold yuan plummeted to the extent that it became worthless scrap paper. The wealth of tens of millions of people suddenly went up in smoke. This heavily affected people's morale and the fate of the nation, and was the chief reason for the loss of the mainland.' With more and more people becoming resentful and disillusioned, KMT rule was doomed to failure.

In conclusion, respective governments' incessant borrowings from BOC resulted in reckless note issue. Excessive note issue shocked public confidence, triggered bank-runs, impacted badly upon BOC's reputation and weakened the Bank's financial strength. Eventually, the hyperinflation in the late 1940s plunged BOC and the whole economy into panic, instigated political movement and brought about regime change.

Policy loans and other special business

One of the major functions of a commercial bank is to accumulate and channel social savings to industrial and commercial establishments. Managing loans was a major part of BOC's business. As with bonds and note issue, governments interfered in the loan operation. This was most obvious under the Nationalist government.

Policy loans

In September 1939, the government decreed 'An Outline of Measures for Reinforcing the National Financial Institutions', and ordered the four government banks to form a joint head office to handle special business operations related to the government's wartime financial and economic policies (CAB 1993). In fact, this scheme later also covered the Central Trust Bureau, the Postal Savings and Remittance Bureau, and the Central Cooperative Treasury (Hong 2001). Chiang Kaishek, in the capacity of chairman of the board of the Farmers Bank of China, assumed the chairmanship of the Joint Head Office. Other important figures of the KMT, also relatives of Chiang, like Kung and Soong, were appointed managing directors of the new organization. The Joint Head Office was given extensive power, ranging from wartime finance to every important aspect of economic policy. As a result, the Joint Head Office became a key decision-making organization and an administrative agency overriding the four government banks, directing and manipulating them, especially with regard to the loan business. Essentially, nothing is wrong with government intervention in bank loan practice, if it is for the purpose of economic development, for industrial policy, or for wartime necessity. But loans should be divided into commercial and policy loans. The government indeed established some special banks (policy banks) for particular purposes. However, banking specialization never advanced in China and all banks generally transacted any type of business (Tamagna 1942: 168). As a result, BOC shouldered the responsibility of both commercial and policy loans. The conflicting objectives obviously distorted manager incentives and confused BOC's performance targets. In December 1940, the deputy chief auditor, Huo Baoshu, on behalf of BOC, attended the Joint Head Office meeting. Later he wrote, 'Among business instructed by Joint Head Office, we are eager to do those which comply with BOC regulations and for BOC benefits. But some business is incompatible with BOC principles, although I tried my best, due to the current situation, I had no way to resist. I apologize for this and ask for punishment . . .' (BOC 1995: 575).

Supposing that all loans to state enterprises were policy-oriented, the ratio of policy loans of the four government banks was no less than 54.8 per cent (Hong 1990: 310). Loans to SOEs were not bad per se, but many loans went towards poorly-performing enterprises. Why the SOEs performed so badly at that time is a complicated issue and goes beyond the scope of this study. Basically, as Coble (1980: 8) correctly summarized, 'Chiang's relatives directed most of the economic programmes and often used their official position for private gain. Government-established enterprises frequently suffered from poor management and over-staffing'. Since it was subordinate to the Joint Head Office, BOC had no option but to support state enterprises. For example, BOC was ordered to undertake special foreign exchange loans and advances to support enterprises affiliated with the National Resource Commission (NRC) directly under Chiang. In 1947, BOC made loans of US$5 million to the Taiwan Sugar Co., which was co-run by NRC and the Taiwan Provincial Government (BOC 1995: 672). Although being reorganized on the basis of four well-functioning Japanese companies, the Taiwan Sugar Co. was problematic (Chen Zhen 1961a: 904–5). First, it was overstaffed. The total fixed staff of the company and four subsidiary sugar factories was as high as 23,200 people. Even so, during the peak sugar-making season every year, lots of temporary workers were also employed. The sugar-making periods for various factories varied from half a month to five months. During the rest of the year, the fixed staff became idle. But they received a good salary for 12 months, as well as allowances and subsidies. Second, it suffered from bad management. The sugar company did not adopt a modern management style with carefully defined job responsibilities and work flows. The businesses of the four factories overlapped and the decision-making and implementation mechanisms were rigid and time-consuming. Third, it was guilty of huge waste. Machinery and equipment were scattered here and there, without proper records being kept. Furthermore, they were not properly maintained or repaired, but were subject to erosion by wind and rain (ibid.: 1457). Due to overstaffing, confusing management and huge waste, the performance of the company was poor. Under Japanese rule, the annual sugar output was originally 1,200,200 tons, but with more people and higher costs, under the KMT, the actual sugar output fell to only 123,000 tons (ibid.: 1459).

Another telling example was the China Textile Corporation (CTC). Under the direction of the Ministry of Economic Affairs, actually under premier T.V. Soong, CTC was one of the biggest state enterprises after the Sino-Japanese war, and held a monopoly position in producing cotton yarn and cloth in China's market (Feuerwerker 1995). CTC was supplied with ample working capital by BOC and received preferential treatment in the allocation of foreign exchange for the purchase of raw cotton. For example, in December 1947, the BOC opened a Letter of Credit of more than 1 million Indian Rupees for CTC under barter trade, which represented about 20 per cent of this kind of business in that month (BOC 1991c: 2362). In 1948, BOC provided a Letter of Credit and made advances of US$10 million to CTC to buy American and Brazilian cotton (BOC 1995: 672). However, the operation and efficiency of CTC was not satisfactory. Feuerwerker (1995: 107) commented that:

> the CTC mills had a definite advantage over the private mills – a position analogous to that of the Japanese cotton mills in China whose heirs they were; except that the Japanese were more efficient. The CTC management looked primarily for short-term profits, for themselves and for the KMT government.

In 1948, the *Xingqiwu Huabao* (5 January 1948) published an article criticizing CTC: 'The China Textile Corporation suffered consecutive losses . . . because the high level officials were running this big enterprise. They recruit many relatives and friends, who know nothing about spinning and weaving. With promotion, they hold posts without adequate qualifications. Meanwhile, they get a good salary. This, of course, wastes a huge amount of money . . .' (Chen Zhen 1961a: 905). On the other hand, capable technicians and textile experts had no opportunities for employment (*Zhengyibao* 16 July 1947). On another occasion a bulb factory director complained about the low efficiency of state enterprises: 'In running a private bulb factory, 22 employees could produce 10,000 bulbs. Now in this state factory, with 70 staff, only 3,500 bulbs are produced' (ibid.: 1451). In other words, the staff tripled, but the output reduced by two-thirds. These were enterprises that BOC was instructed to serve. The loans provided by BOC were of large amounts, with long maturity and low interest. Especially with the sharp depreciation of currency, most loans in fact became free gifts or subsidies.

Special business

Besides policy loans, BOC was commanded to handle special business to support the civil war. For example, following directives from the Joint Head Office, in 1946 BOC purchased grain in Hankou, Changsha, Hangzhou and Lanchang to the value of C$20.4 billion; in 1947 BOC purchased grain in Hankou and Hangzhou totalling C$8.2 billion; and in 1948 BOC bought basic necessities and steel, cement and machinery, etc. totalling C$160.1 billion (BOC 1995: 673–4). Here, BOC Shanghai, Chongqing, Tianjin, Beijing and Qingdao were all involved.

In other words, under Nationalist rule, especially after the Joint Head Office was established, BOC was subject to the strict intervention of the government in loan practice. Funds were directed towards inefficient and politically connected SOEs. What's more, BOC was instructed to carry out quite a number of special businesses, which were certainly not within the Bank's business scope, but were forced upon the Bank to support the civil war. Heavy government intervention definitely distracted BOC from its normal operation, and had an adverse impact on its profit-making capability.

Local government intervention

Regardless of whether it was in the Qing Dynasty, the Northern Warlords or KMT periods, local governments or regional Warlords were an ambitious and influential force, both politically and militarily. Since the BOC branches were situated in areas administrated by these local powers, local governments and Warlords interfered in BOC business, and conveniently used BOC as a cash cow through all kinds of borrowings.

Local government borrowings in the late Qing period

Following the establishment of Daqing Bank, local governments often turned to the Bank for money. Ideally, the viceroy set up a contract with the Bank, submitted a report to the Ministry of Finance, specified a type of local income, such as the salt tax as security, and paid back principal and interest over the following years (Kong 1991).

Hall (1917) noted that in 1906 the leadership of the Daqing Bank favourably impressed the business community in China by its firm refusal to lend to the viceroy of the Liang-Guang provinces without security. However, in most cases it was impossible to resist local government pressure. The *History of Daqing Bank* revealed many previously unknown details (Kong 1991: 89–101).

In 1907 the Liang-Jiang viceroy borrowed 4.50 million taels to repair the Huangpu River; in 1908 the same viceroy borrowed 400,000 taels to finance the autumn military exercise; the viceroy of Northeastern provinces borrowed 400,000 taels to repay external debts; the Liang-Jiang viceroy in 1909 borrowed another 200,000 taels; and the Hu-Guang viceroy borrowed 200,000 taels for famine relief; in 1910, the Hunan government borrowed 200,000 taels for repaying external debts; Anhui borrowed 200,000 taels for a local mine lawsuit; and Fujian borrowed 800,000 taels for administrative expenses; and so on. During the revolution against the Qing Court, the Jiangxi provincial government, in the name of clearing up finance, took over 800,000 taels from Daqing Bank which it never returned (Kong 1991: 360).

At the end of the Qing Dynasty, when Daqing Bank straightened out its accounts, it found that the overdue debts from private business was only 15 million taels, but from local governments the debt was as high as 18 million taels, compared with 5 million taels from central government (Kong 1991: 342). The huge local borrowing imposed a heavy burden on BOC operations.

Local government borrowings during the Warlord era

The situation in the Warlord era became even worse. 'The age of the Warlords was a period of general insecurity and exploitation' (Bergère 1986: 218). The Warlords believed that banks had ready money and were the best target for extortion (Yang Peixin 1985). BOC, as the largest bank in China, was the main victim. For example, to meet fiscal expenditure, the three North-eastern provinces borrowed heavily from the Bank. It was impossible for the Bank to refuse the loans or to ask for repayments. In 1914, the Warlord Zhang Zuolin in Fengtian took C$500,000 with force from the BOC's Fengtian branch (Cheng 2003: 132). The Helongjiang government took C$1 million from BOC in 1915, which, with a previous borrowing, totalled C$2 million (BOC 1995: 357). Even so, the local governments often caused problems for BOC. For one thing, the notes of the Bank of China in circulation were popular with merchants and the general public, but the Fengtian provincial authorities alleged that the Bank was expanding its influence and affecting the growth of local banks. They therefore time and again banned the use of notes issued by the Bank (BOC 1999).

The reports of BOC were full of complaints about extortion by local powers. Besides the Northeastern provinces, the Guizhou provincial governor took C$1.3 million from the BOC's Guizhou branch in 1916 (Cheng 2003: 132). The Kulun (today's Mongolia) government forced a loan of C$300,000 to pay the military salary in 1921 (BOC 1991c: 1886). In 1912, Chen Qimei, the military governor of Shanghai, asked for a loan of 500,000 taels for military provisions. When the manager of the BOC Shanghai branch, Song Hanzhang, refused, he was arrested and detained for two weeks (Shanghai archives). From 1925 to 1927, BOC was required to lend money to support the Northern Expedition army: C$500,000 to Guangdong; C$800,000 to Changsha; C$1.47 million to Wuhan; C$700,000 to Fuzhou, and so on (BOC 1995: 133). In 1927, the Wuhan government forcibly took more than C$30 million from BOC, as a result of which the Hankou branch of BOC had to go into liquidation. Not until the beginning of 1932, after a lapse of five years, did the Bank reopen (BOC 1999: 43). Indeed, the Shanghai Bankers Association in its 1927 proposal complained, 'In recent years Warlords in the north and the south frequently extort and forcefully borrow money from banks, and devastate finance without any reservation' (*Yinhang Yuebao* 26 April 1927).

Local government borrowings under the Nationalist government

Forceful borrowings from local governments, whether it be for local construction projects, for military purposes, for famine relief, or for administrative expenses, brought a heavy burden on BOC. Under the Nationalist administration, beginning in 1931, the Head Office of BOC devised a set of measures to cope with the overdue government loans (BOC 1995). Local governments were asked to pay back by instalments (such as the Wenzhou government borrowing for soldiers' pay and provisions), or pay back by government bonds (such as the Zhejiang government borrowings). Some government borrowings, in fact, were owed by individuals for private purposes. BOC required that the specific persons should be identified, sought after and even brought to court. In 1932, the BOC Head Office notified its branches, 'Unless no alternative exists, try your best to excuse yourself from official borrowing'. The Head Office also pointed out that 'It is understood that small sums of borrowings are inevitable, but those branch managers who approve huge lendings must be held accountable' (BOC 1995: 250).

However, these warnings and regulations were not as effective as expected. The amount collected was negligible, and new loans were more than the Bank could handle. By the end of 1933, overdue debts from local governments reached C$17.08 million, accounting for 15 per cent of total BOC overdue government debts (BOC 1995: 251). Accordingly, BOC issued a report, warning 'We must double efforts to clear up those overdue debts; meanwhile, be extremely cautious about new loans. It is easy to grant loans but difficult to get them back. If the bad debts are on the rise, the hidden losses of the Bank must be mounting' (BOC 1991b: 1082). Zhang Jia'ao (1958) admitted that although BOC wanted to extend into the interior, where the Bank could operate without competition from the foreign banks, BOC was not prepared to take the risk in the absence of legal checks to local government borrowings. Up to the end of 1936, the amount owed by local governments was still over C$10 million (*BOCAR* 1936), and the Bank admitted that there was no way to get these debts back.

In summary, since its birth, BOC had been beset by local government intervention, especially with regard to borrowings. These kinds of loans did not usually have enough security but were enforced and often arbitrary. More often than not, they became bad, which imposed a heavy burden on BOC, and directly worsened its profit returns.

Comparison with Taiwan

The above discussions cover government intervention in BOC in bond business, note issue, loan practice and local government borrowings, as well as its adverse impact on BOC's operations and performance. However, a conclusion cannot be rashly made that intervention in banks is definitely bad. After the KMT's retreat to Taiwan in 1949, the same KMT strongly intervened in the banking system, as well as in the economy as a whole, with successful results. The puzzle is: how could the KMT, which failed so miserably in the mainland, achieve such success in Taiwan? To begin with, let us briefly consider Taiwan's economic success and its general economic and financial structures.

Taiwan's success under the KMT

Certainly, the success story of Taiwan has stimulated a combination of worldwide admiration and fascination. For four decades since 1950, real growth had averaged 9 per cent a year; GNP per capita had multiplied many times from just over US$100 to US$3,000 (Clark 1988: 108); and the economy had been transformed from an agricultural one to a sophisticated industrial society. Taiwan had displayed a 'phoenix-like recovery' from the failure, devastation and humiliation of the Chinese civil war (ibid.). Indeed, Taiwan's economy had been 'shot from a cannon, achieving in the last two decades what most countries could not attain in a century' (Kelly and London 1989: 185). Together with Korea, Hong Kong and Singapore, they are known as 'East Asia Miracle' countries.

Taiwan makes an interesting case study of state intervention. Wade (1990) analysed Taiwan's performance and characterized Taiwan's industrialization from the 1950s to the 1980s as state-led. The state established state enterprises and played the dominant role in Taiwan's industry by confiscating former Japanese assets. Indeed, the Taiwan state generated one of the largest state-owned sectors in the non-Communist world (Field 1995). The state enterprises were in petroleum, aluminium, iron and steel, electric power, shipbuilding and so on. The Taiwan government aggressively promoted the industrial policy, 'which was essentially sectoral policy – choosing certain industries for support using sector-specific measures' (Patrick 1994: 361). Correspondingly, the financial system in Taiwan had been under central and provincial government control since the end of the Second World War (Yang Ya-Hwei 1994). Banks in Taiwan encompass the central bank, government-owned banks, private commercial banks and local branches of foreign banks. Government banks, including commercial and specialized banks, were the core of the system. Chang Hwa Commercial Bank, First Commercial Bank and Hua-nan Commercial Bank were the three largest commercial banks and were the market leaders (ibid.: 298). Even after a series of financial liberalization measures in the mid-1980s, the state banks continued to maintain a dominant role. In 1990, the state banks held 82.3 per cent of total loans and 84 per cent of total deposits in Taiwan (Table 4.6).

Besides owning most of the banks, the government strongly intervened in the banking system, through strict entry regulation, interest rate control, selective credit allocation, administrative guidance, moral persuasion, etc. (Shea 1994). Compared to the failure on the mainland, the intervention was a great success. The following factors go some way to explaining why:

- the transformation of the party-state
- a change of policy objective
- a competent and disciplined bureaucratic organization
- the setting up of appropriate institutions
- strict performance standards.

The transformation of the party-state

When Chiang retreated to Taiwan, some distant regional Warlords, such as General Li Tsung-jen of Guangxi province, did not join him. The 'bureaucrat-capitalists' whom Chiang had difficulty in controlling on the mainland, such as T.V. Soong and H.H. Kung, stayed in America and did not go to Taiwan (Vogel 1991). Chiang Kaishek brought to Taiwan a more unified leadership. In Taiwan, the KMT decided to reorganize itself. Chiang, in August 1950, established a central reform committee charged with implementing the 'Reform Programme of the KMT' (Shieh 1970). The KMT admitted past errors and waged a fundamental overhaul of the party, including purging bad elements, recruiting new members, and strengthening discipline and indoctrination to reinvigorate the party. For example, party members who had cooperated with the Communists, had a definite record of

Table 4.6 The dominant role of government banks in Taiwan, 1962–90

	Percentage of total loans		Percentage of total deposits	
	1962	*1990*	*1962*	*1990*
Total government banks	97.0	82.3	99.5	84.0
(3 major government-owned commercial banks*)	(23.7)	(29.4)	(32.5)	(29.7)
Private banks	3.0	12.5	0.5	14.2
Foreign banks	0.0	5.1	0.0	1.8
Total	**100.0**	**100.0**	**100.0**	**100.0**

Notes:
Postal savings system data are excluded.
* The three major government-owned commercial banks are First Commercial Bank, Hua-nan Commercial Bank and Chang Hwa Commercial Bank.

Source: Yang Ya-Hwei 1994: 302–3.

corruption, or had fled abroad, were expelled from the party (Domes 2000: 115; Eastman 1984: 209). Besides, in order to prevent any challenge from opposition forces, Chiang used emergency powers to impose a ban on the formation of new political parties and outlawed strikes and demonstrations (ibid.). From 1950 until 1988, Chiang Kaishek and his son Chiang Chingkuo dominated the KMT party, the military and the government. The KMT had control over Taiwan to a degree which they had never achieved on the mainland (Gold 1986). Vartiainen (1995) points out that effective state intervention requires the existence of a state which is politically autonomous and able to effectively formulate and carry out its policies and not succumb to particular interests. In Taiwan, the relative autonomy of the state enabled it to put into effect a succession of policies that placed national growth above powerful vested interests.

A change of policy objective

In their analysis of why they lost the mainland, KMT leaders acknowledged that public support had eroded because of their failure to provide for the common people's livelihood (Vogel 1991: 18). The KMT was determined to do better in Taiwan. Meanwhile, the Taiwanese political elite represented an immigrant minority on the island, and they hoped to achieve something to gain support at home. Consequently, economic development was taken as the island's overriding objective. Like in the model of the developmental or 'plan-rational' state discussed by Johnson (1982), the Taiwan government gave the highest priority to economic development, and concerned itself mainly with managing land reform and upgrading domestic industries. Through government intervention, financial resources were channelled to productive investment instead of unproductive military campaigns. In the 1950s, Taiwan was faced with the challenges of mainland China and an economic disaster could have resulted in the demise of the Taiwanese state. However, national security can change the payoffs to the agents in a society, as illustrated by Vartiainen (1999: 224) using the prisoner's dilemma model. Consequently, rather than being tempted to defect, as in the classic prisoner's dilemma model, the public had the will to cooperate for the good of the nation's survival and development. Hence, it was easier for the government's intervention polices to be delivered and carried out.

A competent and disciplined bureaucratic organization

In Taiwan, the government emphasized building up a high-quality bureaucratic organization. The government aggressively recruited college students to serve in the public sector, which offered a grand array of prestigious, well-paid and satisfying jobs (Gold 2000). These talented youths were given wide-ranging training and experience in many different positions before being assigned major responsibilities. Equally important, the USA helped in training political leaders and government technocrats to guide economic development (Vogel 1991).

In their analysis of why they lost the mainland, besides failing to improve people's livelihoods, the KMT leaders also acknowledged that public support had eroded because of the government's failure to stop corruption (Vogel 1991: 18). Therefore, very strict internal discipline was imposed on bureaucracy to guard against the pursuit of individual interests at the expense of collective goals (Evans 1995: 54). Economic policy-makers in Taiwan, for example, were not allowed to engage in their own businesses (Vogel 1991: 18). Chiang Chingkuo further instituted a crackdown on corruption in the bureaucracy. He issued a set of stern dos and don'ts, dubbed 'The ten commandments', to state cadres (Gold 1986: 92). Government bureaucrats not only refrained from accepting presents and dinner invitations from businessmen but avoided any social functions at which members of the business community attended (ibid.: 33). Vogel (1991: 33) commented that 'Although these detailed regulations were considered annoyingly strict by many participants, they did curtail corruption and helped maintain a level of public support and trust.' Wade (1995: 127) also noted that officials were subject to monitoring from centres of expertise and influence outside the core bureaucracies, namely the research and service agencies, and the press was fairly free to make economic (but not political) criticisms of the government. All these institutional arrangements constrained the improper behaviour of public officials.

In government banks, the strict and highly competitive recruitment process attracted the best talent. Besides receiving adequate compensation for their work, bank staff 'considered professional pride and public reputation to outweigh concern for personal material gain' (Vogel 1991: 32). As a general rule it was difficult for bank managers to quit and find comparable or better jobs elsewhere (Patrick 1994). On the other hand, the bank managers were under the strict monitoring of the Ministry of Finance, the Central Bank of China (CBC) and Control Yuan (Shea 1994). Therefore, bank managers had good reasons to fit in, perform well and follow orders. The main reward was promotion to higher positions, which of course meant higher salaries as well as greater status and power.

The Weberian professional bureaucracy consists of career civil servants who are committed to their tasks and prestigious enough not to be easily corrupted by outside interests (Weber 1947). A capable and motivated bureaucracy is able to effectively make policy and deliver services. Evans (1995: 70) commented that, 'the state ability to facilitate industrial transformation in Korea and Taiwan, like its ability in Japan, has been fundamentally rooted in coherent, competent bureaucratic organization'. Such a meritocratic bureaucratic organization is also able to reproduce itself, since its prestige makes it possible to recruit from the best talent (Vartiainen 1995).

The setting up of appropriate institutions

In Taiwan, the government established the central bank, the Central Bank of China. The CBC was under the direct supervision of the president of Taiwan. It enjoyed a high degree of independence and usually dominated the Ministry of Finance (Shea 1994: 225). CBC carried out the monetary policy and maintained a low inflation rate. In order to accommodate the financing needs of specific industries and economic activities, the Taiwan government was sensible enough to set up seven specialized banks: the Land Bank of Taiwan, the Farmers Bank of China, the Bank of Communications, the Export–Import Bank of China, the Cooperative Bank of Taiwan, the Central Trust, and the Medium Business Bank of Taiwan (Shea 1994: 226–7). These banks specialized in industrial, agricultural, real estate, medium and small business and export–import financing, etc. Nevertheless, even though specialized banks provided low-interest loans to strategic users, especially SOEs, there was no free lunch for receivers. Singh (1995) pointed out that the government, in return for the protection and subsidies being afforded to the firms, set them various performance standards, most notably in relation to exports and world market shares. As a result, with competitive and aspiring clients, the performance of specialized banks was not bad at all.

Through institutional build-up, the CBC exclusively exercised the functions of a central bank and maintained a stable money supply. Specialized banks could provide professional and targeting services to important and strategic clients. Here, precisely in line with the late development thesis of Gerschenkron (1962), state intervention remains essential to establishing investment priorities and to creating an institutional framework accommodating the new needs of economic activity. Furthermore, since commercial and policy loans were separated, the state commercial banks could operate according to economic principles, and they could be effectively evaluated and monitored.

Strict performance standards

The government imposed strict performance standards on government commercial banks. State commercial banks were encouraged to pursue profit maximization and bad-debt minimization (Yang Ya-Hwei 1994: 290). Those banks with higher profit ratios usually received higher evaluations from administrative authorities. To ensure the soundness of the financial system, the monetary authorities set restrictions on bank portfolios, especially on loan standards. For example, the ratio of liquid assets to deposits had to be 7 per cent or more; the ratio of 'risky' assets to owner equity had to be less than 8 per cent (ibid.: 294); the total loans to a specific customer had to be less than 25 per cent of a bank's net worth (ibid.). The ministry of audit examined the loan process to check whether rules were violated. The bad loan ratio was also strictly set. A higher ratio than was allowed attracted the scrutiny of the banking authorities, especially at government-owned banks, and the bankers involved could face serious penalties. 'These include requiring the individuals who made a bad loan to repay it; some bankers who could not make restitution have been jailed' (ibid.: 312). Under such a system, loan officers paid much more attention to stable and healthy practices, rather than jumping into dubious projects.

Anti-interventionist scholarship argues that state enterprises are inefficient due to ineffective monitoring of the self-seeking agents (Niskanen 1973; Peacock 1979; Rowley 1983). The World Bank (1995) simply concludes that large SOEs can hinder economic growth because they face contradictory goals (such as profit-making, social stability, full employment), which distort manager incentives. But in Taiwan's case, state commercial banks were operating according to market principles and they were monitored on specific criteria, requirements and discipline.

All in all, the banking system in Taiwan since the 1950s had been 'very successful from a 40-year perspective: whatever the problems, difficulties, deficiencies and costs' (Patrick 1994: 364). Government intervention played a crucial role in transforming Taiwan from an agricultural society to an industrial economy, upgrading industries from labour-intensive to capital-intensive ones, particularly information and high-tech industries. More significantly, rapid economic growth was achieved with social and political stability and equitable income distribution (Gold 1986).

The mainland's failure under the KMT

The factors contributing to Taiwan's successful intervention also mirror the failure of the KMT on the mainland.

First, regarding the party-state, although the mainland was ostensibly the KMT's republic of China for much of the first half of the twentieth century, Chiang Kaishek was constantly challenged by the Chinese Communist Party, while continuously fighting Warlords who refused to surrender their power (Cheng 2003: 4). In this regard, Sheridan (1966: 14) coined a term – 'residual Warlordism'. The Nanjing government never effectively controlled much more of China than the Yangtze River delta and some other large cities. Following the Japanese invasion in 1937, even that degree of political control was sharply diminished (Eastman 1984). Chiang Kaishek had been dependent on distant allies over whom he had little leverage (Vogel 1991: 16). As a result, the state had insufficient autonomy to impose the 'right' policies and to prevent group demands.

Second, the purpose of KMT's intervention in the mainland banks, especially its interference in bond business and note issue, was not for economic growth, but was mainly for increasing government revenue and then for wasteful military drives. It was suggested that part of the bond revenue 'went for troop provision, part to buy weapons, part to buy the loyalty of troops, and part into the private purses of Chiang Kaishek and T.V. Soong'

(*Zhongyang Daobao* 9 September 1931). This kind of intervention could not have a positive outcome. As Nolan (1993: 206) cautioned, 'If interventions are more in response to wasteful military purpose or vested interests than in the interests of the overall accumulation process, then state interventions may in the end produce a worse result than the free market'.

Third, the incessant civil wars and the Japanese war in China disrupted the build-up of a capable and disciplined bureaucracy (Young 1965). Eastman (1984: 2) observed that the regime 'never developed a governmental adminis-tration capable of implementing the KMT's policies and programmes, or political institutions firmly rooted in Chinese society'. Even worse, during and after the War, the corruption became rampant and systemic, which stifled the public administration's efficiency and morale (see Chapter 6). Gold (1986: vii) commented that the ruling Chinese Nationalist Party was notorious for 'heading one of history's most corrupt, violent, and incompetent regimes'. It is no wonder that civil servants lacked the skills, capability and motivation to successfully formulate and carry out economic policies.

Fourth, there was a lack of institutional construction. No central bank which could exclusively exercise a central bank function was in any real sense set up on the mainland; no real policy bank which could provide professional and targeted services to strategic industries or special economic activities was established.

Fifth, performance standards were low. Due to the inadequate institutional setup, government banks, including BOC, were burdened with government bonds, note issue, policy loans and commercial loans. Multiple objectives definitely impacted adversely on BOC's efficiency and performance. What's more, it was impossible for the government to impose performance standards and enact disciplinary procedures against BOC.

With a factionalized party-state, a dominating military objective, incapable and corrupt bureaucracy, an oversimplified banking structure, and a lack of performance standards, it was hardly surprising that KMT's intervention in mainland banks failed.

Conclusion

'Financial institutions ought to stay independent of politics. If they are exploited by careerists, the nation will suffer. If by political factions, people will take a dim view of them' (BOC 1999: 25). This is quoted from Zhang Qian, the president of the Private Shareholders Association of BOC in the Warlord era.

Whether it was in the late Qing Dynasty, Northern Warlord or KMT periods, the chronic deficit in the central budget, the expanding military expenses and bureaucratic self-seeking activities stimulated the governments' excessive intervention. As Zhang Jia'ao lamented in his Autobiographical Note, 'for the dignified authorities, why should they always get sulky with the Bank of China? This is because the military understands nothing about finance, yet tries to interfere in every respect – disheartening political future' (BOC 1999: 42). Excessive floating of government bonds, inflationary note issue, enforced policy loans and local government borrowings distracted BOC from normal business, weakened the Bank's financial strength and finally led to the Bank's takeover by the Communists.

A coin has its other side. Under the same KMT leadership, the Taiwan state after 1949 heavily intervened in banking and the whole economy, and achieved amazing success. The difference of intervention in the mainland and Taiwan mainly manifested itself in the state capacity, intervention purpose, bureaucracy quality, institutional setup, and the performance standards of agents. Taiwan's intervention is 'instrumental', to borrow a term from Nolan (1995a: 238). 'The important issue, therefore, is not whether governments should have overall responsibility for the economic performance of their countries but under what conditions they are likely to discharge it most effectively' (Panić 1995: 52).

5   Foreign competition

Introduction

For a long time, there has been a heated debate about the role of foreigners in China's early economic development from 1840 to 1949. There are two popular theories which attempt to explain China's failure to modernize. The first, Lenin's theory of imperialism, gave Chinese intellectuals and revolutionaries 'a general framework for understanding and interpreting China's modern historical experience' (Dernberger 1975: 22). Among the revolutionaries, the classic statement comes from Mao Zedong in 'The Chinese Revolution and The Chinese Communist Party':

> ... in their aggression against China the imperialist powers have on the one hand hastened the disintegration of feudal society and the growth of elements of capitalism, thereby transforming a feudal into a semi-feudal society, and on the other imposed their ruthless rule on China, reducing an independent country to a semi-colonial country.
>
> (Mao 1965: 312)

Other western-trained Chinese scholars, such as Chen Hanseng (1939), H.D. Fong (1936), Fei Hsiao-Tung (1939), Franklin Ho (1939), and even some non-Marxists, also believed that western investment, technology and trade upset the local economy, disrupted agriculture, drained wealth out of China and oppressed local enterprises. In other words, westerners were detrimental to the development of China's economy.

The second popular explanation about why China failed to modernize focused on the unique characteristics of China's traditional economy and society. Levy (1953) held that the family in 'traditional' China was remarkably stable and produced a protective and anti-development behaviour pattern. As a result, China did not make much progress with modernization. Feuerwerker (1958: 8) believed that the Chinese failed to build up enough momentum to break through the 'barriers' inherent in the traditional agrarian economy. These impediments included government weakness, inadequate savings, technical backwardness, and deficient motivation. As a result, China was prevented from benefiting from western influences.

Dernberger (1975), Perkins (1975) and others critiqued the above two theses and re-evaluated the role of the foreigner in China's economic development. By the end of the nineteenth century, China's agriculture was caught in what Elvin (1972) defined as a high-level equilibrium trap. What worked well in the past, increasing output to support an expanding population, was no longer possible without significant changes in technology or adding arable land. It is, therefore, unjustified to assign China's agricultural impasse to the foreigner (Dernberger 1975). What's more, the relative stagnation of Chinese agriculture was extended to the rest of the economy as well (Riskin 1975: 62). In fact, on the eve of the Opium Wars, China was not breaking into capitalist industrialization independently; on the contrary, the rapid growth of the early/mid Qing period had stopped and 'the Chinese economy was in a state of crisis' (Nolan 1993: 23).

Against this background, foreigners, as the carriers of modern technology, 'served as the vital catalyst for the disruption of China's high-level equilibrium trap and the ensuing search for economic development' (Dernberger 1975: 36). Demonstration effects are the effects on the behaviour of individuals caused by observation of the actions of others and their consequences. The term is particularly used in political science and sociology to describe the fact that development in one place will often act as a catalyst in another place. The proven success of foreign business in China in the late Qing period motivated Chinese businessmen and bureaucrats to emulate that success. At the turn of the twentieth century, a wave of new Chinese industries (using modern machinery and techniques) and organizations mushroomed: modern banks and shipping firms, insurance companies, textile mills, tobacco factories, flour mills, chemical companies, railway companies, Chinese stock market, joint-stock companies with limited liability, even a Chinese chamber of commerce (ibid.). Herein, the foreigner played an especially important role in two ways.

The first way was by the transfer of technology and new modes of production. From the latter half of the nineteenth century onwards, China could import modern science and technology (Perkins 1975), and could begin to establish modern industries. 'Through Shanghai and other points of contact with Europe and America came much of the technology and equipment which made possible the industrial efforts of Chinese promoters' (Feuerwerker 1958: 8). The treaty of Shimonoseki in 1895 permitted foreigners to establish factories inside China. Although the Chinese producers would lose the natural protection, the learning process for local producers could be substantially shortened simply because the model for imitation was now right next door (Chao 1975: 169). What's more, imported producer goods were another source of transferred technology, since the largest share of these imports after 1900 was directed towards Chinese enterprises (Dernberger 1975). Foreign engineering firms trained Chinese technicians. Also, western experts and firms were hired by the Chinese government for projects that the

Chinese could not carry out themselves (ibid.). After 1872, the Qing government began to sponsor students abroad to study western technology and science. About 10,000 students studied in America and Europe, not to mention those in Japan and elsewhere (Yao Linqing 2004: 1). The transfer of western technology helped remove the 'single most important barrier to modern economic growth' in China (Perkins 1975: 2).

The second way in which the foreigner played an important role was in the transfer of entrepreneurial behaviour. Dernberger (1975) commented that the Chinese had rich administrative and organizational experience thanks to the long history of bureaucratic rule in the largest country in the world. Once exposed to modern enterprises, the Chinese people demonstrated themselves to be quick and capable learners. Among them, a new class of compradors stood out, and were employed by foreign businesses to deal with language barriers, distribution networks and the complex monetary systems in China. Compradors functioned as a bridge between East and West (Hao 1970: 48), and learned and engaged in western business activities quite successfully. Later, they became the largest sources of investment and management in modern Chinese enterprises (Dernberger 1975: 31), such as in Guandu Shangban enterprises or private factories. 'In the early twentieth century, western culture and education was advocated by enlightened Chinese people, and more and more young persons were able to be educated in a new way consonant with China's need to survive in the modern world' (Yao Linqing 2004: 1). With more factories and firms being established by foreigners, compradors and overseas returnees, there was a ripple effect, i.e. the entrepreneurial spirit spread to more people, who were enthusiastic to organize, operate and assume the risks of a modern business venture. This was possibly the greatest positive effect of foreigners in China. In fact, in treaty ports, especially in Shanghai, due to contact with foreign commercial expertise, several generations of Chinese businessmen had already enlarged their experience and perspectives (Bergère 1981). Professor Howe (1981: 166) observed that, even after 1949, experienced managers and skilled workers in Shanghai were assigned to help other Chinese cities.

Interestingly, if Karl Marx's theories are carefully studied, it is not hard to find that his proposition is surprisingly different from the pessimistic neo-Marxists, who believed that foreigners led to the underdevelopment or deindustrialization of China, echoing Dernberger's viewpoints. Marx and Engels' *Communist Manifesto* (1888) emphasized the achievements of capitalism in overcoming and controlling nature for the good of humanity, through the rapid development of science, agriculture, industry and technology. The bourgeoisie or capitalist class, declared the *Manifesto*, 'has been the first to show what man's activity can bring about' (ibid.: 16). Meanwhile, 'The need of a constantly expanding market for its products chases the bourgeoisie over the whole surface of the globe. It must nestle everywhere, settle everywhere, establish connections everywhere' (ibid.). China, in the eyes of Marx, was 'barbarous and hermetic, isolation from the civilized world' (Marx

1853a: para 3). Although Marx felt sympathy for China's commoners: 'In China the spinners and weavers have suffered greatly under this foreign competition, and the community has become unsettled in proportion' (ibid.: para 5), Marx still viewed the violent intrusion of western colonialism in a positive light, liberating Asian peoples from 'Oriental despotism' (Marx 1853b: 94). Marx believed that international economy and free trade could provide the stimulus to poor countries:

> The bourgeoisie, by the rapid improvement of all instruments of production, by the immensely facilitated means of communication, draws all, even the most barbarian, nations into civilization. The cheap prices of its commodities are the heavy artillery with which it batters down all Chinese walls, with which it forces the barbarians' intensely obstinate hatred of foreigners to capitulate. It compels all nations, on pain of extinction, to adopt the bourgeois mode of production; it compels them to introduce what it calls civilization into their midst i.e. to become bourgeois themselves. In one word, it creates a world after its own image.
>
> (Marx and Engels 1888: 17)

No matter what the terms of trade or what the extent of unfair advantages and special privileges foreign businesses and investment enjoyed (Dernberger 1975: 46), whatever foreigners did in China, the demonstration effect, voluntary or forceful, helped China absorb modern technology and realize entrepreneurial potential, and started the Chinese economy on the road to modernization. In this sense, foreigners played a net positive role in China's early economic development, though some negative features existed (Dernberger 1975). The fact that Chinese modern industry developed and grew after the turn of the century cannot be denied. Chinese modern banking is one vivid example. Motivated by the foreign banks, Chinese banks appeared, became established, expanded and gained prosperity. Through great effort, Chinese banks, in particular BOC, succeeded in catching up and even overtaking their foreign counterparts.

Entry of foreign banks into China

The Opium Wars opened up China to the western world. The expansion of foreign trade in the wake of the treaties of 1842, 1858 and 1860 with foreign countries created fresh demands for credit and transfer facilities, which encouraged the creation of foreign banking outlets in the treaty ports (Rawski 1989). A British–Indian joint-venture, called the Bank of Western India (later renamed the Oriental Bank), led the way in setting up in China. Established in Bombay in 1842, the bank opened a branch in Hong Kong and an agency in Guangzhou in 1845. It expanded to Shanghai in 1848 (Huang Guangyu 1995: 336). Other British or British–Indian banks followed suit and established their operations in China one after another. Among them, the Commercial Bank of India was established in 1851; the Chartered Mercantile Bank of India, London and China in 1857; the Chartered Bank of India, Australia and China (hereafter Chartered Bank) in 1858; and the Hongkong and Shanghai Banking Corporation (hereafter HSBC or Hongkong Bank) in 1865 (Wang Jingyu 1983).

The treaty of Shimonoseki in 1895 gave westerners further rights to set up industrial businesses in China (Bergère 1986), created more sophisticated demands for banking services and led to the second wave of foreign banks' coming to China. Before the end of the nineteenth century, altogether, a total of 21 foreign banks with 101 branches had begun to operate in China (Wang Jingyu 1999: 299). At the beginning of the twentieth century, all the world powers had a banking operation in China (Table 5.1).

Foreign banks had high expectations about the market in China. The prospectus of the Chartered Bank clearly stated its intention to extend the 'legitimate facilities of banking to the vast and rapidly extending trade between the Australian Colonies, British India, China and other parts of the Eastern Archipelago' (Mackenzie 1954: 5). In China, besides Hong Kong, the bank was determined to carry out activities 'in any port, town, city or place in China where a Consulate is or may hereafter be established' (ibid.: 21). The Chartered Bank was likened to 'a great financial battleship' (ibid.: 263) and was the most powerful foreign bank before HSBC to set foot in China.

Table 5.1 Major foreign banks in China at the beginning of the twentieth century

	Nationality	Head office	Initial registered capital	Year of founding	Year of entry into China
Chartered Bank of India, Australia and China	British	London	644,000 British pounds	1853	1858
Hongkong and Shanghai Banking Corporation	British	Hong Kong	5 million Hong Kong dollars	1865	1865
Banque de L'Indo-Chine	French	Paris	8 million French francs	1875	1899
Deutsch-Asiatische Bank	German	Shanghai	5 million silver taels	1890	1890
Russo-Asiatic Bank	Russian	St Petersburg	6 million rubles	1895	1896
Yokohama Specie Bank	Japanese	Yokohama	3 million Japanese yen	1880	1893
National City Bank of New York	American	New York	2 million US$	1812	1902

Source: Wang Jingyu 1999: 299; Cleveland 1985: 8; King 1988b: 368.

If the purpose of the Chartered Bank was to draw China into its sphere of activities (Baster 1934), the HSBC target was more specific: China itself. The Provisional Committee of the bank consisted of representatives of the best-known British and Continental China Agency Houses (Baster 1935). The famous author King commented: 'The Hongkong and Shanghai Bank . . . has had nothing but China's interest at heart ever since it was started' (King 1988b: 66). The Hongkong Bank was unique in retaining its head office in the east, giving it a sense of permanence, a deep understanding and quick response to the requirements of the region it was founded to serve (King 1987). By the end of nineteenth century, from the north of Tianjin to the south of Beihai, from the island of Taiwan to the hinterland of Hankou, HSBC had spread out a huge financial network (Wang Jingyu 1999: 167). Beyond functioning as a commercial bank, HSBC issued banknotes, dealt extensively in government loans for political indemnities, national railways, and even for military campaigns (Ji 2003). What's more, Hongkong Bank's exchange quotations were used as the basis for all other foreign exchange rates quoted in China's market (Baster 1935: 177). By 1868 HSBC was already regarded as 'the most important public company in China' (Allen and Donnithorne 1954: 108). For more than half a century, HSBC was the most prominent and powerful foreign bank, and the de facto central bank of semi-colonial China before indigenous modern banks came into being (Wang Jingyu 1999). Indeed, one English newspaper in Shanghai commented on the prestige and influence of HSBC:

In England, when people say 'The Bank', they refer to the old nanny on the Threadneedle Street (i.e. the Bank of England). Likewise, in China, as long as we say 'The Bank' or 'Bank', no more explanation, everyone immediately knows we are talking about Hongkong and Shanghai Banking Corporation.

(North China Herald (NCH) 15 August 1890)

The development of modern Chinese banks

Long before western banks arrived, China had two types of traditional financial institutions – Qianzhuang and Piaohao. Not until 1897 did Chinese banks modelled on western practices (corporations of limited liability, relatively impersonal relationships with customers, and secured loans) begin to appear (Coble 1980). 'Although it indicated a new era for China's banking industry, it lagged about 725 years behind the Venice Bank in Italy, 202 years behind the Bank of England' (Kong 1991: 61), and even half a century after the British bank set up its first branch in China. Nevertheless, the activities and expansion of foreign banks had a vivid 'demonstration effect', gave Chinese officials and merchants a good understanding of the functions and profitability of commercial banks and motivated the emergence of Chinese modern banks (Chesneaux *et al.* 1977a).

The founder of China's first bank, the Imperial Bank of China, Sheng Xuanhuai, was an entrepreneur and bureaucrat and his varied career taught him the advantages of western methods and gave him a desire to compete with foreign financial institutions (Rawski 1989: 132). Sheng's prospectus promised that 'all business methods pursued by the [Imperial] Bank will be entirely on the foreign plan, as has been the case with the Hong Kong and Shanghai Bank, which is to be made the model of this Bank in everything' (ibid.: 133). Although the Imperial Bank failed to achieve the stature and power to which Sheng aspired, its inauguration was 'a breath of fresh air' and initiated a new epoch in the domestic financial market (Cheng 2003: 26).

Several years later, in 1905, Daqing Bank was founded. It functioned as both the central bank and a commercial bank and soon became the biggest Chinese bank (Kong 1991); it was the predecessor of the Bank of China. Another government–private bank, the Bank of Communications, organized in 1908 by the Ministry of Posts and Communications, also expanded quickly (Hong 2001). After the Qing Dynasty was overthrown, an enthusiastic imitation of western institutions spread throughout the country. Modern private and official banks mushroomed. Statistics, although incomplete, show that a total of 37 Chinese banks were operating by 1911, at the end of the Qing Dynasty; by the end of the Northern Warlords era in 1927, the number had risen to 160. Meanwhile, the total paid-up capital of these banks achieved a six-fold increase (Cheng 2003: 42).

Since the very beginning, the Chinese banks faced the superiority and dominance of foreign banks. The founder of Imperial Bank, Sheng Xuanhuai, in 1898 clearly realized that 'HSBC has been establishing for over thirty years, with enormous power and a strong foothold. Not only foreign firms do business with HSBC, also the big Chinese firms have established long-term relationship with the Hongkong Bank. It is extremely difficult for domestic banks to grab the market share' (Hong 2004: 176). There was no doubt that foreign banks owned a distinct competitive advantage in China's financial market.

The competitive advantages of foreign banks

Government support

'Foreign banks in China all received the support from their governments' (Wang Jingyu 1999: 333). The overseas financial activities of Comptoir d'Escompte de Paris, the first French bank in China, were always granted 'official support' (Attfield 1893: 32). Although the sponsors of the Deutsch-Asiatische Bank were mainly bankers and entrepreneurs, the German government, from the very beginning, gave it enormous care and consideration. Whether it was the Deutsch-Asiatische Bank itself, or the Deutsch-Asiatische Bank as one member of an international banking consortium, as long as it was necessary, the German government would immediately stand up and encourage the bank's efforts to gain financial interests in China (Feis 1930).

Japanese and Russian banks had a more distinct government background. The Yokohama Specie Bank was the chief foreign exchange bank of Japan and 'had a privileged position in the foreign exchange market' (Allen and Donnithorne 1954: 214). In this bank, the Japanese government allocated one-third of the capital and placed with the bank several million yen of the Treasury Reserve Fund (Sarasas 1940: 160). All these measures were to 'strengthen the institution' and 'maintain the public confidence' (ibid.). Like the Yokohama Specie Bank, the Russo-Asiatic Bank was the product of the Czarist government carrying out its Far Eastern policy (Wang Jingyu 1999). Within two years of its founding, the government, even if in financial difficulties, twice invested in the bank, a sum totalling 2 million rubles (Quested 1977: 6). Under the direct influence of the Czarist government, the bank gained privileges in China, including managing Qing government funds, collecting duties, issuing banknotes, building railways and establishing telegraph lines around railway construction areas (ibid.: 30).

Although British banks always professed that 'the tradition of Great Britain' was 'not to interfere in private enterprises' (*NCH* 7 January 1898), the famous financial historian Baster (1935: 37) pointed out that 'in cases of obvious and immediate need', this government's support was 'prompt and energetic'. Indeed, the members of the British government 'were constantly looking over their shoulders' to see what was happening in China (Endicott 1975: xiii). The Treasury in London approved HSBC's incorporation under a special Hong Kong ordinance. This allowed the Hongkong Bank to maintain a head office in Hong Kong without losing the privilege of issuing banknotes and holding British government funds (Collis 1965). HSBC maintained a close friendship with Robert Hart, the inspector-general of China's Imperial Maritime Customs. The Customs deposited all of its income in HSBC, including 'balances of office expenditure, fines and confiscations, tonnage dues, fees and other special monies (it did not include the customs revenue itself, though some twenty years later this was also deposited with the bank)' (Collis 1965: 60), and the bank established branches where the Customs had local offices. Likewise, the Hong Kong government gave special support to HSBC, whether the bank was applying for registration, expanding its right to issue banknotes, or asking to delay capital submissions (Collis 1965: 164). In the words of Baster (1935: 182): 'The Hongkong Bank looked to official support for its operations, and was constantly guided by official suggestions.'

As a latecomer to China, American banks received the US government's special encouragement and support (*FRUS* (*Foreign Relations of the United States*) 1899: 129–30). The first task of the National City Bank of New York in China was to be entrusted with 'the agency of American treasury in China' (*NCH* 12 February 1902). Specifically, the bank was empowered to handle China's Boxer indemnity to America. Due to this support, National City

Bank of New York could take further steps in expanding its branches in the East, and in carrying out other banking business (*NCH* 31 February 1902). Furthermore, the US government approved legislation in 1913 to aid international trade and overseas banking (Westerfield 1947). In particular, the American government spared no effort in helping American banks compete in the Chinese market. For example, even after Britain, Germany and France formed the first banking consortium to handle loans to the Chinese government, America was invited to join in by the Chinese government after the personal intervention of US President Taft (*FRUS* 1916: 134). More significantly, the government encouraged mergers and acquistions by the American banks. As a result, the National City Bank of New York, the biggest American bank in China, took over the Asia Banking Corporation, which was the second largest in China (Lee 1926). Being commented as the 'most decisive strategy' by the famous financial historian Wang Jingyu (1999: 243), this acquisition remarkably concentrated American banking resources, and helped National City Bank enjoy economies of scale and strong competitiveness in China's financial market.

It was with the 'special encouragement' and 'active help' of home governments that foreign banks built up their financial strength, expanded their influence, gained privileges from the Chinese government, and had a strong momentum to enter, grow and expand in China.

Capital strength and banking network

Foreign banks boasted strong capital strength. Take HSBC as an example: in 1905, its paid-up capital reached HK$10 million (roughly equivalent to C$10 million) (King 1987: 7), almost equal to the combined paid-up capital of China's two existing modern banks, the Daqing Bank and the Imperial Bank of China (Kong 1991: 62–70). HSBC alone had, in 1908, assets of HK$384 million and net profits of HK$3.64 million (King 1988a: 56), many times greater than those of the entire Chinese modern banking industry combined (Daqing Bank, Imperial Bank of China and the newly founded Bank of Communications).

In 1905, when Daqing Bank was established, foreign banks had been operating in China for more than half a century, and had built up a widespread network. By the end of the nineteenth century, Chartered Bank had six outlets in China; HSBC had fourteen; Russo-Asiatic Bank had nine; and Yokohama Specie Bank had four, and so on (Wang Jingyu 1999: 299). They were scattered from the north of Harbin to the south of Haikou, including Shanghai, Tianjin, Hankou, Guangzhou and covered altogether more than 20 big cities, forming a huge network. What's more, foreign banks were mostly internationally-oriented. At the beginning of the twentieth century, HSBC, Chartered Bank, National City Bank, etc. were already operating in Asia, America and Europe (Wang Jingyu 1999). Numerous outlets in China and all over the world gave foreign banks advantages regarding foreign trade and related business – fund transfer, brand building, risk diversification, amongst other things.

Modern management

The joint-stock companies appeared in Great Britain after the 1820 industrial revolution, and spread quickly into the financial industry. By 1865, Britain already had 250 joint-stock banks (Hong 1990: 67). These banks were owned by many stockholders rather than by one or a few persons, and were operated by a group of salaried managers rather than individual owners. Foreign banks operating in China were based on this modern corporate system, which had the advantages of accumulating large amounts of capital, dispersing risks and being managed professionally. Although some western banks in China failed due to speculation or gross mismanagement, such as the Agra Bank and the great Oriental Banking Corporation (Baster 1935: 176), HSBC and the Chartered Bank weathered several financial storms, benefited from the collapse of their competitors and became much stronger and more mature (Allen and Donnithorne 1954). While Chinese banks were in their infancy, foreign banks had already established modern and effective corporate governance structures, which set and enforced clear lines of responsibility and accountability throughout the organization. Foreign banks had also established a complete set of regulations regarding business operations and work flows. No wonder that western banks' scientific management and modern operation greatly improved their efficiency and competitiveness (Hong 2004).

Custodians of China's customs and salt revenues

Before the 1870s, foreign banks usually provided small loans with short maturity to the Qing government. In 1874, HSBC changed this situation and lent the Qing government 2 million taels with a ten-year term (Liu Di 1998: 181). This was the first big imperial government loan arranged by a foreign bank, and was to be followed by many others. Big items included the Franco-Russian loan of 1895 for 15.8 million pounds at 4 per cent interest, the Anglo-German loan of 1895 for 16 million pounds at 5 per cent, and another Anglo-German loan for the same amount at 4.5 per cent in 1898 (Ji 2003: 69). From 1910 onwards, various foreign banks formed a banking consortium to bargain collectively with the Chinese government and in 1913 they made a 'Reorganization Loan' to the Northern Warlord government (25 million pounds, or 248.27 million taels) (Liu Di 1998: 134). The above loans were mainly handled by HSBC, the Russo-Asiatic Bank, National City Bank, Banque de L'Indo-Chine, Deutsch-Asiatische Bank and Yokohama Specie Bank.

Handling Chinese government loans gained foreign banks an international reputation as well as considerable profit. The director-general of China Customs, Robert Hart, once commented on one of HSBC's loans to the

Chinese government: 'The Bank made hugely by it' (Collis 1965: 66). More significantly, many loans were secured on the customs and the salt revenues (Allen and Donnithorne 1954). From 1912, it was proclaimed in writing that customs revenue that was earmarked as a guarantee for a loan had to be deposited with creditor banks to service the amortization of indemnities (Cheng 2003: 72). The custodian banks were the Hongkong Bank, the Deutsch-Asiatische Bank and the Russo-Asiatic Bank. The payments due on these loans were subtracted from the revenues before the net surplus was handed to the Chinese government. In the same way, under the Reorganiza-tion Loan Agreement of 1913, the revenues of the newly established Salt Administration were to be paid into several designated foreign banks (Allen and Donnithorne 1954: 115), including HSBC, Deutsch-Asiatische Bank, the Russo-Asiatic Bank and Yokohama Specie Bank.

Through granting loans to the Chinese government and in connection with the servicing of foreign debt, the 'foreign banks came to undertake another function normally entrusted to a central or government bank, namely the holding of certain of the Chinese public revenues' (Allen and Donnithorne 1954: 115). This provided a cheap and convenient fund supply to the foreign banks. For example, the average balance of deposits from customs and salt revenues in HSBC every year was as much as 10 million silver dollars, and HSBC could use some of the money without paying any interest (Arnold 1926: 173). In fact, the regular inflow of large sums into the custodian banks enhanced their financial power and put them in a favourable position com-pared to their Chinese counterparts.

Foreign trade and international financial business

Before the 1840s, China's foreign trade was monopolized by the East India Company and the agency houses (Wang Jingyu 1999). After the foreign banks came to China, trade financing became a strong feature of foreign banks' business (Allen and Donnithorne 1954). Most of the advances of the foreign banks for financing trade were made to foreign firms. Credit was also given, however, to Chinese merchants. For example, loans from foreign banks to Chinese tea dealers at Fuzhou appear to have been customary around 1881 (Allen and Donnithorne 1954: 111).

The foreign banks, by virtue of their monopoly of foreign trade, also con-trolled the foreign exchange market (Feuerwerker 1995). They engaged heav-ily in international remittances, foreign exchange transactions, buying and selling money orders, currency swaps, etc. Indeed, the characters chosen for HSBC were pronounced by the British 'Wayfoong' and meant 'Abundance of Remittance' (Collis 1965: 20). In particular, through the widespread inter-national network, foreign banks had an overwhelming control on overseas Chinese remittances (Allen and Donnithorne 1954; Liu Di 1998). At the beginning of the twentieth century, 7.6 million Chinese were estimated to be living abroad (Bergère 1986: 42). Their remittance back to China was an important source of foreign exchange for western banks, while at the same time being an important tool through which foreign banks extended their influence into inland China (Allen and Donnithorne 1954). Large parts of these remittances came from the South Seas and Southern Asia, and were made through HSBC, the Nederlandsch Indische Handelsbank (Belgium) and the Banque de l'Indochine (France), while those from Taiwan and Japan were made through the Japanese-funded Bank of Taiwan, and those from the United States through the National City Bank of New York (Tamagna 1942: 112). In 1886, a report from Xiamen said that from the middle of November to the middle of December 1886 alone, 'overseas Chinese remitted back C\$1.2 to C\$1.3 million', all of which was handled by HSBC (*Shenbao* 14 January 1887).

In short, western banks maintained an absolute monopoly over foreign trade and international business, out of which, 'they were obtaining hand-some profits' (Tamagna 1942: 47). Even as late as 1930 it was estimated that at least 90 per cent of China's foreign trade was financed through foreign banks (Allen and Donnithorne 1954: 110). For more than half a century the foreign exchange rate which HSBC quoted every day was adopted as the standard in China's financial market (Allen and Donnithorne 1954: 111; Hong 2001: 102).

Note issue

Extraterritorial rights mean privilege of immunity from local laws and taxes. After the 'peace' treaty of Nanjing in 1842 and subsequent treaties, foreign powers were granted extraterritorial rights by the Chinese government. By virtue of extraterritorial rights, foreign banks were unrestricted by the regulations of the Chinese government, and they had the freedom to circulate their own banknotes in China's territory (Hong 2001). Notes were issued in terms of the tael, the Chinese dollar or the Hongkong dollar (Allen and Donnithorne 1954). Foreign banknotes were welcomed by urban Chinese as trustworthy and reliable, and their circulation in China soared from C\$ 66.5 million in 1911 to C\$121.5 million by 1925 (Rawski 1989: 378). *NCH* (29 November 1889) commented that 'Chinese people would rather want HSBC banknotes than the notes of local Qianzhuang'. Some business dealings 'specially stipulate that only HSBC banknotes are accepted' (*NCH* 8 July 1892). In 1873, on a ferry from Macao to Guangzhou, among the 300 passengers, almost all of them used the HSBC banknotes to pay the fare (*NCH* 13 February 1873).

'The right of a government to issue paper notes, which foreigners should not be allowed to infringe, is a general rule in every country' (Lee 1926: 103). The note-issuing right of foreign banks did not proceed from the Chinese government, but from the charters which they had received from their home governments (Allen and Donnithorne 1954). The note issue was profitable both as a status symbol and as a source of interest-free funds (King 1968: 65).

Through issuing banknotes in China, western banks not only enhanced their reputation, but also secured an important source of funds. As a consequence, foreign banks had a greater capacity to extend loans and make investments.

Deposits

The foreign banks in China had a large deposit business. Apart from accounts opened by foreign businesses and individuals in China, the wealthy Chinese also found it convenient to place their liquid resources with those banks. In particular, when conditions were uncertain in China, there was an obvious advantage in holding deposits with banks that enjoyed extraterritorial rights (Allen and Donnithorne 1954). In the late Qing period, it became a common practice for rich people to put their private savings in foreign banks (Cheng 2003). The very insecurity of the Warlord era boosted this trend. High-level officials and wealthy merchants, some afraid to deposit their money in local banks subject to raids by the Warlords, and some anxious to conceal illegal fortunes, sent their money to foreign banks (Collis 1965).

The reputation of HSBC attracted numerous private deposits. As early as the third year after the founding of HSBC, the English newspaper in Shanghai observed that 'the most satisfying evidence of Hongkong Bank's superior position' was 'the deposits of local merchants' (*NCH* 25 August 1866). Besides merchants, Qing Court prince I'kuang deposited 1.2 million taels in HSBC (Shou 1996: 8), while Qing high official Li Hongzhang put at least 1.5 million taels in the HSBC Tianjin branch (ibid.: 18). According to statistics regarding fixed deposits from Chinese people in HSBC, five people owned deposits above C\$20 million respectively; 20 people each above C\$15 million; and 130 people each above C\$10 million (Liu Di 1998: 179). Similarly, the National City Bank stood out in drawing on Chinese deposits. Prince Qing had C\$300,000 in the National City Bank and was happy to accept an annual interest rate of 5.25 per cent, instead of the 8–9 per cent offered by the Chinese banks (Yan Pingzhong 2004: 59). Jiangsu Warlord Li Chun kept 150,000 taels in the National City Bank (ibid.: 59). Big Warlord Cao Kun was an important depositor of the National City Bank Tianjin branch. By the end of 1919, National City Bank's worldwide deposits were US\$91 million, whereas deposits in China reached US\$42 million, which accounted for 46 per cent of the total number (Wang Jingyu 1999: 249). Put another way, the deposits of the National City Bank in China almost equalled the total amount attracted from other parts of the world, including Britain, Japan, British India, Dutch India, the Straits colonies, the Philippines, Panama and New York.

In short, the extraterritorial rights and strong financial power of foreign banks made them advantageous in attracting deposits. In 1911, the deposits of Chinese banks were about C\$135 million (Cheng 2003: 43), whereas foreign banks' deposits in China had already reached more than C\$218 million (Rawski 1989: 392). Foreign banks, through taking deposits, amassed huge liquid resources and in turn could fuel other businesses.

Bank–client relationship

One motive for the foreign banks' coming to China was to serve foreign firms operating in China. Due to the bank–client relationship back in the home country, or due to the financial strength and quality of products and services, the foreign banks contracted close relationships with foreign clients. The foreign businesses often kept accounts with foreign banks, and in turn, banks provided comprehensive services, such as loans, bill discounting, trade financing, international remittances, foreign exchange transactions, consulting and the underwriting of enterprise bonds (Hong 2004).

The success of the National City Bank (the Citibank of today) in China rested on a close relationship with American big firms operating in China, such as the American Trading Co., the Shanghai Telephone Co., the Standard Oil Co. and the British American Tobacco Co. (Liu Di 1998: 167). William Rockefeller was the largest single stockholder of National City Bank before 1918. Rockefeller was associated with the Stillman family of the Standard Oil Co., due to the dynastic marriage of his two sons to Stillman's daughters (Stanley 1989). The National City Bank and Standard Oil became two extremely influential American enterprises in China. Their close bonds and intimate relationship on the one hand supported Standard Oil's operations in China, and on the other, opened many business opportunities for National City Bank.

Likewise, HSBC had an intimate relationship with British enterprises in China, which numbered 401 in 1900; 590 in 1913; 1,027 in 1930; and 1,031 in 1936 (including all branches) (Hong 1990: 111), 'The entire British business community in China', it was remarked in 1919, 'was dependent in some degree on the credit facilities of the Hongkong and Shanghai Banking Corporation' (Allen and Donnithorne 1954: 114). In particular, Shanghai's most important 40 British enterprises had a loan relationship with HSBC (Hong 2001). The famous three big groups (Jardine, Matheson and Co., E.D. Sassoon and Co. and Swire Pacific Ltd) were the most influential and long-standing British companies in China (Hong 2004: 161). Swire Pacific Ltd owned sugar making and oil paint industries. Sassoon and Co. had a huge investment in real estate, warehousing, wharfs, insurance and railways and was the sponsoring shareholder of HSBC. Jardine Matheson and Co. owned textile mills, silk factories, together with machine-building, food and 20 other industrial enterprises. These three groups were the most devoted clients of HSBC. Furthermore, Jardine, Matheson and Co. and HSBC in 1898 jointly founded the British and Chinese Corporation, where Jardine, Matheson and Co. acquired railway contracts and provided materials and carried out the work, while HSBC advanced the money: 'British and Chinese Corporation became the most powerful foreign company to contract and build-up railways in China' (Collis 1965: 58).

Western banks were also involved in some promising and profitable Chinese undertakings (Allen and Donnithorne 1954). From 1885, HSBC made loans to the China Merchant Steamship Co., which was China's first western-style enterprise. After the Shimonoseki Treaty, foreign capital obviously strengthened their relationship with Chinese enterprises. In particular cotton milling was a major interest. The Yujin Cotton Mill was a client of the Russo-Asiatic Bank, the Tongyigong Cotton Mill secured loans from Japanese banks (Wang Jingyu 1999: 219), and HSBC cooperated with the Shenxin Textile Mill (Liu Di 1998). The Decennial reports of Hankou Customs observed that 'Chinese businessmen have increasing trust towards foreign banks' (Wang Jingyu 1999: 188). Through establishing and strengthening the bank–client relationship, foreign banks could grow with the growth of clients. Powerful clients brought western banks a secure market share and a source of wealth.

In summary, foreign banks, externally, possessed extraterritorial rights and received strong home government support; internally, they had established massive capital strength, huge networks and modern management methods. Compared to Chinese banks, foreign banks boasted prominent competitive advantages in foreign trade and exchange business, note issue, deposits and client relationships.

The challenging efforts of Chinese banks

Facing such a formidable rival, Chinese banks were not daunted. In fact, the desire to compete with foreign banks was one of the most important reasons for the founding of modern Chinese banks. The first Chinese bank, and indeed many of the others, declared that one of their goals was to recover the profits that were now going to foreign banks (Cheng 2003). The target of BOC was much more explicit and straightforward: 'One day BOC is to replace the role of HSBC' (BOC 1995: 395). Through great efforts, Chinese banks experienced vigorous growth, and expanded their business in the face of foreign competition. Correspondingly, the influence of foreign banks declined after the 1920s, and their dominance over the Chinese financial market was shaken. The efforts made by the Chinese banks to challenge the foreign competition includes the following aspects.

Government support

As mentioned above, foreign banks received their respective government's support to establish and grow in China. In the late Qing Dynasty, in order to protect China from economic exploitation and invasion by foreign powers, the Qing Court made efforts to support modern banks. As early as 1904, the Qing Court issued China's first company law. Daqing Bank was set up as a limited liability company, imitating the western model (Cheng 2003: 222). More importantly, Daqing Bank was organized in line with the Guandu Shangban system (see Chapter 3). The privileges granted to the Guandu Shangban enterprise were intended to put Daqing Bank in a stronger position in response to foreign competition. For example, Daqing Bank's banknote was granted an exclusive privilege to be used in all public and private fund transfers (Kong 1991: 171). Daqing Bank also received the exclusive right to run the state treasury (Kong 1991). The Bank was entrusted to handle many other official transactions, such as the Salt Surplus Tax and the government's diplomatic expenditures (ibid.). As a result, Daqing Bank made rapid progress and became the largest domestic bank in China (BOC 1999).

Although the Northern Warlord government was constantly troubled by political turmoil, the government proclaimed the 'National Currency Regulations' which explicitly specified the coin's monetary unit, denomination, weight, fineness, right of coinage and the way by which the coins were to circulate (BOC 1999: 13). The issuing of a national currency greatly advanced the process of unifying the previous disorderly currency and improved the macroeconomic environment in which the banks could operate (Xu Jiansheng 1996). More significantly, the government supported BOC to undertake foreign trade and exchange business, and helped BOC break the monopoly of foreign banks (BOC 1995: 193). When BOC sent staff to make a business investigation in the Malay Archipelago, Singapore and Java, the government instructed Chinese consuls in those areas to give them special support and consideration (BOC 1991b: 1,551–3). It was the government support that helped BOC establish overseas networks.

China's political unification under the Nationalist government in 1928 provided a good opportunity for modern banks to develop. During the Nanjing decade (1928–37), the Nationalists attempted to build up 'a healthy financial system' as the necessary base for China's economic construction (Zhou Kaiqing 1951: 52), including the creation of a central bank, the establishment of a special office to supervise financial affairs and the promulgation of a series of laws and rules to regulate banking activity (Cheng 2003). Meanwhile, 'Rights Recovery' taken by the Nationalist government had a huge impact on the foreign banks (King 1988b). The Nationalist government in 1928 entrusted the Central Bank of China to take over all Customs and Salt revenues and to deal with all foreign indemnity and debt affairs (Cheng 2003). Loss of this huge source of cheap or even costless funds undoubtedly weakened the foreign banks' financial power in China. In 1935, the Chinese government formally abandoned the silver standard, nationalized silver stocks and set up a managed currency (Allen and Donnithorne 1954). Afterwards, the foreign banks gradually stopped issuing banknotes in China. Equally important, the role of HSBC in setting China's official foreign exchange rate was taken by the Central Bank of China (Hong 2003).

With the respective governments' support, it was possible for BOC to enhance capital strength, expand the scope of its business and boost its reputation. Meanwhile, foreign banks gradually lost their former privileges. As a result, BOC and other Chinese banks were in a better position to challenge foreign competitors.

Capital strength and network build-up

When Daqing Bank was established in 1905, its paid-up capital was 4 million taels, or C\$5.6 million, much less than the C\$10 million owned by HSBC. In the late nineteenth and early twentieth centuries, the corporate form was new and strange to most Chinese people. In order to attract investors, Daqing Bank used a special method to guarantee investments – the 'official interest' (guanli) system (Kong 1991). In addition to getting dividends, which varied according to a company's profits, a shareholder could expect a certain fixed percentage of interest for his stock share. The guanli of Daqing Bank was set at 6 per cent annually (DBCO 1915: 83). In three years' time, the capital of Daqing Bank increased to 10 million taels. Later, BOC top management took a road-show to Shanghai and encouraged private banks and institutions to purchase BOC stock (BOC 1995). At the end of 1925, the paid-up capital of BOC reached C\$20 million and almost equalled that of HSBC. By the end of 1935, BOC had increased its paid-up capital to double that of HSBC (BOC 1995; King 1988b).

Meanwhile, BOC speeded up the build-up of its network. By 1911, six years after its birth, BOC had established 35 branches in provincial capitals and trade ports (BOC 1999). In the 1920s, learning from British and American banks, BOC further restructured and expanded its network. The previous practice of setting up units according to administrative regions was changed into setting up units based on the economic importance of each area (BOC 1999). The capital city, various commercial centres, transportation centres and goods trading hubs were particularly emphasized. In 1934, BOC's total bank outlets in China numbered 157 (BOC 1995: 170), compared with 14 HSBC outlets in China (King 1987: 501). BOC operations were also set up abroad, in London, Osaka, Singapore and New York (BOC 1995); later, they spread to, for example, Burma, Batavia, Penang, Kuala Lumpur, Hanoi, Rangoon, Calcutta, Bombay, Sydney and Havana (BOC 1995). Operating in Asia, Europe and America, BOC had a similar overseas network to HSBC's.

The enlargement of paid-up capital is an indication of the increase in BOC's strength and potential to conduct business. The expanding domestic and overseas network provided BOC with more business opportunities and elevated BOC to the ranks of the other international banks.

Modern management

As discussed in Chapter 3, since its establishment, BOC adopted a western-style corporate system, believing that only by imitating western corporate structures could Chinese enterprises hope to compete with their western and Japanese counterparts. This corporate structure was one of the most important features that distinguished BOC from traditional Chinese financial institutions (Cheng 2003: 221). In subsequent years, BOC further modernized its corporate governance (see Chapter 3). Furthermore, at the end of the 1920s, senior managers at BOC spent ten months visiting banks in 18 countries, including France, Germany, Great Britain and the United States. Learning from western experience, BOC devised a series of internal reforms, which greatly improved BOC's overall competitiveness.

Standardization of business procedures

BOC formulated a unified system for business procedure and work flows and laid down corresponding operational rules (BOC 1999). These were all-encompassing and included 'general rules', 'banking documents', 'tele-graph rules', 'warehousing', 'deposits', 'loans', 'remittances', 'inter-banking transactions', 'customer services', 'accounting', 'treasury', 'cashiers' and 'note issues' (BOC 1991c: 2635–51). They were named 'Working Procedures' in general and 'Key Points' for specific operations (BOC 1999: 63). Take the deposit business as an example: the regulations included more than 20 detailed work flows and binding rules, covering who should accept the money or cheque and how it should be done, as well as who should verify the money (cheque), make the voucher, stamp the seal, give out the deposit certificate, keep the business record and cross-check it, etc. (BOC 1991c: 2639–41). Every staff member's duties and responsibilities were clearly defined. In so doing, the work was systematized and standardized, which strengthened professionalism and efficiency, as well as reducing job-shirking and fraud.

Accounting

'A bank's accounting expertise reflects its standard of management and its scientific way of administration' (BOC 1999: 62). BOC invited E. Nicols, Deputy Chief Accountant of the Midland Bank, to help the reform of the Bank's accounting on the patterns of British and American systems (ibid.: 61). BOC adopted the latest accounting methods such as double-entry and back-up journal vouchers and loose-leaf accounting books. After that, cus-tomer service was improved; accounts of every branch were squared up daily; and the Head Office could receive, on a daily basis, reports showing balances of assets and the liabilities of branches and their accumulated profits and losses. The modern accounting system increased information transparency, improved the Bank's service quality and strengthened the financial control on branches (BOC 1999). Soon, BOC's accounting practice was followed by many other Chinese banks.

Emphasis on surveys and research

The importance of surveys and research was not realized by the general public in the 1930s, but the Bank of China took the initiative and achieved remarkable results (BOC 1999). In 1930, F.W. Gray, deputy secretary general of the British Institute of Bankers, was appointed acting director of the Economic Research Department (ibid.: 64). Consisting of a group of learned scholars, the Research Department became the Bank of China's brain trust, the strategist and advisor for decision-making. A number of periodicals, articles and yearbooks were published, such as the *Bank of China Monthly*, the fortnightly *Life at the Bank of China* and *Financial Statistics Monthly*. There were also the *Yearbook of Banks in China* and the *Bank of China Annual Reports*, published for external distribution (BOC 1999: 65). The Annual Reports, following the pattern of the big foreign banks, were issued in the name of the general manager in both Chinese and English, and kept shareholders and customers informed of the international and domestic economic situation and BOC performance (BOC 1995: 187).

The emphasis on research and surveys benefited the Bank in the formulation of its management policies and in the development of its business; through publication and circulation of various research reports and periodicals, BOC led the way in economic and financial research in China, thus winning for the Bank a lasting reputation both at home and abroad.

Human resource management

BOC realized that, in banking, as in all service industries, staff quality was a key to success, as staff members were crucial in winning business, delivering services and maintaining reputation. BOC set up a modern personnel system, which depended less on personal and family ties than had the old-style Qianzhuang and Piaohao system.

BOC attracted talent from foreign banks. Foreign banks in China provided much-needed human capital to the Chinese banks. Here, compradors played a major role. Almost all foreign banks in China employed compradors and a small number of Chinese staff. For example, HSBC hired its first comprador, Wang Huaishan, a former Qianzhuang employee, almost immediately after the bank opened its first office in Shanghai in 1865 (Ji 2003: 55). Wang had come from Shaoxing of Zhejiang province, and he introduced many natives to the foreign banks, thus becoming one of the first generation of compradors in the banking business (ibid.). After gaining work experience in foreign banks, many compradors opened up their own banks, while others brought their management skills to Chinese banks (Ji 2003: xxxii). For example, Wang Kemin, president of BOC in the 1910s, was once the 'Chinese manager' of the Banque Franc-Chinois pour le Commerce et L'Industrie (BOC 1995: 896); Xi Demao, director and general manager of BOC, used to be comprador of the Italian Bank for China (Shou 1996: 284); Xi Songping, having worked in the Chartered Bank of India, Australia and China for six years and the Russo-Asiatic Bank for five years, joined BOC's Shanghai branch (ibid.: 282).

Besides attracting able people from foreign banks, every year BOC sent staff to the most prestigious Chinese universities and high schools to recruit outstanding students through open exams (BOC 1995). Meanwhile, returning students from abroad were welcomed. Among the 42 branch managers and department directors at the BOC's Headquarters in 1932, more than half had studied overseas. Thirteen of them had gained postgraduate degrees, including three doctorates from Harvard, Stanford and the University of Pennsylvania (Yao Songling 1968: 25–8; Cheng 2003: 172). Foreign financial experts were especially valued in BOC. BOC invited a German banker to advise its foreign exchange business, a British banker to take charge of BOC's economic research and a British accounting expert to help with accounting reform (BOC 1995: 181).

Besides recruiting high quality people, BOC paid much attention to staff training and development. Training courses and seminars were regularly held. Staff members were encouraged to take courses at night school, with BOC paying for the tuition (BOC 1995: 184). When people returning from abroad were recruited, BOC often gave them special training to absorb knowledge from other staff members who were experienced in Chinese banking (Cheng 2003).

In order to retain and stimulate talent, BOC had built an effective incentive mechanism. Following the practice of foreign banks, BOC offered their staff, in addition to relatively high salaries and bonuses, other benefits, such as vacation and pension rights, which were rarely heard of in China's business firms at that time (Cheng 2003: 178–80). High salaries and good benefits promoted the devotion and diligence of staff. Meanwhile, BOC also worked out a strict system of rewards and punishments. Rewards were given to those who gave outstanding performance, while violators of the Bank's regulations, especially those who engaged in malpractice for private gain, or those who were corrupt or depraved, were penalized mercilessly (BOC 1999: 234).

By imitating western banks, BOC established a modern corporate system. Especially through the reform of the accounting system, the standardization of business flows, emphasis on research and surveys, and the setting-up of modern human resource management, BOC greatly improved its efficiency and effectiveness, and provided a sound basis for rapid business development.

Foreign trade and international financial business

Although for a long time, foreign trade and related business was monopolized by foreign banks, BOC challenged foreign domination and vigorously competed for business (BOC 1999: 16). BOC not only established branches or offices in London, Osaka, Singapore and New York (ibid.: 70), but had also established links with 62 foreign banks abroad for money transfer and remittance transactions, and 96 specially arranged foreign correspondent banks spread over 43 countries (ibid.: 73). In order to master the up-to-date foreign trade and international business, BOC often sent staff to correspondent banks for training (BOC 1995).

Most significantly, BOC invited August Rohdervald, the deputy director of the foreign department of Darmstadt Bank of Germany, to be an advisor to BOC on foreign business (BOC 1995: 204). In 1930, the Foreign Department was set up. All management regulations and business procedures were compiled by Rohdervald (BOC 1999). The establishment of a Foreign Department created a precedent in China's banking industry and showed BOC's determination to challenge the foreign banks' monopoly. In 1929, about 33 BOC branches and sub-branches were handling foreign trade and exchange business (BOC 1995: 211). King (1988b: 370) acutely observed that BOC developed a Foreign Department which 'challenged the Hongkong Bank in its own sphere of expertise'. Meanwhile, through comprehensive and intensive training, BOC gradually cultivated a team of foreign business experts. Among them, Bei Zuyi had the reputation of being one of the ablest foreign-exchange experts in the country (Stern 1951: 323).

In this way, BOC's foreign business flourished. BOC increased its market share in foreign trade financing, using up-to-date instruments such as the purchase of documentary bills from importers and exporters, granting packing credit and overdraft facilities to exporters subject to their provision of guarantees to cover the Bank's risks, and providing consultancy and guarantee services (BOC 1999). Meanwhile, BOC explored all kinds of foreign exchange business, such as draft remittance, telegraphic transfer, swap business, and purchasing money orders issued by the big foreign banks (BOC 1999: 66). In the late 1920s, BOC Hongkong branch, under the leadership of Bei Zuyi, taking advantage of its geographic location and frequent business contacts with Southeast Asia, was very active in arbitrage business, and gained handsome profits (BOC 1995: 68).

In particular, BOC tried its best to capture the remittance business of the overseas Chinese in competition with foreigners (Allen and Donnithorne 1954). It was with this aim that BOC established widespread branches in Southeast Asia. Branches and agencies were entrusted with the collection of overseas Chinese remittances on the Bank's behalf. On the drafts it was clearly marked 'To be cashed at the Bank of China' (BOC 1999: 77). At the BOC receipt branches, like Hong Kong, Guangzhou, Shantou, Xiamen and Shanghai, measures were adopted to facilitate payment of overseas Chinese remittances, like taking a short-cut mailing route, simplifying paying-out procedures and improving customer services. In this way, BOC's fame was spread far and wide. Gradually, overseas Chinese remittances that used to go through foreign banks were channelled to the Bank of China. The market share of such business handled by the Bank increased from 7.34 per cent in 1932 to about 14 per cent in 1934 (ibid.: 78), jumping to 50 per cent in 1942 (ibid.: 170).

No doubt, BOC played a crucial role in breaking the monopoly of foreign banks in China's foreign trade and related business. Besides BOC, other Chinese banks also worked hard on foreign business, like BoCOM, SHCS and ZJIB (BOC 1995: 192). Obviously, by the middle of the 1930s, foreign banks had ceased to dominate foreign business, except in the field of foreign trade financing (Allen and Donnithorne 1954: 119). Even in that field they had to face increasingly tough competition from the Chinese banks.

Note issue

For a long time, foreign banknotes were welcomed by Chinese people and circulated widely throughout China as a more secure medium of exchange. Along with BOC's gaining strength, BOC went all out to increase the circulation of its paper currency. 'It was the Bank of China that contributed most to the wide circulation and standardization of paper currency in China' (Cheng 2003: 162). Here, BOC employed innovative approaches to achieve this goal.

Note issue agency system

As early as 1915, the BOC made an agreement with ZJIB whereby ZJIB voluntarily relinquished its own right of issue and served as a secret note issuance agency for BOC. ZJIB could obtain C$1 million in banknotes from BOC by depositing a reserve fund in BOC, and BOC would pay ZJIB 2.5 per cent annual interest on its cash reserve (Cheng 2003: 163). The notes carried BOC's name and had a special mark for reference. To the general public, however, there was no apparent difference between these notes and those directly issued by BOC (ibid.). As a result, BOC increased its note issue more cost-effectively, while ZJIB saved the cost of issuance but also received extra income from its cash reserves. The system was so successful that other banks, including the National Commercial Bank, SHCS, Jincheng Bank and many of the Qianzhuang, signed similar agreements with BOC (*Yinhang Zhoubao* 13 May 1924). By June 1924, 22 banks and Qianzhuang had obtained C$6,140,000 worth of BOC notes (*Yinhang Zhoubao* 24 June 1924). The indirectly issued notes of BOC rapidly grew to represent about a quarter of its total notes in circulation (Cheng 2003: 164).

Public surveillance of the reserve funds

To win the confidence of the public and to prevent unlimited expansion of the note issue, the Bank took the bold step of setting up an Audit Commission of Reserves Against Note Issuance, with representatives from the Ministry of Finance, the Shanghai Chamber of Commerce, the Shanghai Bankers Association, the Shanghai Qianzhuang Association and BOC's directors and supervisors of the board (Zhang Jia'ao 1958: 6). It was stipulated that the Bank should back its note issue by reserves of 60 per cent in specie and 40 per cent in government securities and other bank assets. From May 1928, the reserves were examined monthly and made public in the newspaper (BOC 1991c: 1975). The reputation of the Bank's notes was greatly enhanced after this practice began. Those people who previously only trusted in foreign banks' notes now willingly accepted BOC banknotes (BOC 1995).

On the other hand, foreign banknotes suffered heavy blows. After the First World War, angry with the Treaty of Versailles settlement and the 'Twenty-one Demands' of the Japanese, there erupted the most famous anti-foreign movement in China – the 1919 May Fourth Movement. One consequence was that the whole country boycotted Japanese goods and refused to use Japanese banknotes (Shou 1996). Several years later, a demonstration by Chinese students was crushed by the British-dominated Shanghai municipal police on 30 May 1925. This was the famous 'May Thirtieth Massacre', which intensified the tempestuous anti-imperialist movement in China (Chesneaux 1977b). HSBC and other British banks' notes were rejected in many places (Shou 1996). Thus the patriotism of the Chinese people directly impacted against the issuance and circulation of foreign banknotes.

By the middle of the 1930s, Chinese banknotes gradually dominated the Chinese money market. In 1935, the year-end banknote circulation of Chinese banks was C$1,187 million, whereas the banknote circulation of foreign banks in China (excluding Hong Kong) was only C$225 million (Rawski 1989: 380). The former was more than five times the latter. BOC's notes were so popular throughout China that 'even in the remote hinterland people began to keep it as cash' (Zhang Zihan 1942: 251). By the eve of the fabi reform in 1935, BOC had issued C$187 million in notes, more than any other bank operating in China (BOC 1995: 312). BOC's expanding banknotes business not only improved its reputation, but also provided a convenient source of funds, which promoted the growth of other business.

Deposits

Since the late Qing period, it had been a tradition for Chinese high-level officials and rich merchants to put their savings in foreign banks. However, the situation changed when foreign banks suffered a series of catastrophes in the 1920s (Cheng 2003). The Banque Industrielle de Chine and the Russo-Asiatic Bank successively went bankrupt, destroying the myth of the foreign banks' force majeure (Ji 2003). The Banque Industrielle de Chine was closed down due to bad operational and speculation losses. Some C$400,000 to C$500,000 worth of banknotes could not be cashed, and a huge amount of overseas Chinese remittance was held up in the system. In Beijing, about 3,000 depositors could not withdraw their deposits of no less than C$600,000 (Shou 1996: 121). The bank's general manager Pernote was arrested by the French court (ibid.). Likewise, due to its huge losses in financial speculation in Paris, the Russo-Asiatic Bank was finally closed down in 1926. It, too, brought about huge losses to Chinese depositors (Shou 1996: 58). Their failures taught the lesson that foreign banks were not necessarily a safe place to keep money. In December 1930, the Hong Kong and Guangzhou branches of National City Bank had a bank-run due to a rumour that the bank was bankrupt and the general manager had killed himself. The bank-run lasted several days and lots of deposits were withdrawn (*NCH* 16 December 1930). This kind of bank-run was unimaginable in the past. It indicated the declining confidence of the Chinese people in the foreign banks.

On the other hand, Chinese banks spared no effort in attracting deposits. To this end, BOC laid special emphasis on customers. Foreign banks in Shanghai only paid interest on customers' silver tael deposits in the 1910s, but not on silver coin deposits. However, the Bank of China paid interest on both (BOC 1999: 15). Meanwhile, no fee was charged when the depositors exchanged silver taels for silver coins, or vice versa, and the remittance fee was reduced (BOC 1999: 15). As a creative approach, the silver dollar account won BOC a good reputation and attracted an increasing number of customers.

Meanwhile, BOC endeavoured to improve service by introducing a 'one-teller' practice and door-to-door visits by roving clerks, and by quoting preferential interest rates for deposits of large sums, long-maturity and frequent rollovers (BOC 1999: 68). In important branches, senior staff greeted customers and answered their inquiries in the bank hall. On traditional festivals or holidays, gifts were sent out to customers, and for some key customers, regular visits and contacts were arranged (BOC 1995: 232).

BOC tried its best to identify and seize business opportunities. For example, when the tax money of one Shanghai commercial firm was embezzled by a member of staff, BOC realized the business potential and informed all commercial firms in Shanghai that firms could open current accounts with BOC, and use BOC cheques to pay taxes so as to prevent this kind of embezzlement. This measure attracted many commercial firms, and even some foreign firms which didn't deal with Chinese banks came to open accounts at BOC (BOC 1995: 62). On another occasion, in 1930, the funds of the Christian missionaries in China, which were managed by the Shanghai Missionary Treasury Association, had reached about US$19 million. The funds were deposited in the National City Bank and HSBC, so BOC decided to compete for this business. BOC offered the Shanghai Missionary Treasury Association convenient services and additional facilities, which impressed them so much that deposits of the missionary fund were transferred from the foreign banks to BOC (BOC 1995: 205).

Thanks to the great efforts of BOC, the total amount of deposits rose from C$330 million in 1927 to C$1,130 million in 1937 (BOC 1995: 233). In contrast, the National City Bank Beijing branch complained in 1936 that 'over the past three years, our Chinese currency deposits of both savings and fixed accounts gradually declined' (FRI 1990: 678). In July 1934, the Chinese currency deposit accounted for 85 per cent of the total deposits in the Beijing branch. It declined to 66 per cent by July 1935 and fell further to 50 per cent by July 1936 (ibid.).

'A bank functions as a bank only when it starts to do business with its customers' money' (Cheng 2003: 137). Regarding deposits as the lifeline,

BOC adopted innovative approaches to attract deposits. Other Chinese banks followed suit. At the end of 1935 the deposit holdings of Chinese banks amounted to C$3,931 million, much higher than the C$770 million absorbed by foreign banks in China (Rawski 1989: 392). Indeed, 'There appeared a trend that modern Chinese banks gradually received favour among those Chinese who previously worshipped foreign banks' (Cheng 2003: 76).

Bank–client relationship

Before BOC was founded, foreign banks had already built up a strong relationship with foreign firms operating in China. In order to tap and develop its client group, BOC prioritized Chinese enterprises in modern industry. The First World War provided a unique and magnificent opportunity for expansion for the modern sector in China (Bergère 1986). Since the western powers were occupied with the war, the decline of imports and foreign competition led to the development of substitute industries in China; the increased demand for raw materials and foodstuffs during the First World War stimulated Chinese exports; and meanwhile, the rise of silver on the world market reinforced the buying power of Chinese currency. The period of the First World War, which lasted from 1914 to 1918, and the years immediately following, up to 1921, were known in Chinese business circles as the 'golden age of the bourgeoisie' and the 'golden age of national industries' (Bergère 1986: 63). As a result, Chinese capitalists expanded into modern industries, previously dominated by foreign firms (Coble 1980).

Taking advantage of the 'golden age' expansion, BOC increased loans in silk, textile and flour, which were China's three traditional industries, and the loans in these areas accounted for 80 per cent of BOC's total industrial loans (BOC 1995: 255). Thanks to rising credibility and quality of service, BOC built up important clients, such as the Shengxin Cotton Mill, the Yufeng Cotton Mill, the Meiya Silk Mill, the Maoxin Flour Mill, the Fuxin Flour Mill, the Dafeng Flour Mill and the Shoufeng Flour Mill (BOC 1995: 255–60). Besides loans, BOC provides diversified services to clients, such as remittances, deposits, foreign trade financing, money transfer and exchange transactions.

The relationship between the legendary Rong family and BOC is worthy of mention. In the 1910s, the Rong brothers, Rong Zongjing and Rong Desheng, natives of Wuxi, Jiangsu province, began to create an integrated industrial complex including flour and cotton mills in Shanghai and several other cities (Ji 2003: 113). In 1915, they opened the First Shenxin Cotton Mill, and by 1931 nine factories had been established (BOC 1995: 258). Shenxin Mill was the largest manufacturing company in China's textile industry, indeed in all of modern Chinese industry. The Rong brothers were China's leading industrialists.

During the 1920s, Shenxin became a client of BOC, and the two parties trusted each other and cooperated closely. The Rong brothers used the

Shenxin Company's name to invest C$250,000 in BOC, and became share-holders of BOC (Ji 2003: 113). Later, Rong Zongjing was elected as director of BOC (BOC 1995: 886). From 1923 to 1933, BOC provided more than C$10 million in short- or long-term loans to the Shenxin Mill (Cheng 2003: 87), and provided a package of other preferential services. Besides cotton mills, the famous Fuxin Flour Mill and Maoxin Flour Mill owned by the Rong brothers also dealt with BOC (BOC 1995). In fact, the Rong brother's enterprise group had become the most important client of BOC. In 1935, the Rong brothers wrote an appreciative letter to BOC, acknowledging the support and services received from the Bank (BOC 1995: 261). Of course, the prosperity of the Rong enterprises created business opportunities for BOC and promoted BOC's reputation. This was typical co-branding, namely, BOC and Rong enterprises came together and shared their competencies to get the maximum revenues and customer recognition.

BOC developed clients in other industries as well. Zhangyu Brewery Co. in Yantai was China's most famous brewery, producing various kinds of wine and brandy and enjoying a good reputation both at home and abroad. Zhangyu Co. had a long-term relationship with BOC, which provided various credit facilities (BOC 1995: 264). Yongli Chemical Co. in Tianjin was China's first alkali producer. BOC, with several Chinese banks, formed a consortium to provide loans and other services (BOC 1995; FRO 1983). Yongli Co. broke the monopoly previously held by Britain's Brunner Mond and Co. in the Chinese market to became the largest alkali producer in Asia.

After the Mukden Incident of 1931, Japan occupied Manchuria in China, which provoked much anger and condemnation by the Chinese people. There were waves of widespread boycotts of Japanese goods and increasing sales promotions of national products. In 1932, with the sponsorship of the Bank of China, the 'Chinese Product Production and Sales Co-operative Association' was established with Zhang Jia'ao as the director-general (BOC 1999). The Bank provided both factories and merchants with credit facilities in order to promote production and sales. During the process, the China Chemical Industry Co., the Tianchu Gourmet Powder Factory, the Huasheng Electrical Appliance Factory, the Guanshengyuan Food Co., the Wuhe Weaving Mill, the Zhonghua Iron Foundry, the Yapuer Bulb Factory and the China Enamel Factory, amongst others, established or reinforced business relationships with BOC (BOC 1995: 263). These companies were very influential in their respective industries and their cooperation with BOC brought about mutual benefits.

Through taking advantage of the prosperity of China's modern industry and by promoting national products, BOC had established a close relationship with the big Chinese firms. Along with the growth of clients, BOC could attract huge deposits from these clients, and could recover both the principal and interest from loans, and also gain profits from other diversified services. The mutual benefit made both the BOC and Chinese enterprises bigger and stronger.

Inter-bank cooperation

The top officials at the Bank of China had long ago realized that in order to confront the powerful foreign banks, Chinese banks had to strengthen cooperation in order to tide over crises and enhance group competitiveness (BOC 1999).

Shanghai Bankers Association

Under the initiative of BOC, the Shanghai Bankers Association (SBA) was established in 1918. By 1929, the member banks had increased to 26 from the original 7, and included all the major banks in Shanghai (Cheng 2003: 195). The SBA played an important role in modernizing Chinese banks and improving their quality. It helped various banks issue syndicated loans, popularized standard accounting based on the double-entry system, provided training for staff of member banks, and set up a joint warehouse to promote secured loans (Xu Cangshui 1925). In 1919, the SBA established a joint reserve fund, with a sum of C$300,000, deposited with BOC as a protection against any emergency in any of the banks (Tamagna 1942: 43). Besides this, *Yinhang Zhoubao* (Bankers Weekly), publicized by the SBA, advocated the expansion of modern banks and called for the abolition of foreign banks' privileges in China (Bergère 1986: 134). Certainly, the SBA did a good job in defending the common interests of Chinese banks in meeting foreign competition. For example, when SHCS was promoting its foreign exchange business, it was boycotted by the Chartered Bank, which refused to accept SHCS's foreign exchange contracts. Without yielding to this pressure, SHCS announced that it would refuse to accept the Chartered Bank's contracts as well. With the strong support of the SBA, the Chartered Bank had to change its stand (FRO 1990).

Credit investigation society

In the 1920s, credit investigation agencies were run by Japanese and Americans in Shanghai. In 1932, BOC took the lead, together with six other Chinese banks, in setting up China's first professional credit information service – the China Institute of Credit Investigation (BOC 1995: 188). The institute provided various kinds of information, including a potential customer's family background, property, assets, business connections and credit evaluation, whether for corporate or for individual customers (Zi 2005). Later, the institute was reorganized into the China Credit Investigation Incorporation and set up branches in Tianjin and Hankou. The services were welcomed by a large number of Shanghai banks and other firms. Foreign business people in Shanghai were deeply impressed by the quality of these reports and frequently turned to the institute for services (Cheng 2003: 159). As one Chinese banker observed, 'Since the establishment of the Institute, the disdain of foreign people toward Chinese [banks] has changed' (SHCS 1932). More importantly, by making use of the credit investigation reports, Chinese banks were able to evaluate their potential customers and reduce business risks.

Fighting against financial crisis

When BOC's Shanghai branch led the resistance against the Beijing government's note suspension order in 1916, BOC was fully supported by the managers of SHCS, the National Commercial Bank, ZJIB and others. Later on, when Zhang Jia'ao called for increasing private shares in BOC, the major Chinese banks enthusiastically responded (BOC 1995).

As the largest Chinese bank, BOC felt a sense of duty to help other banks. For example, in 1930, the Bank of China joined hands with the Bank of Communications in providing capital to the Sinhua Trust Savings and Commercial Bank Ltd for its reorganization (BOC 1999: 107). In 1931, the Bank supported SHCS in calming down a bank-run caused by the salt pledged as security for the bank's loan being soaked by water (ibid.). In 1932, loans and overdrafts were extended to the National Industrial Bank of China in Tianjin to defuse a panic deposit withdrawal (ibid.).

The close cooperation among Chinese banks helped them to pursue common interests, boost reputation and tide over financial crises. As a group, they became more competitive in China's financial market.

Change of balance of power in China's financial market

Although foreign banks owned absolute competitive advantages in the nineteenth century and the beginning of the twentieth century, Chinese banks, especially BOC, competed vigorously for business. Through all the above mentioned efforts, by 1935 BOC had already became a serious contender to foreign banks in China's financial market.

When BOC was established in 1905, it was lagging far behind HSBC (see the indicators in Table 5.2). But BOC expanded amazingly. By 1935, its scale of assets and the paid-up capital had already overtaken those of HSBC. The value of banknotes issued by BOC was 2.4 times that of HSBC, in spite of the fact that some HSBC banknotes circulated outside China (in Hong Kong) (Rawski 1989: 375). Deposits in BOC increased 63 times from 1905 to 1935, and reached the level of HSBC. The loan business of BOC also advanced rapidly, jumping from a negligible C$13.4 million to about C$500 million, which was even higher than that of HSBC in 1935.

Regarding net profit and the related return on assets (ROA) and return on equities (ROE), there still existed a big gap, namely, HSBC was far more efficient and profitable than BOC. This indicated that BOC needed to improve its management and efficiency. Meanwhile, political interference had a direct adverse impact upon BOC's profit-earning capabilities, whereas foreign banks in China did not face such a problem. For example, BOC

Table 5.2 Comparison between HSBC and BOC, 1905–35 (C$ million)

	Year	Paid-up capital	Total assets	Banknotes	Deposits	Loans	Net profit	ROA (%)	ROE (%)
HSBC	1905	10.0	290.8	19.0	222.0	91.1	3.16	1.09	31.6
	1925	20.0	703.8	45.3	550.7	267.2	12.50	1.80	62.5
	1935	20.0	1,051.5	119.0	776.2	435.9	12.10	1.20	60.5
BOC	1905	5.6	n/a	0.752	12.04	13.4	0.052	n/a	0.93
	1925	20.0	464.1	127.0	259.00	266.5	1.350	0.29	6.80
	1935	40.0	1,342.2	286.0	766.30	489.0	3.600	0.27	9.00

Notes:
1. The original account unit of HSBC was the HK dollar, which was roughly at par with the Chinese silver dollar, C$ (Wang Jingyu 1999).
2. The original account unit of Bank of China in 1905 was the silver tael, which was exchanged to the silver dollar at: 1 tael=C$1.4.

Sources:
King 1987: 7; King 1988a: 56–7; King 1988b: 126, 176, 182.
Kong 1991: 76, 79, 182, 204, 212, 215, 228, 369.
BOC 1995: 908–18.

was instructed to buy government bonds, but bond prices kept sliding; BOC was forced to lend money to local governments, and these lendings became bad (see Chapter 4). Finally, foreign-owned commercial firms or industries, many of which were more competitive than their Chinese counterparts, were generally better capitalized, more efficiently managed and more technologically organized (Coble 1980). The higher quality of HSBC's foreign clients meant higher profits for HSBC than the Chinese clients did for BOC. Nevertheless, considering the fact that BOC was 40 years younger than HSBC, and that HSBC was one of the most powerful and profitable banks in the world, it is fair to say that BOC had made amazing progress.

As a group, Chinese banks wasted no time in catching up and overtaking their foreign counterparts. As one observer wrote, 'Among all China's ventures over the past decade, the modern banks have made the quickest advance, gained the greatest achievement, built up the best credit, and established the most consolidated base' (Xinong 1922). By the end of 1936, there were 30 foreign banks operating in China with 114 branches (Liu Di 1998: 129). In contrast, there were 164 Chinese banks with 1,627 outlets (Cheng 2003: 70). Chinese banks went beyond major cities to reach all over China, even extending to foreign countries. 'Regarding the number of banks and their outlets, Chinese banks finally became the master in their own house' (Hong 2001: 252).

Chinese economic historians coined a special term, 'capital power' (*zili*), to measure the size of a financial institution. This term shows the resources mobilized by a financial institution. It includes its paid-in capital, the attracted deposits and banknotes issues (Yang Yinpu 1930). Combined, Chinese banks owned about C$7,000 million, accounting for more than

77 per cent of China's total capital power in 1936, having increased from virtually nothing in 1894 (Table 5.3 and Figure 5.1). At the same time, the strong competition of modern Chinese banks severely restricted foreign banks' expansion. Before the interruption of the Japanese invasion of 1937, foreign banks only owned about C$1,200 million, or 12 per cent of China's total capital power, declining from 32 per cent in 1894 (Table 5.3. and Figure 5.1). Chinese banks, as a group, finally changed the balance of power in China's financial markets.

The famous economist Ma Yinchu concluded that:

> The monopoly power of the foreign banks in China has declined considerably in contrast to their previous position . . . It is the result of the efforts of China's new entrepreneurs who run the banking business determinedly and have overcome all sorts of hardships and deprivations because of their belief in the profitability of this new business. Their

Table 5.3 Change of capital power in China's financial market, 1894–1936 (C$ million)

Financial institutions	1894		1925		1936	
	Amount	%	Amount	%	Amount	%
Foreign banks	280	32.5	1,303	36.7	1,236	12.3
Shanxi Piaohao	280	32.5	0	0.0	0	0.0
Qianzhuang	303	35.0	800	22.5	757	8.9
Chinese modern banks	0	0.0	1,453	40.8	6,930	77.7
Total	**863**	**100.0**	**3,557**	**100.0**	**8,924**	**100.0**

Source: Cheng 2003: 241.

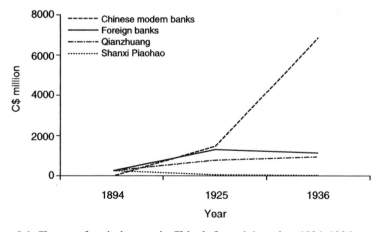

Figure 5.1 Change of capital power in China's financial market, 1894–1936.

activity had substantially recovered China's rights and profits [from the foreign banks] and significantly improved the unequal relationship between foreigners and Chinese.

(Ma Yinchu 1933)

Conclusion

The Opium Wars, which occurred in 1840–2 and 1856–60, were fought primarily to determine the relations between China and the West (Chesneaux 1977a). After the 1840s, 'the western policy towards China had progressed from gunboat policy to financial gunboat policy' (Wang Jingyu 1999: 4). Western banks came in and expanded in the treaty ports under the protection of extraterritoriality. They financed foreign trade, handled foreign exchange and issued banknotes. They possessed financial strength, strong international networks, modern management and high-quality clients. They not only held the official funds derived from Chinese Maritime Customs and other sources to pay off foreign debts and indemnities, but they also served as repositories of the private funds of Chinese politicians and Warlords (Fairbank 1971). Until 1927, the foreign banks enjoyed absolute competitive advantages and dominated the Chinese financial landscape.

On the other hand, 'China was changed by her modern encounter with the west' (Feuerwerker 1995: 181). The opening up of China by foreigners remains 'fundamental to the development of China. It is in relation to that opening-up – in its wake or as a reaction to it – that the various elements of Chinese modernity gradually emerged' (Bergère 1986: 13). Although much smaller and weaker, modern Chinese banks were courageous to face the competition of many types of business (Allen and Donnithorne 1954). Chinese banks broke the monopoly of foreign banks in foreign trade and international exchanges, established close relationships with big Chinese firms, attracted an increasing share of deposits and expanded the note issue all over the country. During this process, Chinese banks greatly improved their financial strength, expanded networks both at home and abroad, and modernized the management. There is no doubt that Chinese banks had grown into viable and self-sustaining institutions, and by the middle of the 1930s they were able, finally, to 'outweigh foreign banks in overall importance' (Nolan 1993: 46).

Several factors contributed to the success of Chinese banks. The example of BOC is an excellent one.

There is, first of all, the demonstration effect. '[T]he foreigner served as a necessary agent to start the Chinese economy on the road to modernization' (Dernberger 1975: 46). The existence of western banks produced demonstration effects and motivated the emergence and growth of Chinese modern banks. Most top and middle-level managers of BOC studied abroad, had an international vision and were willing to learn from foreign competitors. Using the international experience as reference, BOC adopted a western-style limited liability company system. BOC took up the double-entry accounting system used by British and American banks and greatly improved its efficiency and management. BOC recruited western banking experts, who introduced the most advanced business skills and practice. By imitating western big banks, BOC restructured its branches based on the economic importance of each area rather than of administrative regions. The list could go on and on. Learning from the strengths of western banks, BOC bridged the gap and achieved great success. Put in another way, without the presence and competition of foreign banks, it would be hard to imagine the appearance, development and prosperity of BOC. In this sense, foreigners played a decisive role in the early development of Chinese modern banks.

The second point is the government support enjoyed by BOC. The late Qing, the Northern Warlord regime and the early Nationalist government, to some extent and in some aspects, devised an institutional framework favourable to the growth of BOC. Tamagna (1942: 47) commented that, 'modern [Chinese] banking developed by leaps and bounds, with direct or indirect government backing'. The governments entrusted BOC to handle treasury, supported BOC to extend banknote issuance, and encouraged BOC to explore the foreign trade business, for example. The Nationalist government recovered a series of 'rights', from which western banks lost their former privileges and had their power weakened. In a word, government support put BOC in a stronger position to compete with foreign banks.

The third point is the development of BOC's modern corporate governance structure. Since its establishment BOC had been developing western-style corporate governance, which set and enforced clear lines of responsibility and accountability throughout the organization. Professional managers took the chief duties in the bank, auditing was strengthened (see Chapter 6), and accounting was in line with international standards. Recruitment was open to the public through competitive examinations. By 1935, BOC had already been turned into a new type of business institution, somewhat akin to the 'modern enterprise' described by Alfred Chandler. The modern corporate structure helped BOC achieve efficient management, deal with the principal–agent problem, prevent financial malpractices and enhance financial strength.

Last but not least, BOC benefited from innovative approaches and methods. BOC was constantly adjusting itself to the changing business environment and customer demands. For example, BOC adopted a 'note issue agency system' and 'public surveillance of the reserve funds' to expand banknotes. Through paying interest on customers' silver coin deposits and introducing the 'one-teller' practice, BOC increased its deposit business. By virtue of founding the 'Chinese Product Production and Sales Co-operative Association', BOC contracted the best Chinese firms as clients. Inter-bank cooperation, led by BOC, remarkably boosted its capability against financial risks. Indeed, innovation and creativity enabled BOC to capture a larger market share and enhanced BOC's overall power and leverage in the Chinese financial market.

Of course, alongside the above-mentioned competition there was also cooperation between the Chinese banks and their foreign counterparts. Operating in the same economic and market environment, foreign and Chinese banks had all kinds of business connections, such as active inter-bank lending (Du 2002: 81). In particular, in order to maintain the stability of the financial market, the two sides helped each other. For example, in 1916, BOC was ordered by the government to cease the encashment of banknotes. The BOC Shanghai branch suffered a bank-run (BOC 1999). For the sake of the stability of Shanghai's financial market, the Shanghai Foreign Banks Association decided to allow BOC to overdraw credit of C$2 million (BOC 1995: 78), although in the event the Shanghai branch did not need to use it before the crisis had calmed down. In some cases, Chinese banks also gave a hand to their foreign counterparts. During the May Thirtieth Anti-Imperialist Movement in 1925, there was a boycott on Japanese banknotes, and the Tianjin branch of Yokohama Specie Bank suffered a bank-run. The BOC Tianjin branch offered financial support and helped the Japanese bank tide over the crisis (Shou 1996: 316).

However, the head-on competition between Chinese and foreign banks was broken by the Sino-Japanese war (1937–45). During the War, especially after the Pacific war erupted in 1941, the banks of Britain, America and the allied countries in China were closed down or taken over by the Japanese for liquidation (King 1988b). BOC and other Chinese banks relocated to the hinterland. During the War, HSBC opened an agency in Chongqing in 1943, although with very limited business (Collis 1965: 232). After the War, western banks tried to resume their business in China. However, China was undergoing profound changes. On the one hand, the Nationalist government tightened government control on financial business; foreign banks were limited to certain business areas relating to foreign exchange transactions (Ji 2003: 222). On the other hand, China had to contend with the civil war between Nationalists and Communists, and the political and economic environment was extremely unstable. Foreign banks gradually reduced their business, and after 1949 eventually left mainland China. It was not until 30 years later that they staged a comeback. But, by that time, the world had been transformed beyond recognition. Was the current competitive environment the same or even more challenging than the first half of the twentieth century? Could Chinese banks successfully compete against the foreign giants? These questions will be answered in the final chapter.

6   White-collar crimes

Introduction

'The commission of wrongs through fraud is as old as human society' (Weisburd *et al.* 1991: 1). But, the concept of white-collar crime did not come into use until the celebrated sociologist Edwin H. Sutherland coined it. Sutherland's (1940) talk of 'the white collar criminal' changed the study of crime throughout the world in significant ways by focusing attention upon a form of law-breaking that had previously been ignored by criminological scholars. Sutherland argued that members of privilege and status in society were just as likely to commit crimes as those from the lower classes. According to Sutherland (1983: 7), 'White-collar crime may be defined approximately as a crime committed by a person of respectability and high social status in the course of his occupation.' Sutherland especially emphasized such representative corporate offences as antitrust violations, false advertising, theft of trade secrets and bribery in order to obtain special privileges (Geis and Goff 1983: ix).

Following upon Sutherland's scholarship, the study of white-collar crime has become a much wider subject. It includes a variety of criminal activities, such as bank embezzlement, land swindles, price-fixing, fraudulent loans, bribery, mail and wire fraud, and deception. It is not the offenders' occupational position or social status that characterizes these crimes but rather how they are committed (Weisburd *et al.* 1991: 7). Herbert Edelhertz (1970), a US federal prosecutor in the Department of Justice, gave a new scholarly definition, arguing that a white-collar crime was 'an illegal act or series of illegal acts committed by nonphysical means and by concealment of guile, to obtain money or property, or to obtain business or personal advantage'. This conception shifted the major focus from the status of the offender to a particular kind of offence. And it is becoming increasingly influential. Likewise, Weisburd *et al.* (1991: 81) argued that those in positions close to centres of money and power have the chance to commit the 'most consequential white-collar crimes' regardless of their status in society and their occupational prestige. For example, a low-level manager close to the flow of money may have the greatest chance of diverting a large sum even though he is not a board member or a senior manager.

The evolution of the concept of white-collar crime has thus been accompanied by changes in meaning. For the time being, many people employ terms such as economic crime and occupational crime to describe conduct equivalent to white-collar misconduct. The United Nations used the designation 'abuse of power' (Geis and Goff 1983: xxx). To some, the term still refers to crimes committed by individuals of high social status. However, all these terms tend to be similar and cover a number of key aspects of human behaviour (Pickett and Pickett 2002). In fact, it is the contrast between white-collar crime and crime in a common sense that is most significant and thought-provoking.

First, smash-and-grab robbery, rape, murder and other such crimes are easier to describe and categorize (Pickett and Pickett 2002). Violent crimes precipitate a clear response from the general public and law enforcement agencies regarding various quick and effective countermeasures. In contrast, white-collar crime, as it is generally non-violent, appears to be non-traumatic and is easily ignored by police and citizens (ibid.).

Second, white-collar crime may not be prosecuted in court. Paul Tappan (1947) held that only convicted persons ought to be called 'criminals' and studied as such. Sutherland (1983) disapproved of such an idea by contending that it was what the person actually had done . . . not . . . how the criminal justice system responded to what they had done, that was essential to whether they should be considered criminal offenders. Calavita *et al.* (1997: 22) echoed Sutherland's opinion by arguing that, 'The issue here is not whether wrongdoing can be proven before a court of law but whether deliberate insider abuse occurred'. This is particularly the case in the area of the finance industry. The hidden and complex nature of many financial frauds makes them difficult to be detected (Calavita *et al.* 1997). Numerous studies have pointed out the limited capacity of criminal justice agencies to deal with such financial frauds (Benson and Walker 1988), not to mention the fact that political protection and collusion make prosecution more difficult.

Third, in the short term, white-collar crime seems harmless. It is in the longer term that deceitful behaviour has a disastrous impact on business and communities (Pickett and Pickett 2002). The financial cost of 'crime in the suit' is usually many times as great as that of 'crime in the street'. 'The transgressions of these great criminal capitalists were of such magnitude that the receipts of burglars and shoplifters pale in comparison' (Robb 1992: 10). Furthermore, white-collar crime is more likely to 'tear at the core of a social system and render citizens cynical and selfish' (Geis and Goff 1983: x). White-collar crime affects not only individuals but the entire economy and even endangers social and economic stability.

This chapter discusses white-collar crime in BOC. It covers various activities that fall under the broad category of white-collar crime, including insider loans, self-dealing, embezzlement and using public funds for private expenses.

Following the traditional scholarship in white-collar crime, the discussion of wrongdoing is not confined to prosecuted or even prosecutable crimes (Calavita *et al.* 1997). Indeed, this study will use the terms white-collar crime, banking crime, insider abuse, wrongdoing, misconduct, fraud and financial crime interchangeably. Although complicated crimes often involve collusions of insiders and outsiders, this study is primarily concerned with insider fraud.

Emerging white-collar crimes

The white-collar crimes at BOC in the Qing Dynasty were mostly to be found in the handling of loans, which was the major business at that time. After its birth in 1905, Daqing Bank established a form of western corporate system. Compared to old-style Qianzhuang or Piaohao, Daqing Bank was supposed to adopt modern business rules and ordinance. But at its initial stage, the corporate system was only rudimentary, sound management and account-ancy were not established, internal monitoring was weak and old habits of extending credit loans were prevalent. Some branches ignored the risks and blindly expanded their business, and some high executives colluded in order to abuse the Bank.

Unsecured loans

Unsecured loans mean extending loans without asking for proper collateral, securities or guarantees. In 1907, the Guangdong merchant Ye Liangqing ran a store in Yingkou called Dongshenghe, which was the most prosperous store in Yingkou, and he also ran five other chain stores which were also booming (Kong 1991: 229). Dongshenghe ranked first in remittances, loans and other banking dealings amongst all the stores in that area and had a business relationship with many banks. The historical documents do not say what happened to Dongshenghe or why it got into trouble, but, all of a sudden, Dongshenghe and its chain stores went bankrupt, all on the same day in October 1907, and owed a total of 5 million taels to quite a number of banks. Among them, 700,000 taels of debts belonged to the Yingkou branch of Daqing Bank. Unfortunately these debts did not have sufficient securities (ibid.: 230). This obviously went against the 'Business Rules of Daqing Bank', which clearly stated that 'When extending loans, the Bank must require securities or guarantees' (ibid.: 207). In fact, requiring securities essentially differentiated modern banks from Qianzhuang, whose loan oper-ations were based on personal reputation and credit (Hong 1990). The bank chiefs neglected the duty incumbent upon them on the acceptance of such a trust. It is, however, more likely that they might have received kickbacks or other favours from the borrowers. The Yingkou branch monitor (a post appointed by the government), manager and assistant manager were all removed from their posts. A new monitor, Luo Yi, was appointed by the government to rectify the problems besetting the Yingkou branch. But it was Luo Yi and nobody else who was soon to be responsible for the biggest Daqing Bank scandal.

Insider loans

'Insider loans refer to loans granted by an institution to insiders themselves, or to their associates, or to entities in which insiders have a stake' (Calavita *et al.* 1997: 68). After Luo Yi assumed his post as the monitor of the Yingkou branch, he colluded with Gu Siyuan, who was the director of Daqing Bank, and established the 'Houde Bank'. In 1909 this bank was changed to Houde Banking Corporation Ltd.

Daqing Bank soon detected problems. Luo Yi and Gu Siyuan betrayed their positions of trust by utilizing the Bank's credit facilities for themselves. Houde Bank borrowed a huge amount of money from Daqing Bank: over 600,000 taels from the Yingkou branch, 560,000 taels from Shanghai, 170,000 taels from Chongqing, and so on, altogether reaching 1.5 million taels. Luo and Gu ignored the rules of Daqing Bank (Kong 1991: 208–9): loans could not be extended to entities in which insiders had a stake; total loans to one borrower could not exceed 50,000 taels. Luo, Gu as well as two managers in Houde Bank were arrested and dealt with by the Judicial Ministry. The prosecution statement read:

> Daqing Bank was founded by the Finance Ministry. The capital was composed of public funds and private shareholder's hard-earned money. The branch monitor and manager, deputy manager were in charge of extending and recovering loans. They should be risk-sensitive, upright and responsible. It has been found out that the branch monitor Luo Yi has made quite a number of problematic loans. In 1909, he even gave as much as 600,000 taels of loans to his private bank, which was co-founded secretly by him and director Gu Siyuan. Worse yet, Luo and Gu instructed other branches to lend money to Houde Bank, leading to the Bank's nationwide losses. These fraudulent and cheating practices heavily impacted the reputation of the Bank.
>
> (Kong 1991: 231–2)

Luo and Gu used the money to buy stocks and properties for speculation. Some of the money couldn't be recalled promptly, some suffered losses, and some were simply squandered. In fact, the total amount owed to Daqing Bank was later found to be 2.8 million taels (Kong 1991: 233). Of this, only 20 per cent was recovered and the remaining 2.24 million taels was written off (ibid.: 242). Historian Kong Xiangxian suggested that this case must have involved more high-ranking persons in Daqing Bank (ibid.: 235). Director Gu Siyuan dared to instruct many branches to grant loans to his private bank, in doing so he must have got the acquiescence or agreement of top management in the Head Office. That was why Zhang Yunyan, who was the chief person in Daqing Bank, was demoted, although the prosecution letter didn't charge him.

The above cases exposed the weaknesses of the internal monitoring and control of Daqing Bank. At the end of June 1911, the bad loans of Daqing Bank amounted to 16 million taels and the bad loan ratio reached a shocking 25.18 per cent (Kong 1991: 244). At that time, the total capital stock of Daqing Bank was 10 million taels, so, technically, the Bank was bankrupt. Not only would the total capital be gone, but also 6 million taels of deposits had to be absorbed. The position of Daqing Bank became precarious. After the 1911 revolution and the collapse of the Qing Dynasty, Daqing Bank was cleaned up and reorganized into the Bank of China (BOC 1995).

Contained white-collar crimes

From 1912 until 1935, BOC was generally better run than its early Qing counterpart. BOC had constructed a modern and effective corporate governance structure which set and enforced clear lines of rights and obligations throughout the organization. Professional and salaried managers took chief duties in the Bank, and a group of Jiang-Zhe Bankers had the real control of BOC. A number of measures helped increase banking security and contain frauds.

Modern management

BOC formulated a unified system for business procedure and work flows and laid down corresponding operational rules (BOC 1999). The business world was always full of temptations and traps. The setting-up of policies was in essence the institutionalization of a criterion or benchmark for the Bank's business activities in order to minimize risks (Qin 2004: 149). The contents of rules were comprehensive, covering banking business, such as deposits, loans, and remittances, and auxiliary functions, such as documents, accounting, auditing, cashiering, personnel and warehousing (BOC 1995). In so doing, the work was systematized and standardized. The emphasis on standardized methods helped create a business environment where there were fewer opportunities for fraud and where the discovery of fraud was much easier (Robb 1992).

Accounting

A bank's accounting expertise reflects its standard of management and its scientific way of administration. The Bank of China adopted the latest accounting methods such as double-entry and back-up journal vouchers and loose-leaf accounting books. John J. Clancy (1989: 10) noted that the development of double-entry bookkeeping 'first developed to check errors in accounts, became a technique to separate a man's business from his private life . . .'. The modern accounting methods increased information transparency, tightened control on branches and made it difficult for bank insiders to conceal embezzlement and other malpractices.

Auditing

Auditing was made much more rigorous than before. The posts of general auditor and roving auditors were set up (BOC 1999: 62). The position of general auditor was installed directly under the general manager and above all other departments and branches. The auditing included a regular reports check-up and nonscheduled on-site inspections. Auditors were granted access to the Bank's books and records and given power of review and examination over all the Bank's affairs (BOC 1995). What's more, auditors had the authority to punish those responsible for malpractice, including dismissing a sub-branch manager. Due to the importance of the auditing function, the selection of auditing staff thus became extremely strict and rigid discipline was imposed on them, i.e. keeping confidentiality and refraining from abusing power for personal gain. Auditing was increasingly 'used as a weapon to check upon the implementation of business policies and to uphold moral standards and discipline at the Bank' (BOC 1999: 232).

Loan management

Having drawn a lesson from Daqing Bank's loan management, BOC made great efforts to stress material collateral. This can be seen in several of BOC's regulations, which clearly stipulated that the borrowers 'have to provide security of gold, silver, bullion' or 'government bonds or the government securities' (BOC 1991a: 116, 120). BOC's 1928 regulations made the policy more straightforward by prohibiting 'any loans without sound security' (BOC 1991a: 125).

Besides requiring solid securities, there were other detailed rules. For example, BOC staff were forbidden to accept gifts or to be wined and dined by the potential borrower (BOC 1995: 254); loans were not allowed to be made to companies and firms in which the BOC staff had stakes (ibid.: 179); a single client was not allowed to take out overdrafts, take out loans and get discounts simultaneously (ibid.); the credibility of the potential borrower had to be thoroughly investigated, including the nature and potential growth of the borrower's business, manager capability, borrower's default history and life-style (BOC 1995: 254). All these measures strengthened loan management and effectively prevented irregularities in extending loans.

Strict regulations and discipline

BOC offered attractive salaries and good benefits to promote the devotion and diligence of staff. Meanwhile, BOC designed a series of rules and regulations to direct staff behaviour. For example, the staff commandment of the BOC stated: 'No bank employee is allowed to violate his or her supervisor's instruction; to run business outside the bank; to borrow money from the BOC or clients; to leak any commercial secrets' (BOC 1995: 182). BOC employees were also forbidden to engage, directly or indirectly, in any speculation or to use the Bank's name to guarantee any private business transactions (ibid.). Staff members had to abstain from any bad habits (BOC 1995: 183), such as gambling and drug abuse, since bad habits might have pushed them to use the Bank's money illegally.

These rules and regulations were strictly enforced. BOC demanded that staff should take it as a natural thing to obey rules and regulations, like having daily sleep and food (Yao Songling 1982: 100). BOC required its departments or branches to inspect the performance of its staff regularly. Members who failed to obey were subject to citation, salary cut, and, as a last resort, dismissal, regardless of who they were (BOC 1995: 183). In particular, those who engaged in malpractice for private gain, or those who were corrupt or depraved, were penalized mercilessly (BOC 1999: 234). Zhang Jia'ao indicated that he resolutely dismissed those staff who ran private businesses outside the Bank (Yao Songling 1982: 107).

Since managers had more control over money, people and property, the board of supervisors had a key function in monitoring managers on behalf of shareholders. One 'standing supervisor' was elected from five supervisors, and resided in the Bank to exercise daily duties (BOC 1991a: 165). The mechanism of checks and balance was stressed. There were detailed rules regulating manager behaviour. For example, the chief executive (general manager) was forbidden to borrow money or take mortgage loans from the Bank (BOC 1991a: 210). As the general manager, Zhang Jia'ao's salary and social expenditures were transparent (Cheng 2003). Beginning in 1922, a secretary was assigned especially to keep Zhang Jia'ao's personal account. Besides, all of his personal and family expenses were recorded for public scrutiny (Yao Songling 1982: 61). Zhang Jia'ao lived by his salary and never owned any private business in his life (Cheng 2003). Song Hanzhang, who was the Shanghai branch manager and later chairman of BOC, paid rent on a western-style house given to him as a bonus by the Bank (Cheng 2003). Song assumed many other important positions beyond BOC, such as the chairman of the Shanghai's Chamber of Commerce; nevertheless, he did not accept extra pay. Many former employees of BOC described Song as an honest man who never abused his power for personal gain (ibid.: 209). Under strict supervision and accountability, the management of BOC set a good example for their staff by putting personal integrity above selfish pursuits.

Cultivating moral character

Since bank staff deal with money every day, personal honesty and profes-sional ethics are extremely important in the banking business. While strictly enforcing disciplines, BOC required its staff to cultivate a lofty moral character. As Zhang Jia'ao said, 'Morality is even more important than one's life' (Yao Songling 1982: 61). To this end, Zhang Jia'ao set up goals for himself and the staff to follow. Staff members, whatever their positions in the Bank, had to be honest, selfless and be committed to their work (Cheng 2003: 230). Later, Zhang summarized the 'spirit of Bank of China' as nobility (*gao*), flawlessness (*jie*) and strength (*jian*) (Yao Songling 1982: 1332). The Bank published a fortnightly magazine *Life at Bank of China* and arranged regular meetings to spread these ideas among its staff, particularly for newly recruited members (BOC 1995: 187; Cheng 2003: 230). The cultivation of corporate culture by BOC set a precedent in China's banking industry.

Thanks to the improved management, strict discipline and moral education, white-collar crime during this period was effectively curbed. BOC enjoyed financial success and marched towards a strong and modern international commercial bank. Meanwhile, the new image of BOC greatly influenced and improved the general environment of the whole Chinese banking industry (Zhang Jia'ao 1977).

Rampant and systemic white-collar crimes

Causes for rampant white-collar crimes

After the mid-1930s, BOC experienced great changes internally and externally. Financial crimes became rampant and went unchecked. There has been a great deal of detailed study on why people commit fraud and what circumstances are required for fraud to arise (Pickett and Pickett 2002). In the jargon of popular criminology, a criminal needs a motive and an opportunity (Kwong 1997: 133). Four factors are identified to explain why white-collar crime flourished in BOC after the mid-1930s.

The concentration of power in the 'Four Great Families'

In 1927, the KMT headed by Chiang Kaishek ended the Warlord era and established the Nationalist government in Nanjing. According to the constitution drawn up in 1931, the government was officially organized into five powers which Sun Yatsen had defined (Chesneaux 1977b: 187). Accordingly, five supreme government branches (yuan, 'courts') were responsible for legislative, executive, judicial, supervision and examination functions. But their members were appointed, and the Executive Yuan, or Cabinet, was the only one which had real power, since it was composed of the various ministries (ibid.). In contrast to the formality with which these five organs functioned, the actual power lay around Chiang Kaishek and the 'Four Great Families' (Table 6.1).

Among the Four Families, Chiang Kaishek was the Supreme Leader of China. Chiang was thought to be the outstanding individual in a country

Table 6.1 The Four Great Families under the Nationalist government

Family	Relationship	Power
Chiang		
Chiang Kaishek, his entourage, often from his native province – Zhejiang	Married Meiling Soong	Head of party, army and government
Soong		
T.V. Soong, Soong brothers and followers	Brother of Meiling Soong and Ailing Soong	Economy and finance, and foreign affairs
Kung		
H.H. Kung, family members, Kung's favourites and countrymen from Shanxi province	Married Ailing Soong	Economy and finance
Chen		
Two brothers – Chen Guofu and Chen Lifu and associates	Nephews of a militant revolutionary who had helped Chiang in Chiang's early career	KMT party, ideology, and media

Source: Wang Xin *et al.* 1988; Chesneaux *et al.* 1977b.

where 'personalities not principles' were the most powerful factor in politics (Endicott 1975: 14). Both T.V. Soong and H.H. Kung came from eminent families, educated in America (Harvard and Yale respectively) and were related to Chiang Kaishek by marriage. The Chen family (Chen Lifu and Chen Guofu) were from Chiang's hometown. Their uncle was Chiang's close friend and sworn brother (Wang Xin *et al.* 1988). The Four Families controlled the army, party, economy and finance, media and ideology. They represented the most powerful and influential characters in China's pre-1949 modern history. As early as the 1930s, the younger daughter of Kung once furiously claimed, 'Who is the government? We are the government. The Generalissimo is my aunt's husband, the Finance Minister is my uncle, and the Industry Minister is my father. They are the government ...' (Chen Tingyi 2004b: 311). The American Chief of Staff to Chiang Kaishek, Joseph Stilwell, once observed, 'The Chinese government was an edifice which rested on fear and favouritism ... The whole government was interwoven with family and financial attachments and influences' (1948: 103).

'Power tends to corrupt, and absolute power corrupts absolutely', so wrote English nobleman Lord Acton in 1887. This statement has often been repeated, perhaps because so many people see it as undeniably true. In China, the concentration of power in the Four Families and their associates offered them rich social assets, an increased ability to gain from their positions, and plenty of opportunities to indulge in various kinds of fraud.

Ineffective legal and supervision mechanism

Game theory is often used to explain political and economic behaviour. According to this theory, actors are more likely to engage in an activity if the benefits of participation outweigh nonparticipation, the probability of success exceeds that of failure and the chances of getting away with it are greater than those of being caught (Kwong 1997: 60). The concentration of power in the Four Families not only set the stage for fraud, the typically ineffective legal and judicial system and lenient treatment of white-collar criminals offered little deterrence and, more often than not, political protection further encouraged criminal activities.

First, in the KMT government, politicians were so intimately bound up in business activity that they were unwilling to formulate effective laws and regulations to deal with white-collar crime. A large number of government officials were also directors or shareholders of companies. For example, the share-holders of the well-known Qixing Company included the wife of the Finance Minister, the undersecretary of the Finance Ministry, the deputy governor of the Central Bank, and the chairman of the China Manufacturers Bank (Zhang Jianping *et al.* 1997). The private shares of the China Development Finance Corporation were held by 13 KMT statesmen and key officials (Jingji Ziliaoshe (JJZLS) 1948). Moreover, there were no rules governing politicians' associations with trade and business, and no restrictions regarding conflicting interests of public officials.

Second, on the surface, the Supervision Yuan was accountable to the National Assembly. Its functions were 'to exercise the right of supervision and monitoring of KMT officials at various levels, with the power of impeachment, punishment, and auditing' (Qiu 2004: 152). However, the power of the Supervision Yuan was rather limited (ibid.: 138). In most cases, it existed only in name. For example, regarding its auditing function, the accounting book of central and local government agencies had to be sent to the auditing department of the Supervision Yuan within a specified time. But what happened was that, in 1943 and 1944, 'none of the accounting books had been submitted. By the end of 1944, about 500 agencies had delayed submitting' (ibid.: 239). State organizations were required to submit their income and expenses vouchers. But most of these institutions, such as the Central Bank, BOC, BoCOM and the Farmers Bank had not followed the rules. As a result, on-site auditing became impossible (ibid.: 240). These banks were headed by powerful Four Family members and the Supervision Yuan could do nothing about it. Consequently, the fraudulent practices in these banks could not be detected and corrected.

Regarding impeachment and punishment, the Supervision Yuan was a toothless tiger. The actual power and position of the Executive Yuan was higher than the Supervision Yuan (Qiu 2004). Various ministers and top administrative officials often interfered to protect their own corrupt officials. As a result, the big fish got through, and the little ones were caught. For example, it was widely known that many high-ranking officials had committed serious fraud, however, during the ten years from 1937 to 1947, 1,286 middle and low ranking officials were impeached, while only 128 high-level officials were impeached. On top of this, the vast majority of the latter were never prosecuted, and even fewer sent to prison (Chang Zemin 1979: 145).

There were some instances of top leaders greasing the wheels of fraud and offering political protection. In the summer of 1937, Wu Dingchang, the Minister for Industry, tried to stop excessive speculation in Shanghai following a major panic on the Shanghai Cotton Goods Exchange. The investigation report charged that 'certain influential persons' were involved in an attempt to break prices and manipulate transactions on the exchange' (Coble 1980: 249). When Chiang Kaishek read the confidential report, he discovered that the 'influential person' responsible for the scandal was none other than Chiang's own sister-in-law, Mme Kung. The accusation infuriated Chiang. He dismissed Wu as Minister for Industry and instead appointed him governor of Guizhou, which was a demotion. After several lower officials were arrested as scapegoats, no further investigation was allowed and the case was closed (ibid.).

Another well-known incident happened in 1948. On the eve of the KMT downfall, inflation was rising swiftly, and the government tried to stamp out black-marketing in an effort to stabilize the nation's currency. Several hundred speculators in Shanghai were arrested and one civilian was executed for economic crimes (Eastman 1984: 187). Yangtze Company, headed by David Kung (the son of H.H. Kung), was found illegally hoarding 20,000 tons of goods. David was arrested and goods were confiscated (Zhang Jianping *et al.* 1997: 779). But soon David was set free and flown to the US, obviously rescued by his aunt Madame Chiang. Those confiscated goods were released and transported to Hong Kong and Taiwan (Qiu 2004).

Under the weak legal and judicial system and with an ineffective supervision mechanism, the top leaders protected their family members and relatives. In turn, these family members and relatives would cover for their friends and intimates. For example, Gao Bingfang, the director-general of the National Taxation Bureau, was initially sentenced to death for embezzling C\$7 million tax income. Due to the interference of Kung, Gao was released after serving four years in prison (Qiu 2004: 273–5). 'The resulting collusion or cooperation could only contribute to the culture of silence and what the Chinese called *baohu shan*, or protective umbrella' (Kwong 1997: 101). This could partly explain why financial crime was so widespread and rampant under the KMT regime, as well as explaining the audacity of many officials in exploiting their positions for private gain.

Compensation mentality

Another key reason for rampant fraud in the later stage of KMT rule was related to the outbreak of to the Sino-Japanese war. During the War, some officials in Chongqing (the wartime capital city) began to make fortunes from the national calamity. They received kickbacks from military purchases, dealt in foreign exchange in Hong Kong and smuggled goods to the remote, unoccupied areas (Qiu 2004). After the victory in 1945, the KMT sent officials to take over the assets of the Japanese. These officials felt that they had suffered eight years' hardship and difficulty in the remote areas and that now they should be compensated. This 'compensation mentality' also reflected what Ma (1990) called 'negative adjustment', through which bureaucrats compensated for loss, regardless of any consequences for society at large. In fact, once officials arrived at the Japanese-occupied areas, like Shanghai, Nanjing and other coastal cities, without proper restrictions and discipline, they behaved like a broken dam, set their eyes on the 'five zi', i.e. a house (Fang zi), gold (Jin zi), money (Piao zi), a car (Che zi) and women (Nü zi) (Qiu 2004: 346). Author T.B. Gold (1986: 52) called them 'corrupt, vindictive, and rapacious KMT liberators'. They openly engaged in frantic looting, seizure, illegal occupation and stealing. If one only takes into consideration the selling-off of Japanese assets nationwide, it can be seen that C$2.5 trillion was lost because although the total market price was C$5 trillion, the assets were sold at far below their market prices to important/related persons (Qiu 2004: 350). Later, even the director of the 'Takeover Investigation Team' to Shanghai admitted that '[T]he takeover is indeed looting' (ibid.: 356).

When elucidating his theory of structuration, sociologist Anthony Giddens (1984: 2) emphasizes the 'recursive' nature of social activities in social institutions. The social environment prompts individuals to act in certain ways. Through their actions individuals alter and transform the environment which in turn will influence or change their way of thinking and behaviour, as well as those of others. The takeover looting directly affected the behaviour of Chinese officials and stimulated a culture of corruption. After the Sino-Japanese war, there was a four-year civil war between the Nationalists and the Communists. With the Nationalists losing one battle after another, the KMT officials expected doomsday. The 'compensation mentality' further influenced officials to seize fortunes by any means they could before the regime collapsed. In particular, hyperinflation in the late 1940s provided opportunities for fraud and other illegal activities, such as the black market, speculation and hoarding (Young 1965: 317). Corruption occurred on a wide scale, involved a large number of officials at every level and eroded the government from the inside. Fairbank (1986: 264) acutely commented that the Nationalist government 'represented the worst form of "bureaucratic capitalism", in which officials feathered their nests at the expense of the public'. Indeed, toward the end of the Republican period, 'many public officials became primarily servants of the rich' (Kwong 1997: 81). The individual actions in turn made corruption a social phenomenon, both systemic and widespread, and it became the most distinct characteristic of the later stages of the KMT regime. The widespread corruption culture further worsened individuals' behaviour such that, unsurprisingly, financial crime in BOC and other banks became rife.

Decline of the modern corporate governance of BOC

Before 1935, BOC was controlled by the Jiang-Zhe Bankers and enjoyed healthy development and rapid growth. Following the notorious banking coup in 1935, the government took over BOC (see details in Chapter 3), which was then directly managed by the leading figures of the Four Great Families: Soong and Kung successively. On the surface, BOC was still under the administration of the Finance Ministry (BOC 1995), but in reality, the Finance Minister Kung and BOC leader Soong were brothers-in-law. It is hard to imagine that the Finance Ministry could exercise any proper monitoring and supervision of BOC. After 1943, Kung himself held the positions of Finance Minister and BOC chief executive concurrently. The checks and controls from above were therefore completely non-existent.

More fatally, inside BOC, the modern and sound corporate governance structure which had been in operation under the Jiang-Zhe Bankers since the 1920s was no longer workable. The new boards of directors and supervisors were dominated by closely related government officials. BOC was subject to the desires of a small handful of families. The proverb says that 'The left hand cannot control the right hand'. The supervisory board's primary role of monitoring management on behalf of the shareholders became futile. For example, BOC regulations clearly stated that loans were not allowed to be given to the companies and firms in which the BOC staff had stakes, nor were BOC staff allowed to run another business (BOC 1995: 179–82). In contravention to these rules, not only did the new BOC leaders make loans to their own companies but they also ran lots of businesses outside the Bank (which will be examined later in this chapter).

To sum up, the concentration of government power in the Four Great Families set the stage for fraud, and an ineffective legal and judicial system and supervision mechanism offered little deterrence. The compensation mentality flourishing during and after the Sino-Japanese war led to the formation of a culture of corruption. Most significant, the decline of the modern corporate governance structure of BOC provided few checks and balances against fraud. No wonder that financial crime in BOC went out of control. On the other hand, after 1935, besides the Bank of China, the KMT government also controlled the Central Bank, BoCOM, and the Farmers Bank, which became commonly known as the Big Four Banks. The Big Four had government status, held the monopoly on issuing banknote, and controlled nearly three-quarters of China's banking resources (Chen Zhen 1961a: 738). As in BOC, although these institutions had so-called boards of directors and supervisors, the Four Great Families occupied prominent positions. It was widely believed that BOC, Central Bank and BoCOM were controlled by the Soong and Kung families, and that the Farmers Bank belonged to the Chen family (Hong 1990). Since the Four Families and the Big Four Banks were bound together, white-collar crimes often went beyond BOC and involved other government banks and financial institutions. Hence, the following financial crimes are examined from a broader perspective, focusing on but not confined to BOC.

White-collar crimes in BOC and other financial institutions

Self-dealing

Self-dealing is basically a transfer of funds to institutional insiders. This could involve, for example, direct investment by the institution in subsidiaries or limited partnerships in which institution insiders have a stake (Calavita *et al.* 1997: 68); it can also include favourable contracts or privileges for the related companies.

CHINA DEVELOPMENT FINANCE CORPORATION (CDFC)

Even though the BOC charter and regulations in 1935 stipulated that BOC could not engage directly in investment activity (BOC 1991a: 128), the rules were circumvented (BOC 1995). Wang Zongpei (1937) suggested that BOC was used as the basis for wide-ranging investments and activities. Here, the chief executive – Soong – took advantage of his position to increase his private investments and those of his relatives and gained control of a substantial number of enterprises (Coble 1980: 213).

The China Development Finance Corporation (CDFC) was the most important enterprise associated with the Soong family. Established in 1934, CDFC was China's first investment company (*Dagongbao* (of Tianjin) 19 September 1947). The capital of the CDFC amounted to C$10 million, consisting of one million shares of C$10 each (*Shenbao* 1 June 1934). About half the shares were purchased by major Shanghai banks, among whom BOC held an impressive C$2.1 million (BOC 1995: 283). The other half of the shares, C$5 million, were held by individuals, mostly by 13 KMT elder statesmen and key financial officials, as shown in Table 6.2. Among them were T.V. Soong (chairman of BOC), H.H. Kung (Finance Minister), T.L. Soong (younger brother of T.V. Soong) and Xu Kan (undersecretary of the Finance Ministry). Kung was elected chairman of CDFC; Kung and T.V. Soong were both on the executive board to direct the new company; T.L. Soong was named general manager (*Dagongbao* 3 June 1934).

Shehui Xinwen (6 June 1934) suitably commented that although CDFC proclaimed itself a 'purely business concern', the company relied on self-dealing with government institutions and banks. For example, the Finance Ministry in 1934 made CDFC the wholesale agent for C$30 million in tobacco revenue tax stamps, for which CDFC received an 8 per cent commission (Coble 1980: 219). What's more, the Finance Ministry went through CDFC

Table 6.2 The major private shareholders in the China Development Finance Co., 1934

Name	Shares (C$)
Wu Weiqing	1,760,000
Li Shufen	530,000
T.V. Soong	350,000
Xi Demao	310,000
Li Shizeng	300,000
Jia Yuesen	300,000
T.L. Soong	250,000
Zhang Renjie	250,000
Chen Qikang	250,000
Bei Zuyi	250,000
Xu Kan	200,000
H.H. Kung	200,000
Ye Zhuotang	200,000
Total	**5,150,000**

Source: JJZLS 1948: 8.

to borrow money. In 1937, the Finance Ministry borrowed C$60 million from the CDFC (*China Weekly Review* (*CWR*) 13 February 1937). With little capital of its own, CDFC borrowed the money from the associated banks, including BOC, the Central Bank and BoCOM. Hence, 'H.H. Kung, as Minister of Finance, borrowed money from government banks he controlled by going through a private corporation of which he was chairman and a leading stockholder' (Coble 1980: 220).

Later, with the full support of BOC and the major Shanghai banks, CDFC took over the Capital City Power Plant, the Qishuyan Power Plant and the Huainan Mining and Railroad Company, all of which were the most prominent large-scale enterprises at that time (Zheng Huixin 2004).

Through all these active investments, CDFC's assets expanded from C$12.6 million at the end of 1934 to C$115.0 million in June 1936, although nearly C$90 million of the latter figure consisted of loans made on behalf of the syndicated banks (Tamagna 1942: 182). Put another way, with limited capital itself, CDFC depended on huge government banking resources to make investments, and then used government connections to ensure the success of the invested projects. Coble (1980: 220) commented that the government officials who granted business to the CDFC and the shareholders and managers of the CDFC were essentially the same individuals. In such typical self-dealing, these persons acted as both buyers and sellers of the services and made deals which were 'advantageous' to their personal company (Sutherland 1983: 155). As a result, CDFC earned substantial profits for its shareholders. In 1936, the corporation gained net profits of C$1.9 million with a return of nearly 20 per cent on the invested capital (Coble 1980: 220). Even when the fixed interest, or guanli, of 7 per cent was deducted, the dividend could be 13 per cent (Chen Zhen 1961a: 1023). This was much higher than the dividends declared by even the most successful Chinese enterprises: BOC with 7 per cent, the Commercial Press with 7.5 per cent, and the Nanyang Brothers Tobacco Company with 5 per cent (Coble 1980: 168). During the War, CDFC was moved to Hong Kong. It purchased various materials on behalf of the government. Although the accounts for the Hong Kong period went missing during the War, profits were understood to be attractive (Chen Zhen 1961a: 1034). Soong's 'operations in the large corporations . . . built up for him a powerful fortune' (*The Times* 27 April 1971).

YANGTZE DEVELOPMENT CORPORATION

H.H. Kung, Soong's brother-in-law, was equally as active in running private businesses. After the Sino-Japanese war, imports were encouraged and local currency was kept overvalued (Zheng Huixin 2004). Kung took this chance and founded quite a number of companies to engage in foreign trade and across-the-board speculation. Among them, the Yangtze Development Corporation became a superstar. Established in 1946, the company had a registered capital of C$1 billion. Kung's son, David Kung, was general manager and concurrently chairman (Chen Zhen 1961a: 1000). Backed by the rich and powerful Kung and Soong families, the Yangtze Company banked with BOC, China Industrial Bank and the Commercial Bank of China and became a gigantic import–export company.

Yangtze was given preferential treatment by BOC. At one time, the official exchange rate was US$1 to C$12,000, but soon, the black market rate rose so that US$1 was equal to C$40,000 (Zhang Jianping *et al.* 1997: 773). In 1946 alone, the Yangtze Company borrowed US$1.9 million at the official rate from BOC (*Pinglunbao* 11 April 1947). Later, David Kung presented two modern foreign cars to the foreign exchange department director of BOC who frequently sold US dollars cheaply to the Yangtze Company, which then speculated on the black market, raising fabulous fortunes (Zhang Jianping *et al.* 1997: 773). Later, even KMT's newspaper, *Zhongyang Ribao* (29 July 1947), admitted that some privileged companies (including the Yangtze Company) breached import–export regulations and used political connections to illegally obtain official foreign currency exchanges.

BOC not only carried out self-dealing with Yangtze, but also urged other government agencies to do so. When the Transportation Ministry tried to buy materials from America, it was suggested that they used Yangtze as an agent with 5 per cent commission, otherwise, the BOC refused to grant US dollars for the imports (Chen Zhen 1961a: 1001). Similarly, Yangtze acted as the agent when the Chinese government purchased cotton from abroad (ibid.).

According to albeit incomplete statistics, Soong controlled 7 financial institutions, 12 commercial houses, 22 large factories, and 1 transportation company (Chen Zhen 1961a: 1043). Soong's investments were often organized as private or state–private concerns whose private stockholders happened to be government officials (Coble 1980). As to the value of Soong's total capital stock in these companies, this will never be known. In the same manner, Kung directly participated in industry and commerce, and ran no fewer than 28 companies, ranging from banking, textiles and coal mining to Chinese medicine and steel (Chen Tingyi 2004a: 320). Through self-dealing with BOC and other government banking institutions, or through receiving special privileges or monopoly powers from the government, these enterprises prospered and brought lucrative returns to the Soong and Kung families.

Embezzlement

Embezzlement in this study refers to taking money or other financial resources or properties for one's own use in violation of a trust. The embezzlement described here, to borrow a sentence from Calavita *et al.* (1997: 183), 'is different from traditional bank robbery only in its magnitude and destabilizing effect on the rest of the economy'.

EMBEZZLEMENT OF US DOLLAR BONDS

The scandal which forced Kung to step down was related to embezzling US dollar bonds. In 1942, the American government granted US$500 million loans to China in support of the war with Japan. Among them, US$100 million represented reserves for issuing US dollar bonds (Chen Tingyi 2004b). At the beginning, the Chinese public showed no interest in US dollar certificates, because the government had issued too many bonds, and bonds had lost their credibility and attraction (see Chapter 4). Therefore, the market price of US dollar bonds fell from the official price of C$20 to C$17 and even as low as C$10 (Chen Tingyi 2004b: 437). Later, some news sources said that this batch of bonds had actual US dollar reserves, so the bonds became popular and the market price rebounded from C$17 to C$30, and kept rising (Chen Tingyi 2004a: 330). Seeing this lucrative prospect, Kung, then the Vice Premier and Finance Minister, in 1943 ordered sales to the public to be stopped. Lu Xian, the treasury department director of the Central Bank, and Guo Jingkun, the business department director of the Bank, followed Kung's instruction: the remaining US$50 million bonds were purchased by the Central Bank at the official price – C$20 yuan each (ibid.). Instead of keeping these bonds in the Bank, Lu Xian sold US$3.5 million of the bonds to Kung himself at the official price. Soon, Kung and Lu purchased the second set of US$8 million (ibid.). Within several months, bonds worth US$50 million were all purchased by individuals at the official price (Zhang Jianping *et al.* 1997: 543).

According to Chongqing *National Gazette*, in January 1944, the lowest market price of US dollar bonds was C$250 on 20 January, and the highest was C$273 on 16 January (Chen Tingyi 2004a: 331). If only the first and second batches of bonds purchased by Kung, amounting to US$11.5 million, are taken into consideration, and with a conservative calculation of market price, the profits could be in the region of C$2.6 billion. That is to say, Kung alone could have embezzled as much as C$2.6 billion (Chen Yageng 1990: 146). This is equal to the total annual savings of Sichuan province at that time (Zhang Jianping *et al.* 1997: 544).

Paper cannot wrap fire. At the KMT national conference, Kung's dealings with US dollar bonds became an open secret. Many delegates were indignant and demanded that Kung should be severly punished. The government's investigation revealed that certificates to the value of US$50 million were completely sold out. Most of the names and address of buyers were faked and could not be verified (Zhang Jianping *et al.* 1997: 730). Later, it disclosed that, among the US$50 million worth of bonds, Kung and his wife had acquired 70 per cent, Lu Xian and Guo Jingkun together had acquired 25 per cent, and the remaining 5 per cent had gone to other key people in the banks and Finance Ministry (ibid.: 732).

This scandal shocked the nation, stirred the international community and led to angry student demonstrations. Kung became notorious both at home and abroad. The American government severely criticized Kung and attacked the corruption of the Chinese government. The American media also pointed out that during the War, over 170 sons and daughters of Chinese high-ranking officials had evaded military service and lived comfortably in the US (Qiu 2004: 270). Among them were the children of Kung and of Xu Kan (the undersecretary of the Finance Ministry). After intense domestic and international pressure, in early 1945, Kung was removed from his posts in the Finance Ministry and the Executive Yuan (Qiu 2004: 322) and he later resigned from his other government posts and went to stay in America. Several other officials implicated in this scandal also fled abroad (ibid.).

DIVERSION OF FOREIGN AID

During and after the War, China received credit and material aid from America, Britain and various international organizations. The manipulation of aid grants and credits became truly big business, dominated by the Soong family (Kerr 1965). It eventually came to be seen as a gigantic black hole.

At first, America provided purchase credits to China, which BOC guaranteed (Young 1965). After 1941, the US also extended lend-lease materials to China. It was said that these credits and lend-lease materials totalled US$3.5 billion (Zhang Jianping *et al.* 1997: 676). From the beginning, T.V. Soong had insisted that the 'dignity of the Chinese people' required that full legal control of aid supplies must rest in Chinese hands (Kerr 1965: 158). As the chairman of BOC, and also as Chiang's private representative, Soong was dispatched to the US to speed the flow of American aid. Soong set up a number of companies, foremost of which were the Universal Trading Corporation and China Defence Supplies, both staffed with Chinese employees and based in the US (Seagrave 1985). The movement of US aid passed through several stages. Funds were sought by China Defence Supplies, then were used by Universal Trading to purchase materials, and thereafter these purchases were transported to China. According to FBI documents declassified in 1983, 'The Soongs have always been money-mad and every move they made was prompted by their desire to secure funds'. Because of this, 'there was a gigantic conspiracy afoot to defraud the Chinese from materials they would ordinarily receive through [lend-lease] and to divert [a] considerable [part] of this money to the Soong family' (Seagrave 1985: 407).

One way of diversion was to send reports to Chongqing, the wartime capital of the Nationalist government, that a freighter, for example, carrying 60 new American battle tanks and other very expensive war material supplied by lend-lease had been sunk. As a matter of fact this:

> Freighter never left the west coast with any tanks; the tanks were never made . . . this is a positive illustration of the manner in which the Soongs have been diverting funds from lend-lease inasmuch as the money was allocated for the 60 tanks.
>
> (Seagrave 1985: 408)

The second way of diversion happened on the other side of the Pacific Ocean. Coincidently, since the very beginning, T.L. Soong, as the director of the Southwest Transportation Company, had been in charge of American materials in China (Seagrave 1985). For whatever reasons, there were frequent warehouse fires and sabotage which was blamed for the vanishing of large quantities of US war supplies (Pearson 1951). However, the goods were sometimes sold on the black market; at other times, they were just mysteriously missing. Either way, little reached the soldiers in the field. Stilwell – the senior American lend-lease administrator – condemned official corruption for being responsible for its being siphoned off (Seagrave 1985: 410).

Kung once declared that war is a bad business for everyone, but this is only half true. It was a bad business for everyone in China except those associated with the Four Great Families. Ma Yinchu, then dean of the School of Commerce at Chongqing University, pointed out that the Kung and Soong families actually took advantage of China's national calamity to illegally obtain huge amounts of money (Zhang Jianping *et al.* 1997: 706). Later, when told what had happened to the American aid, US President Truman angrily declared:

> I discovered after some time that Chiang Kaishek and the Madame and their families, the Soong family and the Kungs, were all thieves, every last one of them, the Madame and Him included. And they stole 750 million dollars out of the [US$3.5] billion that were sent to Chiang. They stole it, and it is invested in real estate down in Sao Paulo and some right here in New York.
>
> (Miller 1974: 289)

Truman couldn't hold back his anger, 'I never change my mind about Chiang and his gang. Every damn one of them ought to be in jail, and I'd like to live to see the day they are' (ibid.: 283).

Insider trading

Insider trading refers to using confidential information to gain advantages in transactions or trading for private benefits. In the 1930s and 1940s, Shanghai had established quite a number of exchanges for gold, government bonds, commodities and foreign currencies. Due to the unstable political and economic situation, any major events or news affected the market. Meanwhile, rules regulating the financial market were few and those in place were often ignored. It is widely known that the Soong and Kung families used confidential financial information for insider trading, and made 'speculation a way of life' (Young 1971: 97).

QIXING COMPANY

In Shanghai's various exchange and stock markets, the most active and notorious company could be the Qixing Company. As early as 1936, with the support of T.V. Soong, H.H. Kung, Madame Kung, who was 'a financier in her own right' (Hahn 1974), Xu Kan, the undersecretary of the Finance Ministry, Chen Xing, deputy governor of Central Bank, and Madam Kung's younger brother, T.L. Soong, also the chairman of China Manufacturers Bank, the Qixing Company in Shanghai was created (Zhang Jianping *et al.* 1997: 536). Obviously, Mme Kung worked closely with Du Yusheng, the Green Gang boss who held important positions in BOC, BoCOM and a number of Shanghai stock and commodity exchanges (Coble 1980).

It was an open secret that the Qixing Company organizers used their privileged information to engage in 'scandalous speculations in exchange, government bonds, and cotton yarn' (Endicott 1975: 17). At one time, while the Chinese blamed Japan for disrupting the economy, the US Treasury Department agent in Shanghai, Martin R. Nicholson, said, 'It is Mme Kung, not Japan, who is killing the Chinese dollar' (Seagrave 1985: 262). Perhaps this was a slight exaggeration. But one widespread charge directly pointed to the export tax on silver which was implemented in 1934 (Russell 1972). The policy, meant to hold back silver outflow, caused the price of gold to rise considerably. Russell (1972: 81) observed that 'Persons in the immediate entourage of H.H. Kung', including Madame Kung, had taken a long position in gold prior to the tax announcement and made substantial profits.

On some occasions, the Qixing Company got tacit support from the Finance Ministry to make money. Before the full eruption of the war with Japan, the situation was sensitive and unstable. In 1936 the Qixing Company spread a rumour that the government was planning to issue a new bond to replace old bonds and would stop paying interest on the old bonds. As a result, small investors panicked and dumped bonds, and within a few days, bond prices plummeted to about half their face value (Zhang Jianping *et al.* 1997). The Qixing Company then bought a huge number of bonds at a low price and the Finance Ministry formally made an announcement to dispel the original rumour. All of a sudden, the bond price rose sharply. The Qixing Company sold the bonds with favourable timing and made a profit of C$30 million (Zhang Jianping *et al.* 1997: 537), and in the phrase of economist Qian (1955: 130), 'easily made a killing'. Immediately after that, the bond market collapsed again. The crash brought disaster to thousands of small investors as well as prominent merchants and tradesmen. Some even committed suicide. But the Qixing Company, taking advantage of inside information and a large supply of banking capital, continued to manipulate the market and create storms on the Shanghai exchanges (Leith-Ross 1968).

T.V. SOONG'S GOLD SCANDAL

T.V. Soong was also implicated in insider trading – the infamous gold scandal. Since 1943, the US had been lending gold to China (Seagrave 1985). Ideally, the gold was to be sold by China's government banks in order to help check inflation. On 28 March 1945 the government secretly instructed the government banks that the official price of gold would be raised from C$20,000 to C$35,000 per ounce on 30 March, 29 March being a bank holiday (*Time* 28 May 1945). The information, however, was leaked out. Before the bank holiday, insiders bought up, and even used public money to buy up large stocks of gold. As a matter of fact, the sale of gold on 28 March was double the average of preceding days (*Time* 28 May 1945). The dramatic rise of the gold price over the bank holiday allowed those privileged people to buy cheap and sell dear. The alleged fortunes made by insiders amounted to C$45 billion (*New York Times* (*NYT*) 16 May 1945).

The gold scandal astounded China and aroused sharp criticism from the foreign media. America commented that 'The US$200 million certification and bonds and the gold sold in China have gone into relatively few hands with resultant large individual profits and have failed to be of real assistance to the Chinese economy' (*FRUS* 1945: 2083). Chinese *Zhoubao* (Weekly Report) critically stated that: 'Under the cover of the gold policy, the market experienced lots of ups and downs. Only those people who are close to inside information can make such quick profits' (Zhang Jianping *et al.* 1997: 530). Although called the 'worst scandal of the war' by the American press (*Time* 28 May 1945), only two junior officials of the central government's Central Trust Bureau were arrested for their part in the gold sales (Seagrave 1985: 421). On the other hand, no misconduct or even negligence of duty was filed against Soong, who was the premier of the government, and a director of this Central Trust Bureau. No accusation was made towards BoCOM or the Central Bank, even though, strangely, both those banks had extended their normal closing time that Friday from 5 p.m. until 9 p.m. to 'handle the sudden demand' from gold buyers (Seagrave 1985: 422). Still, it was crystal clear that this scandal arose 'from insiders, with high government connections' (*Time* 28 May 1945).

Siphoning-off funds

The last but not least white-collar offence is siphoning-off, which refers to the diversion of public funds for personal use by highly placed insiders (Calavita *et al.* 1997: 69). Since the Four Families were closely connected to national power and politics, their family riches were also, to some extent, mixed up with the government-controlled banks. More often than not, they utilized the government banks for their own private purposes.

Kung apparently wrote to Central Bank, for example, and instructed them to 'make payment to Chiang Kaishek C$30,000 every month from July to December 1936 for special expenses, drawn on the account of the national treasury' (Coble 1980: 204). In 1938, Kung issued another order, saying that the allocation to Chiang was become automatic and that he was not going to issue any further order regarding it (Chen Zhen 1961a: 768). Kung himself followed suit, and took C$400,000 from the Central Bank from 1938 throughout 1939 in the name of secret funds (Chen Zhen 1961a: 1010).

Besides directly taking money from government banks, Soong, as the first president of the Central Bank, set a precedent by regarding the bank as 'his' bank. And the Central Bank paid the expenses of his whole family (Chen Zhen 1961a: 1041). 'In Chongqing each evening, when journalists were not around, he dined on Kansas City steaks flown in exclusively at the great cost for him' (Seagrave 1985: 420). Once, when Soong's wife was ill, Soong sent a plane from Nanjing all the way to Connecticut in America to hurry back with a cargo of dogwood, of which she was particularly fond. The bouquet must have cost between twenty and thirty thousand dollars (Greene 1965: 47). Although Greene did not say who paid the money, he commented that Soong had 'a flair for exotic and expensive gestures' (ibid.). When Kung led the Central Bank, all the expenses of Kung family were reimbursed by the Bank (Zhang Jianping *et al.* 1997). Among them, the expenditures of Kung's extravagant mansions were covered, including his mansions in Shanghai, Nanjing, Beijing, Guangzhou and Hong Kong (Zhang Jianping *et al.* 1997: 419), as the Kung family preferred to live in different locations according to the change of weather. What's more, big items such as private cars for Kung, Kung's wife, daughters and sons, or even small items like toilet soap imported from Britain, were all paid for by the Central Bank (Zhang Jianping *et al.* 1997: 539). Surprisingly, Kung, who was always keen to broadcast his skills as a great financier, did not keep proper accounts and records in the Central Bank. At a meeting of the Executive Yuan, Kung flew into a rage: 'Some people want to check the accounts of the Central Bank, they must be mad. . .' (Chen Tingyi 2004a: 326).

In 1943, the war with Japan entered into the most difficult time, prices were rocketing and people could barely survive. When Kung's eldest daughter got married in America, Kung used an airplane to send eight big cases containing the dowry, but the airplane crashed (Chen Tingyi 2004b: 304). This incident brought harsh criticism from the media. The newspaper *Dagongbao* of Changsha commented that 'The loss of the airplane alone could have sustained 2,000 war victims, not to mention other expenses' (Zhang Jianping *et al.* 1997: 759). Kung resent another six cases of dowry by air to America. Of course, all these expenses were borne by the Finance Ministry.

In retrospect, for about 20 years from 1927 to 1947, the Soong and Kung families dominated China's economy and finance, and through all kinds of self-dealing, insider-trading, embezzlement and siphoning-off of funds amassed huge fortunes. There was a household doggerel – 'Chiang family owns China, Chen family owns Party, and Kung and Soong own wealth' (Chen Tingyi 2004a). After the KMT retreated to Taiwan, the Soong and Kung families lived comfortably in America. The *Encyclopaedia Britannica* (Britannica website) asserts that T.V. Soong alone was 'once reputed to have been the richest man in the world'. Likewise, H.H. Kung was rated 'the richest person in China' (Chen Tingyi 2004b; Chesnaux *et al.* 1977b: 272). The Soong and Kung families, according to Seagrave (1985: 416), collectively amassed a fortune probably well in excess of US$2 billion, possibly even more than US$3 billion.

Conclusion

White-collar crime is an illegal act or series of illegal acts committed by nonphysical means and by concealment or guile, to obtain money or property, or to obtain business or personal advantage. Between 1905 and 1949, changes in the frequency of BOC financial crimes, the overall monetary value, the nature of the complexity and variety of the crimes, and the scale and scope of their impact, could perhaps be best represented by a U-curve.

The initial point of the U-curve was high in the Qing dynasty. The financial crimes at BOC were most exposed in its loans, since sound management and accountancy practices had not been established, internal monitoring was weak and old habits of extending credit loans were still prevailing. Bank managers and high-level officials extended unsecured loans and insider loans for the benefits of themselves and their friends, which led to nationwide scandals.

After Daqing Bank was reorganized into BOC, a group of professional Jiang-Zhe Bankers took real control. Thanks to improved management, strict discipline and moral education, white-collar crime during this period was effectively contained. In the U-curve, the line dipped gradually in the late 1910s, and reached its lowest point in the mid-1930s.

The best way to rob a bank is to own one (Calavita *et al.* 1997). Through the banking coup of 1935, the KMT government controlled BOC as well as the banking system. The concentration of government power in the Four Great Families, the ineffective legal and judicial systems and supervision mechanisms, the compensation mentality and related seizing of assets, and the decline of the modern corporate governance structure of BOC provided fertile ground for the development of white-collar crime. With other things being equal, the more diverse the access channels, the greater the opportunities to obtain the financial resources, and the smaller the chance of detection, the more likely it is that the individual will indulge in various types of financial crime (Kwong 1997: 110). The U-curve rose rapidly after the mid-1930s, and the final point in the 1940s was much higher than that in the Qing Dynasty. The Soongs and the Kungs are classic actors portrayed by Sutherland (1983: 230): 'men of affairs, of experience, of refinement, and of culture, and of excellent reputation and standing in the business and social world'. Soong was praised as 'China's smartest banker' by *Time* magazine (15 January 1940) and Kung was commented as having 'a shrewd financial mind' (Leith-Ross 1968: 204). They were involved in appalling self-dealing, embezzlement, insider trading and the siphoning-off of funds, and created shocking scandals one after another.

Inspired by Calavita *et al.*'s (1997) categorization of the savings and loan crimes of America, this study summarizes six categories of fraud described in this chapter (see Table 6.3). The classification is made according to the major offence and chief characteristics, as some of these categories overlap, and some complex cases involve several types of wrongdoing.

Table 6.3 Summary of white-collar crimes in BOC and others, 1905–49

Type	Description	Cases
Unsecured loans	Extending loans without asking for proper securities or guarantees	Dongshenghe Store
Insider loans	Loans to insiders themselves, or to their associates, or to entities in which insiders have a stake	Houde Bank case
Self-dealing	Direct investment in insiders' companies; granting favourable contracts or privileges towards related companies	China Development Finance Co.; Yangtze Development Co.
Embezzlement	Taking money or other financial resources or properties for private purpose in violation of a trust	US$ bonds scandal; Foreign aid diversion
Insider-trading	Using confidential information to gain advantages in transactions or trading for private benefits	Qixing Co. speculation; Gold scandal
Siphoning-off funds	Diversion of public funds for personal use	Soongs' and Kungs' family expenses

The danger of white-collar crime is accurately described by Professor Gerald Vinten:

> White collar crime seems like the nice end of criminal activity, since it does not usually involve violence, and the perpetrators are just like the people next door. However, its economic consequences can be devastating, and in the wider scheme of things it can be even more lethal than crimes of physical violence.
>
> (Quoted in Pickett and Pickett 2002: 13)

That is true. Daqing Bank's loan crime made the bad loan ratio as disappointingly high as 25 per cent, created big nationwide cases and seriously damaged the reputation of the Bank. However, in the later stages of the Republican period, besides the serious economic consequences, the political cost of white-collar crime was extremely high. The crimes incited protests from the general public, aroused the indignation of the international media and caused a government reshuffle. The government became 'increasingly unpopular and distrusted' (Tuchman 1970: 505). The ancient Chinese philosopher Mencius warned a long time ago that a state sows the seeds of its own destruction before others finally destroy it. The climate of rampant financial crime and corruption undermined the effectiveness and legitimacy of the KMT, and ultimately contributed to its demise.

7 Conclusion

Summary

Corporate governance

From the outset, and with reference to western models, Daqing Bank was set up as a limited liability company, which distinguished it from the traditional financial institutions such as the Qianzhuang and Piaohao, and laid a fundamental basis for a modern corporate structure. Here, the special Guandu Shangban system ensured the protection necessary for the development of a new industry, and helped make the Bank profitable and competitive.

Through the Northern Warlord and early KMT periods, BOC had constructed a modern and effective corporate governance structure, which set and enforced clear lines of responsibility and accountability throughout the organization. Professional and salaried managers took charge within the Bank, while a group of Jiang-Zhe Bankers had the real control of BOC. In parallel to this, BOC greatly improved its efficiency and enjoyed rapid business growth. BOC was soon capable of challenging the foreign banks in China, and began to represent China by taking its place in the international financial arena.

The 1935 banking coup and subsequent control of BOC by the KMT government terminated this practice. Afterwards, BOC was troubled with party control, multiple objectives and the principal–agent problem. The decline of BOC's modern corporate governance structure adversely affected its operation and performance, and led to BOC's decay and downfall.

Government intervention

In the late Qing Dynasty, and the Northern Warlord and KMT periods, the chronic deficit in the central budget, the expanding military expenses, coupled with bureaucratic self-serving activities, stimulated government intervention in BOC. BOC was put under pressure to buy bonds to finance government budget deficits. It was mainly due to the BOC's disobedience in bond policy that the general manager, Zhang Jia'ao, was expelled and the

Bank taken over by the KMT government. Meanwhile, the government's incessant borrowings from BOC resulted in reckless note issue, which shook public confidence, triggered a bank-run, and plunged BOC into a vulnerable position. Under Nationalist rule, BOC provided policy loans to SOEs, which were connected to or favoured by government officials, but were unfortunately inefficient and loss-making. What's more, BOC was commanded to undertake a number of special business ventures to support the civil war. Besides the central government intervention, BOC had been pestered with requests for loans from local government offices. These kinds of loans were usually without sufficient security, and, in addition, were not ones that could be refused. More often than not, they became bad.

Excessive buying of government bonds, inflationary note issue, instructed policy loans and enforced loans to local government distracted BOC from its normal business operations, weakened its financial strength and reduced its profit returns. In particular, the unrestricted note issue and hyperinflation in the late 1940s plunged BOC and indeed the whole economy into both panic and paralysis, and directly triggered the collapse of the Nationalist government on the mainland.

Foreign competition

Long before China's indigenous modern banks evolved, western banks had set up and developed in the treaty ports under the protection of extraterritoriality. They financed foreign trade, handled foreign exchange and issued banknotes. They were financially strong, operated within international networks, run with modern management methods and attracted high quality clients. Until 1927, the foreign banks had enjoyed absolute competitive advantages and had dominated the Chinese financial landscape.

However, this western incursion is fundamental to the subsequent development of China. The demonstration effect directly motivated the emergence of Chinese modern banks. Although much smaller and weaker, Chinese banks were courageous in the fight against competition in many types of business. Through learning from foreign competitors, seeking government support, modernizing internal management, and adopting innovative approaches and methods and so on, Chinese banks broke the monopoly held by foreign banks in foreign trade and international exchanges. They also established close relationship with big Chinese firms, attracted an increasing share of deposits and expanded the note issue all over the country. During this process, Chinese modern banks were formed, experienced vigorous growth, and held their own in the face of foreign competition. By the middle of the 1930s, Chinese banks were finally able to 'outweigh foreign banks in overall importance' (Nolan 1993: 46).

White-collar crime

The idea of 'white-collar crime' proposed by Sutherland is ground-breaking in modern criminology and sociology. Compared with crimes in the street, white-collar crime is usually non-violent, not easily detected and more disastrous on business and communities in the long term (Pickett and Pickett 2002). Between 1905 and 1949, changes in the frequency of BOC financial crimes, the overall monetary value, the nature of the complexity and variety of the crimes, and the scale and scope of their impact, could perhaps be best represented by a U-curve.

The initial point of the U-curve was high in the Qing Dynasty. The financial crimes at BOC were most exposed in its loans. Without sound management and effective internal monitoring, bank managers and officials extended unsecured loans and insider loans for the benefits of themselves and their friends. After BOC was under the control of professional Jiang-Zhe Bankers, thanks to improved management, strict discipline and moral education, white-collar crime was effectively contained. In the U-curve, the line dipped gradually in the late 1910s, and reached its lowest point in the mid-1930s. Along with the government's control of BOC as well as the whole banking system after 1935, the U-curve rose again, and the final point in the 1940s was much higher than that in the Qing Dynasty. The concentration of power in the Four Great Families set the stage for fraud; the ineffective legal and judicial system and supervision mechanism offered little deterrence; the compensation mentality among officials led to the formation of a culture of corruption; and the decline of modern corporate governance within BOC provided few checks and balances against fraud. High-level executives in BOC and other financial institutions engaged in self-dealing, embezzlement, insider trading and the siphoning-off of funds. One scandal after another seriously damaged the reputation of the Bank and weakened its financial strength. Worse, rampant white-collar crimes and widespread corruption lost the government its public support, undermined the effectiveness and legitimacy of the KMT, and finally led to its collapse.

Policy implications for today

The history of BOC in the first half of the twentieth century is not dead and buried. History repeats itself, but on a more advanced level under new circumstances. In the twenty-first century, China's state banks, including BOC, are facing a series of deep challenges in corporate governance, government intervention, foreign competition and white-collar crime. In solving these problems, BOC's past can be used to serve the present and the future. This is exactly the purpose of business history.

Corporate governance

Corporate governance is the foundation and framework of a modern enterprise. North and Thomas (1973: 1) pointed out that 'efficient economic organization is the key to growth'. China's four state banks are in the process of comprehensive restructuring. So far, BOC has established a corporate governance structure comprising the general shareholder's meeting, a board of directors, a board of supervisors and an executive management. This governance structure is good for its appearance. Nevertheless, on close examination, it is problematic. To some extent, it is similar to the one under the late Nationalist rule. In the 1940s, KMT party members occupied leading positions in BOC, and decided on personnel appointments and dismissals; today, the CPC committee has a paramount position in BOC, and the principle of 'the party manages cadres' is still being adopted. In the 1940s, BOC was burdened with both commercial and non-commercial activities, whereas the contemporary BOC also faces multiple objectives, i.e. serving social goals and seeking profit. In the 1940s, there were no valid constraints against manager behaviour, and the agency problem was rampant. This is exactly what is happening again nowadays.

Only recently, the Asian Corporate Governance Association released its 2005 annual report: Singapore ranked number one regarding good corporate governance, followed by Hong Kong and India; China ranked second from the bottom, only better than Indonesia (*Xingdao Daily* 25 November 2005). Corporate governance is an urgent and important issue which Chinese state banks must address. Although there exists no best-for-all corporate governance model that functions effectively in every condition, the experience of BOC during the 1920s and 1930s under the Jiang-Zhe Bankers is very illuminating for today. The professional Jiang-Zhe Bankers, instead of politicians, managed and controlled BOC, and they focused on BOC's business growth and modernization; there were clearly defined rights and obligations, as well as performance standards throughout the organization; high criteria were used in selecting directors and supervisors; managers were under constant supervision and monitoring to prevent the abuse of power. Besides strict discipline, BOC staff were offered appropriate incentives so that they were encouraged to exert themselves, and pursue corporate interests instead of short-term gains. Sound corporate governance structures made BOC one of the three best-governed institutions in China in the 1930s, and ensured BOC's financial success. Nowadays, for state banks, among many things, appointing a business-oriented chief executive officer (CEO) is crucial. If senior management is still appointed by the Central Organizational Department of the CPC, rather than by the board of directors, the president and senior managers might still be more interested in their political futures than in commercial returns. Considering China's special situation, a feasible suggestion is that the Central Organizational Department should have more communication and coordination with the board of directors, and in particular with the Central Huijing Company (the major shareholder of BOC), in order to choose and appoint a business-oriented president and senior executives. Another important issue is to clarify the duties and relationship between the party committee and the board of directors. The purpose is to make the board truly independent, active and accountable. Otherwise, even though BOC has set up the board of directors and introduced three prominent foreign independent directors (*BOCAR* 2004: 12), it could not be brought into full play, but would end up being nothing but a beautiful showcase.

Today, in order to organize an efficient corporate governance structure, besides the internal arrangement mentioned above, external factors are also indispensable (Iskander 1996). These factors include: a competitive product and capital market; a well-developed labour market; the clarification of companies' legal obligations; and the bankruptcy of banks. For example, if a CEO's performance is not up to par, his or her job is threatened either by replacement by a new manager or by a takeover (Jensen 1986). This imposes a tremendous pressure on executives. China so far has not established a mature capital and product market. Executives of China's state banks, as CPC cadres, even if they are mediocre and incapable, can remain in high positions until their retirement or be transferred to other state banks. China also lacks a sound legal system and effective judicial enforcement. For example, the threat of the bankruptcy of banks due to poor performance is a disciplinary mechanism (Grossman and Hart 1982). However, it is impractical nowadays to use this disciplinary mechanism due to the consideration of massive unemployment and social instability, since China has not established an extensive social security network. It will therefore be a long and complex process to transform state banks into well-governed, modern financial institutions.

Government intervention

China's Commercial Bank Law issued in 1995 required state banks to be responsible for their own operations and to be freed from external interference. However, as in the period before 1949, BOC is still troubled with government intervention. In the past, BOC was treated like a subsidiary of the Ministry of Finance, and was continuously pressed to finance budget deficits by buying government bonds or issuing notes; today's central government tends to treat state banks as a 'secondary budget', a convenient source of funding to support the projects and activities that otherwise should be covered by the state budget – an implicit transfer of budget deficits. The old BOC was instructed to support money-losing state enterprises, many of which were headed or controlled by the Four Great Families; today's BOC shoulders the burden of supporting ailing SOEs and restructuring them. The old BOC was commanded to handle special business, such as purchasing grain and basic necessities inherent in supporting the civil war; today's BOC is mandated to grant a 'stability and solidarity loan', to help rejuvenate the special geographic areas and help needy students to finish their education. In the past, local Warlords treated BOC as a cash cow through enforced loans and arbitrary extortions; nowadays, local governments intervene in bank lending in order to protect local industries and employment.

It is true that the pre-1949 government intervention was mainly for military campaigns and accumulating rulers' personal fortunes, whereas current intervention in state banks is chiefly for economic and social development (Tang 2004). Nevertheless, the current government intervention has led to banks' low efficiency, mounting NPLs, and has also put state banks at an obvious disadvantage against escalating foreign competition. The state should definitely withdraw from the daily operations of the state commercial banks, in particular, policy loans and social undertakings should be taken away from the state banks. Actually, as early as 1978, when China began to reform and open up, the leader, Deng Xiaoping, pointed out that modernization called for many changes 'in the relationship of production, the superstructure and the forms of management in industrial and agricultural enterprises, *as well as changes in the state administration over these enterprises*' (Deng 1984: 146, emphasis added). Only through independent operation, can state banks operate like true commercial enterprises and stick to principles of profitability, security and liquidity, as well as compete with foreign giants without distractions. Meanwhile, it is easier for authorities to monitor and evaluate the performance of state banks. Furthermore, state banks should continue carrying out organizational restructuring, and adopt a matrix and vertical administrative framework, so that the major decision-making powers are concentrated in the hands of the headquarters instead of the branches (Qin 2004), in order to better resist local government intervention.

Since government intervention has already hindered the state banks' moves towards commercialization, will the involvement of the government be relinquished? As the forces of globalization advance, the influence of mainstream neo-classical proposals in Chinese policy-making increases. Leading international institutions, such as the IMF, through 'structural adjustment' and 'stabilization' programmes, call for drastic moves 'towards market economy and a greatly reduced role for the state' (Nolan 1995a: 237). Truly, the state should refrain from intervening in the day-to-day operations of the state banks; but meanwhile, the state must strengthen its functions in other areas (Chang and Rowthorn 1995). Singh (1998: 20) pointed out that the Asian Financial Crisis erupted not because of too much government intervention but because of too little control over the financial liberalization process these countries implemented before the crisis. The Chinese economist Wu Jinglian also emphasizes that the Chinese government is misaligned. In some aspects, it is overreaching; in others, it is absent from duties when it should not be (*Caijing* 27 December 2004).

In this regard, Taiwan's experience is thought-provoking. After 1949, the same KMT leadership intervened heavily in both banking and the whole economy, and achieved striking success. Taiwan's successful intervention lies in a strong state capacity, a development-oriented objective, a competent and disciplined bureaucratic team, an institutional set-up and a strict performance standard on agents. Learning from Taiwan and combining this with China's special circumstances, the Chinese government ought to strengthen its roles in the following areas: improving state capacity, especially constructing an appropriate fiscal budget relationship between the centre and the localities, so that the local governments will not intervene in local banks' lending practices; building a clean and capable (professional) team of bureaucrats to formulate and carry out effective financial policies and banking regulations; strengthening existing policy banks and establishing new ones (the current three policy banks obviously don't have enough capacity to undertake a sufficient number of policy assignments); setting up a nationwide credit rating system to help banks know their clients better and reduce credit risks; reinforcing supervision and monitoring of banks through the CBRC, PBC, and so on, in particular, imposing high industry standards and rules on state banks, and holding managers and people on duty accountable; encouraging and requiring foreign strategic investors to transfer key management skills and banking techniques to local partners, which could help local banks improve international competitiveness. At the same time, it is extremely important for the government to establish an appropriate institutional framework, such as a bankruptcy law of enterprises. The new bankruptcy law, which has been under discussion for ten years, should give better protection to the legal rights of creditors and the security of banking assets (*Caijing* 6 February 2006). At the same time, China urgently needs a social safety network. The absence of such a net means that BOC and other state banks have to sustain insolvent enterprises, and BOC itself cannot lay off its surplus employees. This prevents BOC transforming into a true commercial bank. Obviously, the way out of the present problems lies not in giving up government intervention but in giving it new content (Chakravarty 1987: vii). Here, it requires the enormous wisdom and creativity of the government.

Finally, government intervention is not static. Chang and Rowthorn point out that 'there is no hard and fast rule to determine the optimal degree and the desirable areas of state intervention, and that it can be determined in the concrete historical, institutional and geographic context' (1995: 18). Even within the same country, government intervention should differ as circumstances change. Simply giving up the role of the state is dangerous. 'State improvement, not state desertion, is the only rational goal for Chinese system reform' (Nolan 2004a: 177).

Foreign competition

After 30 years of absence from China's financial markets, foreign banks have staged a comeback, but this time with a much bigger oncoming force. Old 'faces' are back, such as Citibank (the former National City Bank of New

York), HSBC and Standard Chartered Bank (the former Chartered Bank of India, Australia and China). There are also many new ones, such as BNP Paribas, Credit Suisse, the Development Bank of Singapore, the Royal Bank of Scotland and the Union Bank of Switzerland. So far, almost all global big names have established a presence in China and they are bringing fierce competition to China's banking sector as they have done in the past. With a share of 1.6 per cent of total banking assets in China, they have already grabbed 40 per cent of the international settlement and 23 per cent of foreign currency lending (Liu Mingkang 2004b). The annual growth of their assets, deposits and loans all exceed 30 per cent (CBRC 2005c). Under the agreement of WTO entry, most of the restrictions on foreign banks' business scope and geographic expansion by the end of 2006 have been removed. Foreign giants are hungry to penetrate the Chinese market and take the 'cream' of the Chinese financial services market (Nolan 2004c: xix). It is expected that Chinese banks will continue to suffer losses of market share, profits, and quality clients amongst others.

More than half a century ago, China's modern banks under the professional Jiang-Zhe Bankers successfully challenged foreign banks. Will China's banks have a second chance of success? This is hardly possible. In the early half of the twentieth century, although foreign banks operated in the market earlier, had more experience in modern banking, and held remarkable competitive advantages, the banking business was relatively simple, focusing on loans, deposits, remittances and foreign trade business. No complicated banking equipment and techniques were involved, no computers were used to design and deliver services. Although Chinese banks were smaller in assets, loan business and note issues, the gap between domestic and foreign banks was only quantitative, and it was possible for Chinese banks to catch up. However, since the 1980s, the international banking sector has been transformed beyond recognition. Financial liberalization, along with the rapid development of information technology, has caused great changes in the global financial services industry. 'The boundaries of geography and product sectors are disappearing at high speed' (Wu Qing 2001: 837). Foreign banks enjoy massive competitive advantages in scale, scope, innovation capability and productivity (see Chapter 1). In particular, financial innovation has become the indispensable lubricant and driver of global banking development. The strong innovation capability determines the core competitiveness of foreign banks. Through the adoption of new techniques and instruments, such as ATM, POS, bank cards, the internet and satellite communication, foreign banks bring about innovation of products and create brand names. Foreign banks not only have changed the operation methods and environment of banks, but have also re-engineered and restructured business flows and management streams. During this process, more and more new products have been created, including financial futures, options, swaps, bill facilities, e-business, all kinds of derivatives and securitized financial assets. As a result, foreign banks can acquire first-mover advantage, provide full-range and sophisticated services, and are able to attract the most highly valued clients from around the world.

In contrast, Chinese banks are smaller in size, narrower in business scope and with inferior innovation capability. It is possible for Chinese banks to augment their assets and expand their physical international network; it is also possible to expand their business scope with the issuance of governmental new policy. But, it is extremely difficult for Chinese banks to improve their innovation capability. For many years, state banks, under central planning, mainly dealt with SOEs and provided simple and low value-added products and services, primarily concentrating on interest-based business. State banks lack financial and human resources and a competitive environment in which to initiate new products, introduce new methods of production, develop new techniques, and even reorganize the banking industry. For one thing, the product categories offered by Chinese banks only number a few hundred, whereas the innovative products and services offered by foreign banks have reached more than a thousand since the 1980s (Liu Xiliang 2004; Liu Mingkang 2002: 11). The much weaker innovation capability of Chinese banks indicates that the gap between Chinese and foreign banks is qualitative instead of quantitative. It also suggests that Chinese banks will have to cling to their low-end traditional banking products in the global value chain. It further indicates that Chinese banks have lower quality customers, with less opportunity to earn high margins and generate large profits. Consequently, it will be impossible for China's state banks to compete with foreign giants on the global playing field; also, it is highly unlikely for China's state banks to catch up with the global giants in the foreseeable future.

In the 1920s and 1930s, when Chinese banks competed fiercely with foreign competitors, the rise of nationalist sentiment helped Chinese modern banks gain financial power. One consequence of the 1919 May Fourth Movement was that Japanese banknotes were rejected by Chinese people. The 'May Thirtieth Massacre' in 1925 intensified the tempestuous anti-imperialist movement in China. The business of HSBC and other British banks was heavily adversely impacted. Nowadays, it is hard to foresee that this kind of nationalism will again boost China's banks. In addition, the First and Second World Wars and the Great Depression disrupted and affected the development of foreign banks. For instance, the once powerful Deutsch-Asiatische Bank (which established its head office in Shanghai in 1890) was closed down during the First World War. Later, although this bank resumed operation, it never regained its previous power and influence (Hong 2004: 169–70). True, nowadays, worldwide incidents may happen, such as a terrorist attack or a stock market crash, but with the deepening interdependence of the world economy, it is unlikely that one particular bank will be involved without implicating many others. Therefore, it is unrealistic to count on unexpected events in advancing Chinese banks.

Before 1949, although foreign banks held massive competitive advantages over the Chinese market, they were not so aggressive as to participate in or even take over domestic banks. The respective Chinese governments did not invite foreign equity investment in any of the major banks, such as BOC or BoCOM. Since the 1980s, the globalization, deregulation and advancement in information technologies have made more banking giants in high income countries expand into developing markets. And most notably, there is the overwhelming cross-border nature of M&A, 'with increasingly more and more foreign banks taking dominance in the local financial market, taking into their hands those former national champions' (Gao 2001: 2). In China, so far, 18 foreign financial institutions have purchased shares in 16 Chinese banks, with the total investment reaching US$12.6 billion. Foreign capital has participated in state banks like BOC, CCB, and in joint-stock banks like BoCOM, the Shanghai Pudong Development Bank and the Shenzhen Development Bank (Tang 2005). It is true that overseas strategic investors might bring in modern corporate governance structures, up-to-date expertise and international practices to domestic banks; however, by acquiring an existing institution in China, the acquirer gains the ability to develop more rapidly than would be possible with an organic growth strategy (Gao 2001). And foreign banks are eager to achieve more. The latest news is that a consortium of bidders, chief among them Citigroup, tried to gain an 85 per cent stake in the restructured Guangdong Development Bank, a commercial bank where the Guangdong provincial government has a controlling stake (*Caijing* 9 January 2006). If this acquisition is approved, it will break a regulatory cap limiting a single foreign investor's total stake in a Chinese financial institution to 20 per cent, and combined foreign stakes to 25 per cent. Indeed, in the first half of the twentieth century, Chinese domestic banks mainly faced competition from their foreign counterparts; nowadays, the picture is more daunting. Besides fierce competition, Chinese domestic banks also face being controlled and taken over by foreign giants.

Still, for the time being, China's Big Four have maintained a massive physical presence. Owning about 110,000 operating networks (Chang Song 2005: 171), the Big Four have a complicated, multi-tier organizational system throughout China. What's more, the Big Four have long-term commercial and social relationships with their customers (Wu Qing 2001). Many ordinary Chinese people feel foreign banks are mysterious and complicated, and still maintain the habit of dealing with the Chinese bank just around the corner. It will be difficult for multinational banks to replace the Big Four in local retail markets in the short term. In spite of the competition with foreign rivals, Chinese banks still have the chance to develop. Learning from the early Jiang-Zhe Bankers, China's present-day bankers need to take full advantage of the 'demonstration effect', in particular, they should learn from foreign counterparts regarding modern corporate governance structures, up-to-date banking techniques and advanced management skills. The good news is that Chinese banks are trying hard to adopt international accounting standards, improve information transparency and are aiming to establish a well-functioning corporate governance system. More and more Chinese banks, like BOC,

CCB, BoCOM and Shanghai Pudong Development Bank are recruiting foreign experts (*Xingdao Daily* 24 October 2005). Indeed, following the lead of the British Financial Services Authority (FSA), a professional banking supervision agency, CBRC, has been established, although improvement is needed. In the 1920s and 1930s, government support played an extremely important role in putting BOC in a better position to compete with its foreign rivals. Today, facing a powerful and ambitious competitor, China urgently needs to have a clear and active industrial policy for its banking sector. This issue is in essence related to the earlier discussion about strengthening state capacity, and adjusting intervention focus, methods and instruments. All in all, the purpose is to safeguard financial stability, and create and sharpen the competitive edges of China's state banks. If not, in an era of incredibly fast transformation and globalization, it is not impossible that China might one day lose ownership of its domestic banking industry, as have some Latin American and European countries.

White-collar crimes

BOC, as well as other state banks, are now haunted by serious white-collar crimes, from top management all the way down to the very lowest levels. The current banking crimes have similar manifestations to those that happened before 1949:

1   *Unsecured loans* Daqing Bank managers violated bank rules and extended unsecured loans to Dongshenghe Store, with the result that hundred of thousands of taels could not be recovered. Recently, Liu Jinbao and others in Shanghai openly ignored bank procedures, and made huge loans to Wantai Property without collateral or guarantees. As a result, a debt of RMB1.5 billion became bad.
2   *Insider loans* The director of Daqing Bank and the monitor of the Yingkou branch colluded together to make huge loans to Houde Bank, which they had secretly founded themselves. Recently, Xu Chaofan of BOC Kaiping sub-branch established Ever Joint Properties in Hong Kong, and moved a large amount of the Bank's money to his own company and then speculated in stocks and real estate (*Caijing* 5 May 2002). Typically, for insider loans, bank managers don't follow them up or chase repayment, but wait, instead, for the loans to become bad and be written-off by the bank.
3   *Self-dealing* Yangtze Development Corporation, organized by the powerful Kung family, was granted many lucrative business deals from BOC. Recently, Wang Xuebing, as the head of BOC, awarded handsome advertising deals to Re-orient Advertising Company, in which Wang's wife Zong Lulu was a major shareholder.
4   *Embezzlement* Kung accumulated stunning riches through embezzling US dollar bonds, and Soong was implicated in embezzling foreign aid.

Likewise, although on a smaller scale, the high executives of BOC Hong Kong Ltd, Liu Jinbao and others embezzled unauthorized internal cash accounts, and secretly destroyed financial records (*Caijing* 20 August 2004).

5 *Insider-trading* The Qixing Company, under Madame Kung, took advantage of privileged inside information and continuously created storms on Shanghai's stock exchanges. Similarly, Shenzhen Development Bank, from 1996 to 1997, used more than RMB320 million of bank funds to speculate and manipulate the price of its own stocks (Lu 2000: 210).

6 *Siphoning-off funds* The Soong and Kung families were accused of using bank money to live a luxurious life, even when China was suffering the calamity of endless wars. Likewise, when Wang Xuebing was heading the New York branch, he purchased a luxurious mansion next to the United Nations Headquarters and pursued an extravagant lifestyle (*China Securities* 15 December 2003). Liu Jinbao claimed his family's holiday expenses from the BOC, and even included a medical bill for his pet dog (*World Economic Report* 20 August 2005).

Not only are the crimes similar, but also the causes of white-collar crimes prevalent in the 1940s resemble those of today:

1 *Lack of internal control* BOC in the 1940s suffered a decline in the use of modern corporate governance systems, which provided little checks and balances against fraud. BOC today has still not built up an effective and functioning corporate governance structure. It is easy for people with authority, or who are close to the money flow, to abuse their power.

2 *Ineffective external control* Under KMT, the absence of external monitoring and supervision mechanisms offered little deterrence to white-collar crimes. Similarly, in today's China, the 1979 criminal code is 'simplistic and flawed with loopholes' so that managers and officials easily take advantage (Kwong 1997: 132). Anything not specifically forbidden in the legal documents is acceptable (ibid.). Meanwhile, China routinely imposes the death penalty on low-level officials convicted of corruption, while more senior officials tend to be treated less severely (*NYT* 16 August 2002). Furthermore, many staff in the criminal justice system are recruited from the People's Liberation Army or CPC organizations with little legal training and expertise, and their low professional standard directly affects judicial enforcement (Kwong 1997). It is true that China has created the Ministry of Supervision, the Central Disciplinary Inspection Committee and the CBRC to strengthen the supervision of banks. Nevertheless, all these authorities lack sufficient power, resources and independence to effectively check and punish banking criminals. Hu Angang and Guo Yong of Beijing's Qinghua University estimated that only 10–20 per cent of corruption cases were solved and only 6.6 per cent of party officials who were disciplined for

corruption receive any criminal punishment (*The Economist* 15 February 2002).

3   *The example of high-level officials* In the old China, the high-profile KMT officials and their families were engaged in a wide range of business, through all kinds of illegal means, and made fabulous fortunes. In recent years, central government leaders have been exposed as being involved in financial crimes and corruption (see Chapter 1). Chinese people hate the fact that their leaders introduce and impose laws, but break laws themselves. 'If the top leaders and their children could do it, so could they' (Kwong 1997: 131).

4   *Compensation mentality* During and after the war with Japan, KMT officials cultivated a strong 'compensation mentality', that is, bureaucrats compensated themselves for wartime difficulties and hardships regardless of any consequences for society at large. In today's system, state banks have not established an incentive mechanism which is compatible with the manager's responsibilities and performance. 'These people are grossly underpaid by international standards, and *they hate the system for that*. Wang [Xuebing], for example, made well under $1,000 a month in an industry where his international counterparts regularly made 100 times that amount' (*Washington Post* 15 February 2002, emphasis added). Not surprisingly, the huge contrast is damaging to Chinese bankers' enthusiasm and morality. Some bank chiefs even seek opportunities to be corrupted. Like the KMT officials, they are busy pursuing the 'five zi', i.e. house (Fang zi), gold (Jin zi), money (Piao zi), cars (Che zi), and women (Nü zi). Everyone else is doing it. There is no sense of shame or a moral code (ibid.).

White-collar crime is not a simple economic problem, but 'a political matter concerning the public image and political legitimacy' of the government (Gong 1994: 135). KMT leaders in Taiwan acutely acknowledged that one of the important reasons for their losing the mainland was the eroding public support due to the government's failure to stop corruption (Vogel 1991: 18). It seems that pre-1949 corruption was more serious than today, if we think about the 'Great Four Families' and their shocking scandals, but, if today's corruption cases were to be fully exposed, it would be hard to say which were worse. Nevertheless, 'For a party [CPC] which defeated rivals by its reputation for moral rectitude as well as its military power, it is certainly unbearable to be tarred with the same corrupt image as that of pre-1949 KMT' (Gong 1994: 135). The fact that so many big cases in Chinese financial institutions have come to light is precisely because the government has tried to do something to tidy up the banking sector. When Liu Mingkang, then BOC president, talked about the Kaiping case and about problems in other branches, he clearly stated, 'We feel it's our duty to clean up the Bank of China' (*Caijing* 13 May 2002). The existence of the investigative financial journal *Caijing*, well-known for its first-hand reports and sharp comments, also reflects the government's determination to improve transparency and fight crimes.

Fighting white-collar crimes is not an easy task, but a systematic project which involves many aspects. First, establishing modern corporate governance structures for banks is essential, and in particular, effective checks and balances should be put in place. Individuals will not be able to commit fraud without a lapse in the system of internal control (Weisburd *et al.* 1991). Second, external control is also important, such as strengthening the power of the banking watchdog (CBRC), increasing judicial independence, improving the legal system and encouraging the monitoring role of the press. For example, although *Caijing* is praised as an independent and objective magazine, it only selectively reports some cases and usually only after the events have been exposed. Third, in order to correct the unhealthy compensation mentality among bank chiefs, state banks might, in reference to international standards, establish an appropriate incentive scheme to promote managers' devotion and diligence and make them abstain from short-term personal gains. Fourth, in order to curb financial crimes exemplary behaviour is required from high-ranking leaders. Wu An-chia (2000: 155) warned that resistance to anti-corruption measures is coming from 'within the CCP itself, mainly from certain interest groups that have emerged since the beginning of economic reforms'. Hence, a truly effective approach is to punish officials – even at the highest levels – and their family members who have engaged in fraud (Kwong 1997). This will demonstrate the government's determination in fighting corruption.

The former Chinese leader Deng Xiaoping acknowledged that institutions were extremely important. If institutions are well-organized and effective, bad people cannot do bad things; on the contrary, good people may become bad (*People's Liberation Army (PLA) Daily* website). Indeed, improvement of the above-mentioned institutions will make it harder for those insiders and outsiders to steal from the bank. The ideal situation should be that the bank chiefs do not want to commit crimes because they enjoy their salary, prestige and fame; they cannot commit crimes, because internal and external control systems are tight and rigorous; and they dare not commit crimes, because the punishment is severe and they are certain to lose everything.

The above arguments cover comparisons between BOC's status quo and the situation before 1949 regarding corporate governance, government intervention, foreign competition and white-collar crimes, as well as relevant policy implications for today. In fact, the four issues are closely related. Among them, corporate governance is at the core. Corporate governance:

> provides the structure through which the objectives of the company are set, and the means of attaining those objectives and monitoring performance are determined. Good corporate governance should provide proper incentives for the board and management to pursue objectives that are in the interests of the company and shareholders and should

facilitate effective monitoring, thereby encouraging firms to use resources more efficiently, thereby underpinning growth.

(OECD 2004: 11)

With efficient and functioning corporate governance, specifically with clarified responsibility and accountability throughout the organization, business-oriented senior management, independent boards of directors and super-visors, and appropriate incentives and constraints, state banks will become market-driven, client-oriented, and will be on the right track to deliver out-standing performance. Meanwhile, it is possible for the banks to effectively cushion government intervention, vigorously compete against foreign giants and ultimately contain white-collar crime, although not completely eliminate them. Proper corporate governance is an essential condition to safeguard the sustainable growth of banks (Chen Jianjun 2005). Put another way, deficient corporate governance for the time being is at the root of the state banks' problems. In this regard, Mr Tang Shuangning, vice chairman of CBRC said in an interview:

> In the past 20 or so years, China's banking reform has achieved great progress. However, it was mainly focused on curing the symptoms with some effort in dealing with the root cause. But on the whole, tackling the root cause was given scant notice. The core target of the 2003 reforms in state-controlled shareholding commercial banks, is to shift the focus from curing the symptom to curing the root cause. By dealing with both the symptom and the root cause, we expect to bring the banks on the right path.
>
> (Quoted from Chen Jianjun 2005: 25)

Several controversial issues

The task about how to effectively sort out the problems of the state banks has not only commanded the attention of CBRC and the state banks, but has also become a hot topic among various government authorities, scholars and intellectuals. Accordingly, some opinions and solutions have been proposed. Among them, the following four are worthy of special discussion.

Can privatization solve China's banking problem?

Privatization is viewed by many as the 'indispensable process' by which the very institution of private property would be reintroduced in the socialist economies (Borenzstein and Kumar 1991; World Bank 1995). For the Bretton Woods doctrines, 'enterprise reform' is equivalent to privatization. In China, a widespread view among scholars has been that there is only one significant goal for enterprise reform, namely, privatization (Nolan 2004c). When push-ing reforms through, policy-makers usually put a lot of emphasis on changing property rights.

This view is simplistic. There is no necessary causal effect between a private company and good performance. The success or failure of a bank does not necessarily depend on the property rights structure, but mainly relies on how the bank is managed. The American Savings and Loan Association (S&L), made up of private companies, focused on residential mortgage lending. In the 1980s, against a background of federal insurance cover and federal deregulation, S&L in America experienced chaotic management, excessive speculation, collective embezzlement and a liquidity crisis. Hundreds of S&L members incurred enormous NPLs and went broke. This was one of the worst financial disasters in American history and cost American taxpayers US$500 billion (Calavita *et al.* 1997: 1). Barings Bank, the oldest British bank with 233 years' history, was brought down in 1999 by a 28-year-old trader (Nick Leeson) at the Singapore exchange office. Most fatally, Barings allowed Leeson to remain its chief trader while being responsible for settling his trades, a job that is usually separated (BBC website). This made it much easier for Leeson to hide his losses, and allowed him to gamble with large amounts of money unchecked. Finally, he ran up US$3 billion of liabilities which broke the bank (ibid.). S&L's disaster and Barings' collapse vividly demonstrate that without good corporate governance, well-established private banks can get into trouble. On the other hand, with good corporate governance, state-controlled banks can do very well. Besides Taiwan's experience discussed in Chapter 4, the Development Bank of Singapore (DBS) is an often-cited example. DBS is a state-controlled commercial bank. It boasts good corporate governance and operates according to market principles. Specifically, the government sends representatives through the board of directors and special committees to influence DBS's important strategy and policies, but does not send representatives to be the top executive managers, and refrains from intervening in the daily operations of DBS. The board of directors is mainly composed of non-executive directors and independent directors; the management team and staff are recruited from the open market; strict and specific operating targets are set with reference to industry standards; and an incentive mechanism is based on performance (Hu Zuliu 2004). DBS is one of the largest financial services groups in Asia. Its credit ratings are among the highest in the Asia-Pacific region. Among many honours, DBS was awarded 'Bank of the Year' (2005) by *The Banker* and 'Best in Corporate Governance Awards' (2005) by *The Asset* (DBS website).

The above empirical evidence suggests that privatization may not be necessary for a bank's good performance. Even if privatization or ownership diversification is the right policy under some circumstances, how to carry it out it needs careful calculation. Since the 1980s, China has experienced formal and informal enterprise privatization, which is 'highly corruptive' (Zhang Weiwei 2000: 133). Officials rush to fill the ownership vacuum left by the SOEs, and siphon state assets into their own pockets. 'A common practice is to start a joint venture with a foreign partner in which an artificially low price is offered for state assets in exchange for kickbacks from the foreign partner' (ibid.). Furthermore, management buyout (MBO) has in recent years become a popular way to privatize SOEs. In western countries, 'MBO usually works for the spin-off of a side business or as a deterrent against hostile takeovers, and it takes place in an open, transparent system' where it is tightly regulated and closely monitored (*China Daily* HK edition 24 September 2003). Because China lacks a mature legal framework and professional and independent third-party institutions, such as asset evaluation or auction agencies, there is a potential danger that MBO is open to mass abuse. According to a recent survey, MBO prices in China can be undervalued by 63 to 75 per cent compared with market prices (ibid.). The practice of MBO, to some extent, is similar to what happened on the Chinese mainland under the KMT, when confiscated Japanese enemy assets were sold at far below market prices to important relatives or people (Qiu 2004: 350). Or, when Russia undertook privatization in the early 1990s, there was widespread 'insider dealing' in which mangers, bureaucrats and (less often) workers reaped windfall gains, i.e. a 'legalized theft' (Nolan 1995b: 281).

The above arguments are not to suggest that Chinese state banks shouldn't introduce overseas strategic investors or diversify its ownership structure. This will be helpful in bringing in advanced management expertise, new technologies, international talent and improved transparency. Nevertheless, privatization is not a panacea for state banks, and nor does it necessarily guarantee good performance. Also, privatization might lead to huge losses of state assets. How to carry it out requires careful planning and monitoring.

Can strict regulations and rules solve China's banking problems?

The banking sector has been putting increasing emphasis on rules and regulations. In 2005, for example, the CBRC promulgated over 200 supervisory rules and regulatory documents. In particular, the CBRC set out thirteen requirements for cracking down on the number of cases of bank crime (CBRC 2005c). BOC itself also formulated and optimized a set of rules, regarding almost every aspect of its business and functions, such as risk control, money laundering, accounting, auditing and information disclosure (*BOCAR* 2004). Rules and regulations govern the distribution of power and responsibilities, set criteria for employee behaviour, promote business standardization and boost risk-control (Qin 2004).

What matters is that, even if we have comprehensive and well-designed policies and regulations, they must be enforced and obeyed by the banks. For the time being, state banks have many meetings, many inspections, many regulations and many documents. There are several factors that might explain why these alone cannot prevent the frequent occurrence of banking crimes.

1   *The chief bank manager* The bank president, the department director or branch head still has strong authority and power, and is someone on whom it is difficult to impose any checks and balances. This is related to

the long tradition of the 'rule of men' in China's government agencies, enterprises and institutions. Staff from lower down the hierarchy are more willing to listen to their superiors than to obey the regulations, i.e. they are willing to keep loyal to their superiors who are supposed to represent company or organizational values (Ma 1990: 1047). In a few cases, they are forced to be 'yes' men. When Liu Jinbao was the general manager of Shanghai BOC, even BOC had clear regulations and standards regarding the granting of loans, but Liu openly violated the loan procedure. Hence, loans were granted to Wantai Property first, and then the departments concerned were instructed to make up the necessary paperwork, such as writing a duty investigation report and an evaluation report. When Wang Xuebing was the general manager of the New York branch, Wang issued an ordered granting loans to Zhou Qiang's company, in spite of opposition from the risk control department. Today BOC (*BOCAR* 2004) clearly states that the Bank of China has established a 'three-in-one' credit decision-making process for its corporate and institutional lending, including independent due diligence investigation, an assessment of all credit applications by an independent credit review committee, and a strict approval process with clear accountability enforced through follow-up evaluations. However, some loan managers in BOC have voiced their concerns. One manager remarked, when he worked for a Hong Kong bank and wrote the loan evaluation report, that he was required to objectively point out both good and bad points regarding the candidate project, especially about risks and how to avoid them. But now in BOC, the department general manager, even the bank executive, usually hints his approval or disapproval beforehand. Accordingly, the loan officer only puts down good or bad points in the evaluation report. Otherwise, he is asked to do the report again and again until the leader is satisfied. 'A "good" loan officer must be observing and obedient', the loan manager hinted.[1] No wonder, without sufficient restraints against the behaviour of the 'first in command' (yibashou), even with seemingly strict regulations in place, they are rarely implemented in reality.

2 *Psychology of gambling for resurrection* In some circumstances, in the hope of gaining an advantage or a benefit, managers choose to take excessive risks and break rules. A typical case is Zhou Lu, who succeeded Liu Jinbao to become the general manager of BOC Shanghai after Liu moved to Hong Kong. Zhou did not make any loans to Wantai at first. Faced with the over RMB700 million (US$84 million) of bad loans inherited from Liu, Zhou had to make a very difficult decision: do nothing and let the bad loans expose themselves in time, or make further loans in the hope of recovering earlier losses (*Caijng* 5 March 2004). He chose the second option, which can be explained as the theory of 'gambling for resurrection' (Calavita *et al.* 1997: 33). That is, bank managers engage in ever-riskier behaviour, much like a casino gambler, in the hope of even bigger rewards. Zhou continued to offer ten batches of loans

involving RMB700 million to Wantai. Most of the money was diverted to the Hong Kong stock market for speculation. Like gamblers, bank managers hoped Wantai would make extraordinary profits from speculation and pay back the loans. But instead of recovering the previous losses, BOC eventually ended up with bigger losses. Zhou Lu's RMB700 million loans also became bad (*Caijing* 5 March 2004). After Zhou was removed, quite a number of bank managers believed that Zhou was treated unfairly, since his original intention was to recover BOC losses.[2] Obviously, even it is against the prudent principles of banking, this kind of psychology of gambling is not unknown among bank staff. It is not surprising that even though the rules of the CBRC or the bank itself are tough, they can be easily ignored and disobeyed.

3   *Unrealistic deposit quota or target* The grass-root bank employees are usually assigned a deposit quota. In order to reach the target, the rules and regulations are conveniently ignored. In many cases, the crime route is like this: attracting deposits – collusion of insiders and outsiders – make fake documents – swindle bank of money. Not long ago, two CCB sub-branches in Jilin province in Northeast China were defrauded of RMB320 million (Xinhuanet 30 March 2005). To begin with, a person called Zhang Yuji persuaded some big institutions and enterprises to put deposits in CCB, and these institutions were to get 10 per cent kickbacks. Due to this high return (gaoxi lanchu), Zhang attracted a huge number of deposits to the two branches and established a close relationship with bank managers and employees. Since Zhang drew in substantive deposits, he had his own plan. From 1999 to 2001, he applied for loans from the two branches, and the bank manager and employees tried their best to satisfy Zhang in order to keep the deposits in the bank. When making loans to Zhang, the banks were slack in examining the evidence. Even worse, some bank managers and staff colluded with Zhang. They helped fabricate financial documents, such as seals, contracts and letters of guarantee, and altogether withdrew RMB320 million from the two branches. Later, besides Zhang, six bank managers and members of staff were brought to court and sentenced (ibid.). A deposit quota, which is impractical in many cases, is usually linked to employee salary, bonus and even promotion. Under this pressure, employees put the deposit quota first and leave regulations and rules behind. A similar story is that the Enping branch of CCB in Guangdong used 30 per cent high interest rates to attract deposits. When later it could not repay the money it triggered a large-scale bank-run (Nolan 2005: 6).

Regulations, rules and procedures are good per se, but we must make sure that they are actually implemented. In the 1940s, BOC rules and regulations were the same as those in the 1930s, but rules were not obeyed any more. BOC leaders made loans to their own companies, ran lots of business outside the Bank and used its money for speculation. Today, as a long as bank chiefs have the dominating power in the organization, the gambling psychology will still exist among managers and banks will still assign unrealistic deposit quotas or tasks to employees. Even where rules and regulations are perfect, they exist only on paper and are bound to be repeatedly violated and disobeyed.

Can ideological education solve China's banking problem?

The Chinese government and the Communist Party always emphasize political campaigns and education programmes to its party members and officials. It is also expected that through this traditional way of instruction and indoctrination, bank managers and staff will cultivate high moral standards and exert themselves to improve bank performance and contain white-collar crime. The role of ideological education needs to be analysed carefully, within a historical perspective. In 1949, there was enormous popular support for the leadership of the CPC under Mao, who claimed that the Chinese people would 'stand up' at last (Nolan 2004b: 120). Since most high-level officials were trusted party members, they were also subject to the party's behavioural guidelines (Kwong 1997). The good qualities of party members were listed in PRC chairman Liu Shaoqi's 'How to be a good communist', which stressed the need to cultivate high moral behaviour and thought. What's more, 'Chinese citizens look to their leaders for guidance; honesty and dedication especially of the top leaders during the classical socialist period have trickled down to inspire those below to do likewise' (Kwong 1997: 151). In those times, an ideological education was an effective weapon to instruct and encourage party members and government officials to practise self-discipline and work for the socialist construction.

However, subsequent government policies and a succession of political campaigns, such as the Great Leap Forward, the Anti-Rightist Campaign, and the Cultural Revolution, undermined public confidence and commitment to the government. Behind each political campaign were intense power struggles among the top leaders (Kwong 1997). These campaigns, especially the Cultural Revolution, undermined the prestige of the government, and weakened the trust of the general public in the party. More and more people are becoming cynical and skeptical. Once these feelings set in and permeate, ideological education has gradually lost its power (ibid.).

Since the late 1970s, China has undertaken economic reform. Market mechanism, private enterprises and the stock market, etc., are changing people's mindset day and night. 'To get rich is glorious' has become a popular slogan. Meanwhile, opening-up has enabled China to build close contacts with the outside world. Maoist rhetoric seems increasingly out of date in China, which attracts US$1 billion a week in foreign investment, and where branches of McDonald's have appeared even in the smaller towns (*The Times* 2 July 2005). There is a growing materialism and hedonism in China. 'The glorification of the successful by the media encouraged the search for material wealth and the better life until it became a national occupation' (Kwong 1997: 119).

This change in the public's values has also been brought about by the fact that the supreme leaders don't practise what they preach. Many high-level officials and their families are engaged in lucrative businesses, and some are even involved in financial crime and corruption. Many have transferred money abroad, and sent their children to seek foreign citizenship. The Chinese public feel disgusted with this. They lose trust in the party and show no interest in government teachings. So far, the party has carried out a series of ideological campaigns. The latest one requires every party member to look at himself and improve himself. 'In thinking you should be more upright, in working you should be more efficient, in difficulties you should stand on the front line' (*The Times* 2 July 2005). Instead, many party members and officials view the speeches of the central leaders as show-making; some think the discussion groups and personal feedback reports a mere formality. Bank managers jokingly asked questions such as: 'Citibank and HSBC do not have this kind of education, so why are they doing better than us?'[3]

To some people, the only role of these education programmes is to make people double-talkers. Wang Xuebing's article 'Being diligent and upright, and refrain from self-indulgence' was published in an eye-catching position in *Jinrong Shibao* (*Chinese Financial Times* 20 February 2000). Several months later, people were shocked to find out that Wang took bribes, lived a debauched life and broke financial rules. Zhang Enzhao was a member of the Central Disciplinary Committee. At the meeting of the 'Three Stresses' (stress study, stress politics and stress righteousness) discussion at CCB, he passionately declared that: 'Whoever wants to use illegal means to purse money, I, first, will not protect; second, will not let pass; third, will not forgive. I am accountable to the loyal duty and mission of Central Disciplinary Committee'. He continued to say that, 'The final outcome of Wang Xuebing, Zhu Xiaohua, and others are utterly despicable. They lost on insatiable greed, and fell on pleasure and lust' (*Debate* April 2005). Zhang's brilliant speech was repeatedly circulated in CCB internal bulletins and reports; not long after that, however, Zhang himself was removed and investigated for financial crimes.

We admit that moral education is important, especially for bank managers who deal with money every day. In the 1930s, moral education was effective under the Jiang-Zhe Bankers, because the education was aligned with matching institutional arrangements, such as strong incentives and strict punishment. In the 1950s and 1960s, the invisible 'ideology and consciousness' was powerful, since people were enthusiastic about socialist construction, and the dedication and honesty of top leaders inspired the lower levels to behave likewise. Nowadays, the situation is completely different. Without adequate rewards and severe punishment, without top leaders setting good examples, and even though bank managers receive moral education every day, they cannot be expected to do good. Truly, even China's official newspaper, the

Peoples' Daily (12 May 2000), admitted that, 'in developing the socialist market economy, the work of moral education faces many new problems'. Given the poor record of many rounds of China's anti-corruption campaigns, it is safe to say that ideological education may not work out.

Can listing solve China's banking problem?

As early as 2001, the PBC governor Dai Xianglong promised to speed up banking reform, and outlined three steps that the state bank should adopt. They included strengthening internal reform, transforming to joint-stock banks, with the government holding the majority of shares, and floating on domestic and overseas markets (Reuters 20 September 2001).

In recent years, state banks seem to have ignored the first step, but overstressed the second and especially the third steps. From top bank executives to rank-and-file employees, they have set their eyes on listing. CCB was listed in October 2005, and BOC finished its initial public offering (IPO) in both Hong Kong and Shanghai in June–July 2006. ICBC and ABC are anxious to go public soon.

There is a widespread belief that listing is the best way to deal with China's banking problems. The earlier the better. Listing will put state banks under international laws and regulations, improve their corporate governance, and speed up their internal reforms. Listing can elevate Chinese banks to an internationally prominent position and give bank executives peace of mind. This belief is completely wrong. Listing cannot guarantee either sound corporate governance or good banking performance. Actually, lots of problems could arise as a result of becoming a listed company.

First, if enterprises rush headlong toward listing, it may produce a lot of negative incentives (*Caijing* 21 March 2005). The pressure for speedy progress could easily convert into forged books and bigger problems down the line. And finally, companies will get into trouble (ibid.). At the beginning of 2004, just three months after listing in the US, China Life Insurance Company was sued by its American investors. They alleged that the largest life insurance company on the mainland had failed to disclose accounting irregularities when it raised US$3 billion in America (CFOAsia website). Nowadays, empowered by stringent regulations, overseas investors are demanding better corporate governance practices from listed companies, and they will not shirk from bringing to court those companies which fail their standards (ibid.). One of the purposes of China Life's overseas listing was to increase its credibility as a global firm, but the hurried listing and subsequent legal case, instead, adversely impacted on the reputation of China Life, drove down its share price and involved it in a time-consuming and expensive law case.

Furthermore, those advocating an aggressive and quick listing strategy say they need to seize the IPO as 'a window on the capital market' and that doing so will generate additional pressure for banking reforms (*Caijing* 21 March 2005). True, state-owned banks could raise funds through IPOs, but what is the point of having a giant that is flabby, weak and even sick? Listing does not necessarily apply pressure on the listed firm to do better. This has been proven time and again by previous IPOs by Chinese enterprises. For instance, immediately after the Asian Financial Crisis, the Yuehai Group based in Guangdong province was seriously insolvent. Under the Yuehai Group, there were quite a number of red chip companies listed in Hong Kong. Among them, the flagship company Guangnan Co. was very influential in the Hong Kong stock market. But later, Guangnan Co. was discovered to be a collectively 'large-scale swindling company', and a 'criminal firm, creating private riches for managers' (Nolan 2005: 35). The Hong Kong authorities issued arrest warrants for 18 of the leading executives, including the former chairman, six former directors, the finance managers and the assistant to the finance supervisors. Other red chip companies were also problematic. Altogether, Yuehai Group had 35 members of staff who were arrested for 'fraud' (ibid.). The stories of red chips clearly indicate that the myth of improving corporate governance through listing is impractical. The red chips under Yuehai Group, for many years, had international laws to govern them, social celebrities as independent directors, the general managers appointed according to the Hong Kong salary standard, and also world-famous accounting firms as their external auditors (Deloitte Touche, for example, were the auditors of the Guangnan Co.), but they were shown to be responsible for shocking falsehoods, accounting chaos and crime rather than good performance (ibid.: 43).

This is not to argue against planned listings as such, because it represents a crucial step toward reforming China's state-owned commercial banks, but it is wrong to overstress listing and regard it as the symbol of a bank's success, or as the finishing line of banking reform. Listing is by no means a quick or easy solution to poor corporate governance and weak internal controls. Listing itself doesn't necessarily guarantee good performance or halt white-collar crime. A lot of hard work has be done both before and after listing.

These four controversial issues reflect the erroneous, partial or superficial understandings about China's banking reform. Privatization, strict regulations, ideological education and listing might help to solve China's banking problems, but many corresponding measures are needed. At the moment, nothing can be more crucial than focusing on the banks' internal reform, especially building and exercising excellent corporate governance practices.

Concluding remarks

Since the late 1970s, China has achieved remarkable economic progress. In particular, China has weathered the 1997 Asian Financial Crisis successfully and has maintained relatively sound economic performance. However, the Asian Financial Crisis sounds a warning bell to China's policy-makers. Among its many problems, China's creaking state banks are by far the most visible and worrying (Anderson 2003). Banking reform is the 'most sensitive and difficult part of the whole process of system change; if mistakes are made in this area, with its deep roots in the everyday lives of the whole population, they threaten the whole socio-political fabric' (Nolan 2004a: 49). However, banking reform must be continued. There is a general consensus among scholars and practitioners that this reform is central to the continuation of fast stable economc growth in China. The stakes are therefore very high both for the Chinese economy and indeed for the world economy that a sound and efficient banking system should be established which is also compatible with China's obligations under the WTO agreement.[4] No doubt, the challenges facing China's state banks are formidable; yet, the future remains dynamic. History never ends. BOC's pre-1949 history is highly relevant today. The good experiences as well as the grave lessons of the first half of the twentieth century should enlighten us, make us wise, and help us march forward.

Notes

2 The challenges facing China's state banks today

1   I would like to thank Professor Peter Nolan for raising this point.
2   From the author's interview at BOC in 2005.
3   From the author's interview at BOC in 2004.

7 Conclusion

1   From the author's interview at BOC in 2004.
2   From the author's interview at BOC in 2004.
3   From the author's interview at BOC in 2004.
4   I wish to thank Prof. Ajit Singh for highlighting this issue.

Bibliography

Allen, G.C. and Donnithorne, A.G. (1954) *Western Enterprise in Far Eastern Economic Development: China and Japan*, London: Allen and Unwin.

Amsden, A. (1989) *Asia's Next Giant*, New York: Oxford University Press.

Anderson, J. (2003) 'Ruhe xiuzheng zhongguo de yinhang xitong' (How to fix China's banking system), *Caijing*, 5 November.

Arnold, J. (1926) *China, a Commercial and Industrial Handbook*, Washington: Government Printing Office.

Attfield, J.B. (1893) *English and Foreign Banks: a comparison*, London: E.Wilson.

The Banker (2004) Top 1000 world banks, The Banker, website: www.thebanker.com.

The Banker (2005) Top 1000 world banks, The Banker, website: www.thebanker.com.

Barshefsky, C. (1999) 'USTR briefing on the trade agreement reached with China', released by the Office of the USTR, 15 November.

Basel Committee (1999) 'Enhancing corporate governance for banking organizations', Basel: Bank for International Settlements.

Baster, A.S.J. (1934) 'Origins of the British exchange bank in China', *Economic History*, January.

—— (1935) *The International Banks*, London: P.S. King and Son Ltd.

BBC website: http://www.bbc.co.uk/crime/caseclosed/nickleeson.shtml.

Benson, M.L. and Walker, E. (1988) 'Sentencing the white-collar offender', *American Sociological Review* 33, 301–9.

Bergère, M-C. (1981) ' "The other China", Shanghai from 1919 to 1949', in C. Howe (ed.) *Shanghai: revolution and development in an Asian metropolis*, Cambridge: Cambridge University Press.

—— (1986) *The Golden Age of the Chinese Bourgeoisie, 1911–1937*, translated by Janet Lloyd, Cambridge: Cambridge University Press.

Berle, A. and Means, G. (1932) *The Modern Corporation and Private Property*, New York: Macmillan.

Bhagwati, J.N. (1982) 'Directly unproductive profit-seeking (DUP) activities', *Journal of Political Economy*, 90(5).

BOC (Bank of China) (1932) *Zhongguo Zhongyao Yinhang Zuijin Shinian Yingye Gaikuang Yanjiu, 1921–1931 (An Analysis of the Accounts of the Principal Chinese Banks, 1921–1931)*, Shanghai: Bank of China.

—— (1937) *Quanguo Yinhang Nianjian (National Banking Yearbook)*, Shanghai: Bank of China.

—— (1991a) *Zhongguo Yinhang Hangshi Zhiliao Huibian (I) (A Collection of*

Materials on the History of Bank of China, Volume I), Beijing: Dang'an chubanshe (Archives Press).

—— (1991b) *Zhongguo Yinhang Hangshi Zhiliao Huibian (II)* (*A Collection of Materials on the History of Bank of China, Volume II*), Beijing: Dang'an chubanshe (Archives Press).

—— (1991c) *Zhongguo Yinhang Hangshi Zhiliao Huibian (III)* (*A Collection of Materials on the History of Bank of China, Volume III*), Beijing: Dang'an chubanshe (Archives Press).

—— (1995) *Zhongguo Yinhang Hangshi, 1912–1949* (*History of BOC, 1912–1949*), Beijing: Zhongguo jinrong chubanshe (China Financial Publishing House).

—— (1999) *A History of the Bank of China, 1912–1949*, Beijing: Sinolingua.

BOCAR (*BOC Annual Reports*), 1912–2004, various issues, Shanghai and Beijing: BOC.

Boorman, H.L. (ed.) (1979) *Biographical Dictionary of Republican China*, New York: Columbia University Press.

Borenzstein, E. and Kumar, M. (1991) 'Proposals for privatization in Eastern Europe', IMF Staff Papers, 38, Washington DC: IMF.

Bottelier, P. (2001) 'WTO and the reform of China's financial sector', at: www.du.edu/gsis/china/pdf_files/bottelier.PDF.

Brahm, L. (2000) 'Ready or not', *Business China*, 3 January.

Britannica website: http://www.britannica.com/eb/article-9068719.

Broadman, H. (2001) 'The Chinese state as corporate shareholder', *Finance and Development*, IMF, 36 (3).

CAB (Chongqing Archive Bureau) (1993) *Silian Zongchu Shiliao (Historical Materials on Joint Head Office of Four Government Banks)*, Beijing: Dang'an chubanshe (Archives Press).

Caijing (Chinese magazine) http://www.caijing.com.cn.

Calavita, K., Pontell, H. and Tillman, R. (1997) *Big Money Crime: fraud and politics in the savings and loan crisis*, Berkeley: University of California Press.

CBRC (China Banking Regulatory Commission) at: www.cbrc.org.cn.

CBRC (2004) 'Guidelines on corporate governance reforms and supervision of BOC and CCB', at: www.cbrc.org.cn.

—— (2005a) 'Improving corporate governance as the core of reforming state commercial banks', at: http://www.cbrc.gov.cn/index.htm.

—— (2005b) 'Yinjianhui 2004 nian xianchang jiancha chengxiao xianzhu' (The notable result of CBRC's 2004 on-site inspection), at: www.cbrc.gov.cn.

—— (2005c) 'Latest developments in China's banking reform, opening-up and supervision', at: www.cbrc.gov.cn.

CFOAsia (*Chief Financial Officer Asia*) website: http://www.cfoasia.com/archives/200407-07.htm.

Chakravarty, S. (1987) *Development Planning: the Indian experience*, Oxford: Clarendon.

Chan, J. (2005) 'Foreign capital pours into China's bank', at: http://www.wsws.org/articles/2005/oct2005/chin-o08.shtml.

Chandler, A.D. (1977) *The Visible Hand: the managerial revolution in American business*, London: Belknap Press of Harvard University.

Chang, G. (2001) *The Coming Collapse of China*, New York: Random House.

Chang, H.-J. (1999) 'The economic theory of the developmental state', in M. Woo-Cumings (ed.) *The Developmental State*, London: Cornell University Press.

Chang, H-J. and Rowthorn, R. (1995) 'Role of the state in economic change: entrepreneurship and conflict management', in H-J. Chang and R. Rowthorn (eds) *The Role of State in Economic Change*, Oxford: Clarendon.

Chang, Song (2005) 'Consolidation and internationalization in the global banking industry since the 1980s, and the implication for Chinese banking reform', University of Cambridge: PhD thesis, Judge Business School.

Chang, Zemin (1979) *Zhongguo Xiandai Jiancha Zhidu* (*China's Modern Supervision System*), Taibei: Taiwan shangwu yinshuguan (Taiwan Commercial Press).

Chao, K. (1975) 'The growth of a modern cotton textile industry and the competition with handicrafts', in D.H. Perkins (ed.) *China's Modern Economy in Historical Perspective*, Stanford: Stanford University Press.

Chen, Baizhu (2000) 'An overview of China's financial markets: progress, problems and prospects', in Baizhu Chen (ed.) *Financial Market Reform in China: progress, problems and prospects*, Oxford: Westview Press.

Chen, Boda (1947) *Zhongguo Sida Jiazu* (*China's Four Great Families*), Hong Kong: Changjiang.

Chen, Hanseng (1939) *Industrial Capital and Chinese Peasants*, Shanghai: Kelly and Walsh.

Chen, Jianjun (2005) 'China's banking reform in corporate governance', University of Cambridge: MBA dissertation, Judge Business School.

Chen, Tingyi (2004a) *Song Ziwen Da Zhuan* (*The Complete Biography of T. V. Soong*), Beijing: Tuanjie chubanshe (Solidarity Press).

—— (2004b) *Kong Xiangxi he Song Ailing* (*H.H. Kung and Ailing Soong*), Beijing: Tuanjie chubanshe (Solidarity Press).

Chen, Xulu, Wang, Xi and Gu, Tinglong (2000) *Zhongguo Tongshang Yinhang* (*Imperial Bank of China*), Shanghai: Shanghai renmin chubanshe (Shanghai People's Press).

Chen, Yageng (1990) 'Kong Xiangxi jingtun meijin gongzhai yimu' (The case of H.H. Kung's swallowing US$ bonds), in Chongyi Shou (ed.) *Kong Xiangxi Qiren Qishi* (*H.H. Kung and His Stories*), Beijing: Zhongguo wenshi chubanshe (China Literature and History Press).

Chen, Zhen and Yao, Luo (1958) *Zhongguo Jindai Gongyeshi Ziliao* (*Historical Materials on China's Modern Industry*), Volume 2, Beijing: Sanlian shudian (Joint Publishing Co.).

Chen, Zhen (1961a) *Zhongguo Jindai Gongyeshi Ziliao* (*Historical Materials on China's Modern Industry*), Volume 3, Beijing: Sanlian shudian (Joint Publishing Co.).

—— (1961b) *Zhongguo Jindai Gongyeshi Ziliao* (*Historical Materials on China's Modern Industry*), Volume 4, Beijing: Sanlian shudian (Joint Publishing Co.).

Cheng, Linsun (2003) *Banking in Modern China: entrepreneurs, professional managers and the development of Chinese banks, 1897–1937*, Cambridge: Cambridge University Press.

Chesneaux, J., Barbier, F. and Bergère, M-C. (1977a) *China from the Opium War to the 1911 Revolution*, translated from the French by Anne Destenay, Hassocks: Harvester Press.

—— (1977b) *China from the 1911 Revolution to Liberation*, translated from the French by Paul Auster and Lydia Davis; chapters 1 to 3 translated by Anne Destenay. Hassocks: Harvester Press.

Chung, Ching-Yi (2003) 'Management structure and bank performance: an empirical examination of the early Republican Chinese banking industry', at: http://aghistory.ucdavis.edu/chungpaper.pdf.

Clancy, J.J. (1989) *The Invisible Powers: the language of business.* Lexington, MA: Lexington Books.

Clark, C. (1988) 'Dependency, development and constituency appeals as determinants of state entrepreneurship in industrializing nations: the Taiwan case', in C. Clark and J. Lemco (eds) *State and Development*, New York: E.J. Brill.

Clarke, D. (1997) 'State Council nullifies statutory rights of creditors', *East Asian Executive Reports*, April 15: 9–15.

Cleveland, H.B. and Huertas, T. (1985) *Citibank, 1812–1970*, Cambridge, MA: Harvard University Press.

Coble, P.M. (1980) *The Shanghai Capitalists and the Nationalist Government, 1927–1937*, Cambridge, MA: Council on East Asian Studies, Harvard University.

Collis, M. (1965) *Wayfoong: the Hongkong and Shanghai Banking Corporation*, London: Faber and Faber.

Consular Reports (1883) 'Commercial Reports from Her Majesty's Consuls in China', Shanghai: Great Britain Foreign Office.

CPC (Communist Party of China) (2003), at: www.org.cn/english/2003/oct/77302.htm.

DBCO (Daqing Bank Clearing Office) (1915) *Daqing Yinhang Shimoji (The Whole Story of the Daqing Bank)*, Beijing.

DBS website: www.dbs.com.

Deng, Xiaoping (1984) *Related Works of Deng Xiaoping (1974–1982)*, Beijing: Foreign Languages Press.

Dernberger, R.F. (1975) 'The role of the foreigner in China's economic development, 1840–1949', in D.H. Perkins (ed.) *China's Modern Economy in Historical Perspective*, Stanford: Stanford University Press.

Domes, J. (2000) 'State capacity in an Asian democracy: the example of Taiwan', in K.E. Brodsgaard and S. Young (eds) *State Capacity in East Asia: Japan, Taiwan, China and Vietnam*, Oxford: Oxford University Press.

Dornbusch, R. and Giavazzi, F. (1999) 'Heading off China's financial crisis', Bank for International Settlements (BIS) Paper, No. 7, p. 40; http://www.bis.org/publ/plcy07b.pdf.

Du, Xuncheng (2002) *Zhongguo Jinrong Tongshi, Disanjuan, Beiyang Zhengfu Shiqi (The General History of China's Financial Industry, Volume 3, the Northern Warlord Period)*, Beijing: Zhongguo jinrong chubanseh (China Financial Publishing House).

Eastman, L.E. (1984) *Seeds of Destruction: Nationalist China in war and revolution, 1937–1949*, Stanford: Stanford University Press.

Edelhertz, H. (1970) *The Nature, Impact and Prosecution of White Collar Crime*, Washington: Government Printing Office.

Elvin, M. (1972) 'The high-level equilibrium trap: the causes of the decline of invention in the traditional Chinese textile industries', in W.E. Willmott (ed.) *Economic Organization in Chinese Society*, Stanford: Stanford University Press.

EMKT (E-Market) (2002) website: www.emkt.com.cn.

Endicott, S.L. (1975) *Diplomacy and Enterprise: British China policy 1933–1937*, Manchester: Manchester University Press.

Evans, P. (1995) *The Embedded Autonomy: states and industrial transformation*, Princeton, NJ: Princeton University Press.

Fairbank, J.K. (1971) *The United States and China*, third edition, Cambridge, MA: Harvard University Press.

—— (1986) *The Great Chinese Revolution, 1800–1985*, New York: Harper and Row.

Fang, Xianming (1999) *Zhidu Bianqian yu Jinrong Tiaozheng* (*Institutional Change and Restructuring of Financial Sector*), Beijing: Zhongguo jinrong chubanseh (China Financial Publishing House).

FBI (Federal Bureau of Investigation) website: http://www.fbi.gov/page2/april04/042904china.htm.

Fei, Hsiao-tung (1939) *Peasant Life in China: a field study of country life in the Yangtze Valley*, London: Routledge and Kegan Paul.

Feis, H. (1930) *Europe: the world's banker 1870–1914*, London: Yale University Press.

Feuerwerker, A. (1958) *China's Early Industrialization: Sheng Xuanhuai (1844–1916) and Mandarin enterprises*, Cambridge, MA: Harvard University Press.

—— (1995) *The Chinese Economy, 1870–1949*, Ann Arbor, MI: Centre for Chinese Studies, University of Michigan.

Field K. (1995) *Enterprise and the State in Korea and Taiwan*, New York: Cornell University Press.

Fong, H.D. (1936) 'Rural industrial enterprise in North China', *Nankai Social and Economic Quarterly* 8: 4.

FRI (Financial Research Institute (of the People's Bank of China)) (1980) *Zhongguo Nongmin Yinhang* (*Farmers Bank of China*), Beijing: Zhongguo caizheng jingji chubanshe (China Finance and Economics Publishing House).

—— (1990) *Meiguo Huaqi Yinhang Zaihua Shiliao* (*Historical Materials on the National City Bank in China*), Beijing: Zhonghua shuju (Zhonghua Book Co.).

FRO (Financial Research Office (of the Shanghai Branch, People's Bank of China)) (1978) *Shanghai Qianzhuang Shiliao* (*Historical Material of Shanghai's Qianzhuang*), Shanghai: Shanghai renmin chubanshe (Shanghai People's Press).

—— (1983) *Jincheng Yinhang Shiliao* (*Historical Materials of the Jincheng Bank*), Shanghai: Shanghai renmin chubanshe (Shanghai People's Press).

—— (1990) *Shanghai Shangye Chuxu Yinhang Shiliao* (*Historical Materials on Shanghai Commercial and Savings Bank*), Shanghai: Shanghai renmin chubanshe (Shanghai People's Press).

FRUS (*Foreign Relations of the United States*), Washington: Department of State, various years.

Gao, Dingxin (2001) 'Opening up or taken over? future of banking in China', University of Cambridge: MBA dissertation, Judge Business School.

Geis, G. and Goff, C. (1983) 'Introduction', in E.H. Sutherland (1983) *White Collar Crime*, New Haven: Yale University Press.

Gerschenkron, A. (1962) *Economic Backwardness in Historical Perspective: a book of essays*, Cambridge, MA: Belknap Press of Harvard University Press.

Giddens, A. (1984) *The Constitution of Society: outline of the theory of structuration*, Berkeley: University of California Press.

Goetzmann, W. and Koll, E. (2004) 'The history of corporate ownership in China: state patronage, company legislation, and the issue of control', at: http://www.nber.org/books/corp-owners03/goetzmann-koll7-20-04.pdf.

Gold, T.B. (1986) *State and Society in the Taiwan Miracle*, London: M.E. Sharpe.

—— (2000) 'The waning of Kuo Min Tang state on Taiwan', in K.E. Brodsgaard and S. Young (eds) *State Capacity in East Asia: Japan, Taiwan, China and Vietnam*, Oxford: Oxford University Press.

Gong, T. (1994) *The Politics of Corruption in Contemporary China: an analysis of policy outcomes*, London: Praeger.

Greene, F. (1965) *A Curtain of Ignorance*, London: J. Cape.

Grossman, S. and Hart, O. (1982) 'Corporate financial structure and managerial incentives', in J. McCall (ed.) *The Economics of Information and Uncertainty*, London: University of Chicago Press.

Haddock, F. (2000) 'A tough act to follow', *Global Finance*, January.

Hahn, E. (1974) *The Soong Sisters*, Bath: Chivers.

Hahnel, R. (1999) 'Global economy inside: Paul Volcker and third world views', ZNet Commentary, 16, June.

Haier website: www.haier.com.

Hall, R.O. (1917) *Chapters and Documents on Chinese National Banking*, Shanghai: Shangwu yinshuguan (Commercial Press).

Hamilton, Adrian (1986) *The Financial Revolution: the big bang worldwide*, Harmondsworth: Viking.

Hamilton, Alexander (1791) 'Report on manufactures', the report to American Congress.

Hao, Yanping (1970) *The Comprador in Nineteenth Century China: bridge between east and west*, Cambridge, MA: Harvard University Press.

Hayek, F. (1941) *Pure Theory of Capital*, London: Routledge.

Ho, F. (ed.) (1939) *Agrarian China*, London: Allen and Unwin.

Hong, Jiaguan (1990) *Zai Jinrongshi Yuandili Manbu* (*Walking in the Field of Financial History*), Beijing: Zhongguo jinrong chubanshe (China Financial Publishing House).

—— (2001) *Zhongguo Jinrongshi* (*China's Financial History*), Chengdu: Xinan caijing daxue chubanshe (Press of Southwestern University of Finance and Economics).

—— (2003) *Shanghai Jinrongzhi* (*History of Shanghai's Financial Industry*), Shanghai: Shanghai shehui kexueyuan chubanshe (Shanghai Academy of Social Sciences Press).

—— (2004) *Ershi Shiji de Shanghai Jinrong* (*Shanghai Finance in Twentieth Century*), Shanghai: Shanghai renmin chubanshe (Shanghai People's Press).

Howe, C. (1978) *China's Economy: a basic guide*, London: Paul Elek.

—— (1981) 'Industrialization under conditions of long-run population stability: Shanghai's achievement and prospect', in C. Howe (ed.) *Shanghai: revolution and development in an Asian metropolis*, Cambridge: Cambridge University Press

HSBC (Hongkong and Shanghai Banking Corporation) website: www.hsbc.com.

Hu, Zuliu (1998) 'Yinhang wenti yu yazhou jinrong weij' (Bank issues and Asian Financial Crisis), Beijing: working paper, No. 199806, National Centre for Economic Research, Tsinghua University.

—— (2004) 'Zhengfu can/konggu shangye yinhang zhili xu yi shichanghua wei fangxiang' (The participation or control of government in commercial banks must be market-oriented), *Caijing*, 20, May.

Huang, Guangyu (1995) *The Universal Dictionary of Foreign Business in Modern China*, Chengdu: Sichuan renmin chubanshe (Sichuan People's Press).

Huang, Jianhui (1992) *Shanxi Piaohao Shi* (*History of Shanxi Piaohao*), Taiyuan: Shanxi jingji chubanshe (Shanxi Economics Press).

Huang, Jinlao (2003) 'Zhongguo yinhang gongsi zhili yanjiu' (Research of BOC corporate governance), Beijing: The International Finance Research Centre, BOC, unpublished paper.

Huang, Yiping (1998) 'Challenges for China's financial reform', paper presented to China Update, at: http://ncdsnet.anu.edu.au/pdf/china/cu98'N1.pdf.

ICBC (Industrial and Commercial Bank of China): www.icbc.com.cn.

Iskander, M. (1996) 'Improving state-owned enterprise performance: recent international experience', in B. Harry (ed.) *Policy Options for Reform of Chinese State Owned Enterprises*, Washington: World Bank.

Jensen, M. (1986) 'Agency costs of free cash flow, corporate finance and takeovers', *American Economic Review* 76: 323–39.

Jensen, M. and Meckling, W. (1976) 'Theory of the firm: management behaviour, agent costs, and capital structure', *Journal of Financial Economics* 3: 305–60.

Ji, Zhaojin (2003) *A History of Modern Shanghai Banking: the rise and decline of China's finance Capitalism*, Armonk, NY: M.E. Sharpe.

Jiang, Zemin (2001) 'Speech at the meeting celebrating the 80th anniversary of the founding of CPC', at: http://www.china.org.cn/english/2001/jul/15486.htm.

Jiao, Jinpu (2001) *Zhongguo Yinhangye Jingzhengli Bijiao (The Comparison of Competitiveness of China's Banking Industry)*, Beijing: Zhongguo jinrong chubanshe (China Financial Publishing House).

Jin, Pusen and Sun, Shangen (2001) *Ningbo Bang Da Cidian (Comprehensive Dictionary of Businessmen of Ningbo Origin)*, Ningbo: Ningbo chubanshe (Ningbo Publishing House).

JJZLS (Jingji Ziliaoshe) (1948) *T. V. Soong Haomen Ziben Neimu (The Capital Wealth of T. V. Soong Family: an inside story)*, Harbin: Guanghua Shudian (Guanghua Bookstore).

Johnson, C. (1982) *MITI and the Japanese Miracle: the growth of industrial policy, 1925–1975*, Stanford: Stanford University Press.

Johnston, M. (1995) 'China's surge of corruption', *Journal of Democracy*, October.

Jones, G. (2002) 'Business history', in M. Warner (ed.) *International Encyclopedia of Business and Management*, second edition, London: Thomson Learning.

Kagawa, N. (1999) 'The modern enterprise system and corporate governance in China's SOE reform', at: http://gwu.edu/~270/noriko.htm/.

Kelly, B. and London, M. (1989) *The Four Little Dragons*, New York: Simon and Schuster.

Kerr, G.H. (1965) *Formosa Betrayed*, Boston: Houghton Mifflin.

Keynes, J.M. (1936) *The General Theory of Employment, Interest and Money*, New York: Harcourt, Brace and World.

King, F.H.H. (1968) *A Concise Economic History of Modern China (1840–1961)*, New York: Praeger.

—— (1987) *The History of the Hongkong and Shanghai Banking Corporation, Volume I, 1864–1902*, Cambridge: Cambridge University press.

—— (1988a) *The History of the Hongkong and Shanghai Banking Corporation, Volume II, 1895–1918*, Cambridge: Cambridge University press.

—— (1988b) *The History of the Hongkong and Shanghai Banking Corporation, Volume III, 1919–1945*, Cambridge: Cambridge University press.

—— (1991) *The History of the Hongkong and Shanghai Banking Corporation, Volume IV, 1941–1984*, Cambridge: Cambridge University press.

Kong, Xiangxian (1991) *Daqing Yinhang Hangshi (History of the Daqing Bank)*, Nanjing: Nanjing daxue chubanshe (Nanjing University Press).

Krueger, A. (1974) 'The political economy of the rent-seeking society', *American Economic Review*, 64(3).

Kwong, J. (1997) *The Political Economy of Corruption in China*, London: M.E. Sharpe.

Lal, D. (1997) *The Poverty of 'Development Economics'*, London: Institute of Economic Affairs.

Lampton, D.M. (ed.) (1987) *Policy Implementation in Post-Mao China*, Berkeley: University of California Press.

Lardy, N. (1998a) 'China and the Asian contagion', *Foreign Affairs*, Jul/Aug: 78–88.

—— (1998b) *China's Unfinished Economic Revolution*, Washington, DC: Brookings Institution Press.

—— (2002) *Integrating China into the Global Economy*, Washington, DC: Brookings Institutions Press.

Lee, F.E. (1926) *Currency, Banking and Finance in China*, Washington DC: Government Printing Office.

Leith-Ross, F. (1968) *Money Talks: fifty years of international finance: the autobiography of Sir Frederick Leith-Ross*, London: Hutchinson.

Levy, M.J. Jr. (1953) 'Contrasting factors in the modernization of China and Japan', *Economic Development and Cultural Change*, 2, Oct.

Li, Keping (1998) 'Zhongyang caizheng yu guoyou zhuanye yinhang' (Central budget and state specialized banks), in J. Lou (ed.) *Zhongguo Guoyou Zhuanye Yinhang Shangyehua Gaige (The Commercialization Reform of China's State Banks)*, Beijing: Zhongguo jinrong chubanseh (China Financial Publishing House).

Li, Shuguang (2001) 'Bankruptcy law in China: lessons of the past 12 years', *Harvard Asia Quarterly*, 5: 1.

Li, Tiangang (2005) 'Jindai Shanghai: jinrong zhongxin de gushi' (The modern Shanghai: the story of financial centre), *Shanghai Securities*, 15 January.

Li, Xuewen (1998) 'Jindaihua jincheng zhong de zhongguo yinhang' (Bank of China in modern history*)*, Beijing: MA dissertation, Graduate School of People's Bank of China.

Li, Yining (2001) 'Qianzai de jinrong fengxian burong hushi' (Potential financial risks cannot be ignored), *Guoji Jinrongbao (International Finance)*, 20, July.

Lin, Yifu (1998) 'The emergence and evaporation of economic bubbles', *China National Condition and Strength*, 6: 7–9.

List, F. (1885) *The National System of Political Economy*, London: Longman.

Liu, Di (1998) *Kuaguo Yinhang yu Jinrong Shenhua (Multinational Banks and Financial Deepening)*, Shanghai: Shanghai yuandong chubanshe (Shanghai Far East Press).

Liu, Mingkang (ed.) (2002) *Lingdao Ganbu Guoji Jinrong Zhishi Duben (Readings of International Finance for Leaders and Cadres)*, Beijing: Jinji kexue chubanshe (Economics and Science Press).

—— (2004a) 'Managing the reform process, speech at the International Dialogue of New Forms of Governance in the 21st Century', Berlin, published by the CBRC website.

—— (2004b) 'Creating a favourable environment for the further opening of China's banking industry', at International Investment Forum of 2004 CFIIT, Xiamen, China.

Liu, Xiliang (2004) 'Guoyou shangye yinhang gaige zhide yanjiu de bage wenti' (Eight issues relating to China's state bank reform), *Zhongguo Jinrong (China Finance)*, 14 January.

Lo, Chi (2000) 'China's banking reform: the good, the bad and the ugly', paper prepared for the ADB Annual Conference Manila, the Philippines, 27 November.
—— (2004) 'How much time does China have', at: www.chinabusinessreview.com/public/0403/chilo.html.

Lu, Ding (2000) 'Credit quota as a banking risk control in China: a retrospect', in Baizhu Chen (ed.) *Financial Market Reform in China: progress, problems and prospects*, Oxford: Westview Press.

Ma, Jun (1998) 'Shareholding experiment, modern enterprise system, and state-owned enterprise reform', at: http://members.aol.com/junmanew/cover-htm.

Ma, S.K. (1990) 'Chinese bureaucracy and post-Mao reforms: negative adjustment', *Asian Survey*, 30: 1038–52.

Ma, Yinchu (1933) 'Wo duiyu zhongguo xianshi jinrong shiye zhi guancha' (My observations towards China's current financial industry), Shanghai: *Yinhang Zhoubao (Bankers Weekly)*, Nos 797, 798.

Mackenzie, C. (1954) *Realms of Silver, One Hundred Years of Banking in the East*, London: Routledge and Kegan Paul.

Mann, S. (1974) 'The Ningpo pang and financial power at Shanghai', in M. Elvin and G.W. Skinner (eds) *The Chinese City Between Two Worlds*, Stanford: Stanford University Press.

Mao, Zedong (1965) *Selected Works*, Beijing: Foreign Languages Press, Volume. 2.

Marshall, A. (1923) *Money, Credit, and Commerce*, London: Macmillan.

Marx, K. (1853a) 'Revolution in China and Europe', in *Marx on China*, London: Lawrence and Wishart, 1968 reprint.
—— (1853b) 'The British rule in India', in S. Aveneri (ed.) (1969) *Karl Marx on Colonialism and Modernization*, New York: Anchor Books.
—— (1869) *Eighteenth Brumaire of Louis Bonaparte*, New York: International Publishers, 1926 reprint.

Marx, K. and Engels, F. (1888) *The Communist Manifesto*, translated by Samuel Moore, with an introduction by Mick Hume, London: Junius, 1996 reprint.

Mi, Rucheng (ed.) (1963) *Zhongguo Jindai Tielushi Ziliao (Material on the History of Modern China's Railways)*, Beijing: Zhonghua shuju (Zhonghua Book Co.).

Miller, M. (1974) *Plain Speaking: an oral biography of Harry S. Truman*, London: Gollancz.

Monks, R.A.G. and Minnow, N. (2001) *Corporate Governance*, second edition, Oxford: Blackwell.

Muir, R. and Saba, J.P. (1995) 'Improving state enterprise performance: the role of internal and external incentives', World Bank Technical Paper, No. 306.

NAO (National Audit Office) (2004) 'Auditing report', No. 6, at: www.audit.gov.cn.

Narvaez, A.A. (1978) 'White-collar crime deterrents urged', *New York Times*, 2 December.

Niskanen, W. (1973) *Bureaucracy: servants or master?*, London: Institute of Economic Affairs.

Nolan, P. (1993) *State and Market in the Chinese Economy: essays on controversial issues*, Basingstoke: Macmillan.
—— (1995a) 'Politics, planning and the transition from Stalinism: the case of China', in H-J. Chang and R. Rowthorn (eds) *The Role of State in Economic Change*, Oxford: Clarendon.
—— (1995b) *China's Rise, Russia's Fall: politics, economics and planning in the transition from Stalinism*, London: Macmillan.

—— (1996) 'From state factory to modern corporation? China's Shougang Iron and Steel Corporation under economic reform', University of Cambridge: Department of Applied Economics, Working Paper, no. 9613.

—— (2001) *China and the Global Business Revolution*, Basingstoke: Palgrave.

—— (2004a) *China at the Crossroads*, Cambridge: Polity.

—— (2004b) *Transforming China: globalization, transition and development*, London: Anthem.

—— (2004c) 'Foreword', in X. Qin (2004) *The Theory of the Firm and Chinese Enterprise Reform: the case of China International Trust and Investment Corporation*, London: RoutledgeCurzon.

—— (2005) 'Kanshu jiulin: Guangdong huajie jinrong weiji "sanbu zou" '(Cutting the trees to save the forest: 'three steps' in solving Guangdong's financial crisis), translated by Dr Jin Zhang, *Weilai yu Xuanzhe* (*Future and Choice*), No. 2005–23.

North, D.C. and Thomas, R.P. (1973) *The Rise of the Western World: a new economic history*, London: Cambridge University Press.

OECD (Organisation for Economic Cooperation and Development) (2001) 'OECD principles of corporate governance, questions and answers', at: www.oecd.org.

—— (2004) 'OECD principles of corporate governance', at: www.oecd.org.

Pan, L. (1984) *Old Shanghai: gangsters in paradise*, Hong Kong: Heinemenn Asia.

Panić, M. (1995) 'International economic integration and the changing role of national governments', in H-J. Chang and R. Rowthorn (eds) *The Role of State in Economic Change*, Oxford: Clarendon.

Panitchpakdi, S. and Clifford, M. (2002) *China and the WTO: changing China, changing world trade*, Singapore: John Wiley and Sons (Asia).

Patrick, H.T. (1994) 'Comparisons, contrasts and implications', in H.T. Patrick and Y.C. Park (eds) *The Financial Development of Japan, Korea and Taiwan: growth, repression, and liberalization*, New York: Oxford University Press.

PBC (People's Bank of China) website http://pbc.gov.cn/news.

PBC (2001) *Jinrong Guizhang Zhidu Xuanbian* (*Selections of Financial Rules and Regulations*), Beijing: Zhongguo jinrong chubanshe (China Financial Publishing House).

Peacock, A. (1979) 'Appraising government expenditure: a simple economic analysis', in A. Peacock (ed.) *The Economic Analysis of Government*, Oxford: Martin Robertson.

Pearson, D. (1951) 'Washington merry-go-round', *Baltimore Sun*, 16 July.

Pei, Fei and Wei, Muting (1999) *Cong Shanghai Shizhang dao Taiwansheng Zhuxi–Wu Guozhen Koushu Huiyi* (*From Shanghai Mayor to Chairman of Taiwan Province – the Oral Memoir of Wu Guozhen*), translated to Chinese by Wu Xiuyuan, Shanghai:Shanghai renmin chubanshe (Shanghai People's Press).

Perkins, D.H. (1975) 'Introduction: the persistence of the past', in D.H. Perkins (ed.) *China's Modern Economy in Historical Perspective*, Stanford: Stanford University Press.

Pickett, K.H. Spencer and Pickett, J. (2002) *Financial Crime Investigation and Control*, New York: John Wiley and Sons.

PLA (People's Liberation Army) Daily website: http://english.pladaily.com.cn/special/three/content/3.htm.

Posner, R. (1975) 'The social costs of monopoly and regulation', *Journal of Political Economy*, 83/4.

PWC (PriceWaterhouseCoopers) 2004, 'China's new bankruptcy law', at: http://www.pwchk.com/webmedia/doc/1097811935112_cn_bankruptcy_law_oct2004.pdf.

Qian, Jiaju (1955) 'Jiuzhongguo faxing gongzhai shi de yanjiu' (The study of government bonds in old China), *Lishi Yanjiu* (*History Research*) 2.

—— (1984) *Jiu Zhongguo Gongzhaishi Ziliao* (*Historical Material on Government Bonds in Old China*), Beijing: Zhonghua shuju (Zhonghua Book Co.).

Qin, Xiao (2004) *The Theory of the Firm and Chinese Enterprise Reform: the case of China International Trust and Investment Corporation*, London: Routledge-Curzon.

Qiu, Tao (2004) *Zhonghua Minguo Fantanshi* (*Anti-corruption History of Republic of China*), Lanzhou: Lanzhou daxue chubanshe (Lanzhou University Press).

Quested, R. (1977) 'The Russo-Chinese Bank: a Multi-National financial base of Tsarism in China', University of Birmingham: PhD dissertation.

Rawski, T.G. (1975) 'The growth of producer industries, 1900–1971', in D.H. Perkins (ed.) *China's Modern Economy in Historical Perspective*, Stanford: Stanford University Press.

—— (1989) *Economic Growth in Prewar China*, Oxford: University of California Press.

—— (2002) 'Will investment behaviour constrain China's growth?' *China Perspective* 38: 28–35.

Riskin, C. (1975) 'Surplus and stagnation in modern China', in D.H. Perkins (ed.) *China's Modern Economy in Historical Perspective*, Stanford: Stanford University Press.

Robb, G. (1992) *White-collar Crime in Modern England: financial fraud and business morality, 1845–1929*, Cambridge: Cambridge University Press.

Rosenstein-Rodan, P. (1943) 'Problems of industrialization of eastern and south-eastern Europe', *Economic Journal* 53 (3).

Ross, S. (1973) 'The economic theory of agency: the principal's problem', *American Economic Review* 63(2): 134–9.

Rowley, C. (1983) 'The political economy of the public sector', in B. Jones (ed.) *Perspectives on Political Economy*, London: Frances Pinter.

Russell, M.B. (1972) 'American silver policy and China: 1933–1936', University of Illinois: PhD dissertation.

Sarasas, P. (1940) *Money and Banking in Japan*, London: H. Cranton Limited.

Seagrave, S. (1985) *The Soong Dynasty*, London: Sidgwick and Jackson.

Shanghai archives, at: http://202.136.208.148/hshrw/chyqch/200301200184.htm.

Shaw, E. (1973) *Financial Deepening in Economic Development*, London: Oxford University Press.

SHCS (Shanghai Commercial and Savings Bank) (1932) 'Zongjinglichu huiyilu' (Records of the meetings of the general manager's office), SHCS file, No. 76.

Shea, Jia-Dong (1994) 'Taiwan: development and structural change of the financial system', in H.T. Patrick and Y.C. Park (eds) *The Financial Development of Japan, Korea and Taiwan: growth, repression, and liberalization*, New York: Oxford University Press.

Shen, Yunlong (1979) 'Wang Yunlao yu jinyuanquan an zhiyi' (Doubts about Wang Yunlao and the case of the gold yuan), *Zhuanji Wenxue* (*Biographical Literature*), Taibei: Zhuanji wenxueshe (Press of Biographical Literature), 209.

Sheng, A. (1996) *Bank Restructuring: lessons from the 1980s*, Washington: World Bank.

Sheridan, J.E. (1966) *Chinese Warlord: the career of Feng Yu-hsiang*, Stanford: Stanford University Press.

Shieh, Milton J.T. (1970) *The Kuo Min Tang: selected historical documents*, New York: St. John's University Press.

Shleifer, A. and Vishny, R. (1994) 'Politicians and firms', *Quarterly Journal of Economics*, 109(4), 995–1025.

Shou, Chongyi (ed.) (1996) *Waishang Yinhang zai Zhongguo* (*Foreign Banks in China*), Beijing: Zhongguo wenshi chubanshe (China Literature and History Press).

Singh, A. (1992) 'Corporate takeovers', University of Cambridge: paper prepared for the New Palgrave Dictionary of Money and Finance, Faculty of Economics.

—— (1995) 'The state and industrialization in India: successes and failures and the lessons from the future,' in H-J. Chang and R. Rowthorn (eds) *The Role of State in Economic Change*, Oxford: Clarendon.

—— (1998) 'Financial crisis in East Asia: "The end of the Asian model?" ' discussion paper 24, Development Policies Department, International Labour Office, Geneva.

—— (2002) 'Corporate governance, competition, the new international financial architecture and large corporations in emerging markets', University of Cambridge: ESRC Centre for Business Research, Working paper, No. 250.

Smith, A. (1776) *The Wealth of Nations*, Volume II, edited with an introduction and notes by Andrew Skinner, London: Penguin, 1999 reprint.

Soong, T.V. (1932) 'Report for the 19th and 20th fiscal years, July 1930 to June 1932', Nanjing.

Stanley, M.R. (1989) 'The influence of Frank A.Vanderlip and the National City Bank on American commerce and foreign policy, 1910–1920', PhD Dissertation, Ann Arbor: U.M.I. Dissertation Information Service.

Steinfeld, E.S. (2001) 'Moving beyond transition in China: financial reform and the political economy of declining growth', *Journal of Comparative Politics*, July.

Stern, S. (1951) *The United States in International Banking*, New York: Columbia University Press.

Stilwell, J. (1948) *Chinese Adventure*, New York: W. Sloane Assoc.

Sutherland, E.H. (1940) 'The white collar criminal', *American Sociological Review* 5: 1–12.

—— (1983) *White Collar Crime*, the uncut version, with an introduction by Gilbert Geis and Colin Goff, New Haven: Yale University Press.

Tamagna, F.M. (1942) *Banking and Finance in China*, New York: Institute of Pacific Relations Publications Office.

Tang, Shuangning (2004) 'Reforms of China's banking sector and prospects of the banking industry development in Northeast China', speech at Northeast China Rejuvenation and Northeast Asia Cooperation Forum.

—— (2005) 'Yinjin hege zhanlue touzizhe cujin zhongwaizi yinhang "shuangying" ' (Introduce qualified strategic investors, promote the 'win–win' of both parties), at: http: www.cbrc.gov.cn.

Tappan, P.W. (1947) 'Who is the criminal?' *American Sociological Review* 12: 96–102.

Tricker, R.I. (1984) *Corporate Governance: practices, procedures, and powers in British companies and their boards of directors*, Aldershot, Hants: Gower.

Tuchman, B.W. (1970) *Sand against the Wind: Stilwell and the American experience in China, 1911–45*, London: Macmillan.

UIBE (University of International Business and Economics) (2004) 'Zhongguo jianshe yinhang yuanhangzhang wang xuebing yanzhong weiji weifa anjian' (The serious case of former CCB president Wang Xuebing), at: http://www.uibe.edu.cn/upload/up_jcsjc/alfx/200412902.htm.

Vartiainen, J. (1995) 'The state and structural change: what can be learnt from the successful late industrializers?' in H-J. Chang and R. Rowthorn (eds) *The Role of State in Economic Change*, Oxford: Clarendon.

—— (1999) 'Successful state intervention in industrial transformation', in M. Woo-Cumings (ed.) *The Developmental State*, London: Cornell University Press.

Vogel, E.F. (1991) *The Four Little Dragons: the spread of industrialization in East Asia*, London: Harvard University Press.

Wade, R. (1990) *Governing the Market: economic theory and the role of government in East Asian industrialization*, Princeton, NJ: Princeton University Press.

—— (1995) 'Resolving the state-market dilemma in East Asia', in H-J. Chang and R. Rowthorn (eds) *The Role of State in Economic Change*, Oxford: Clarendon.

Wang, Jingyu (1983) *Shijiu Shiji Xifang Ziben Zhuyi dui Zhongguo de Jingji Qinlue (Western Economic Invasion of China during the Nineteenth Century)*, Beijing: Renmin chubanshe (People's Publishing House).

—— (1999) *Waiguo Ziben zai Jindai Zhongguo de Jinrong Huodong (Financial Activities of Foreign Capital in Modern China)*, Beijing: Renmin chubanshe (People's Publishing House).

Wang, Xin and Liu, Hong (1988) *Nanjing Guoming Zhengfu Junzheng Yaoyuan Lu (The Biography of Key Members of Nanjing Nationalist Government)*, Beijing: Chunqiu chubanshe (Spring and Autumn Press).

Wang, Y.C. (1966) *Chinese Intellectuals and the West, 1872–1949*, Chapel Hill: University of North Carolina Press.

Wang, Yeh-chien (1981) *The Development of Money and Banking in Modern China, 1644–1937*, Taibei: Institute of Economics, Academia Sinica.

Wang, Zongpei (1937) 'Zuijin zi Zhongguo Jinrongye' (China's recent financial industry), *Shenbao Weekly* 2 (13 June).

Weber, M. (1947) *The Theory of Social and Economic Organization*, translated from German by A.M. Henderson and Talcott Parsons, revised and edited, with an introduction, by Talcott Parsons, New York: Oxford University Press.

Weisburd, D., Wheeler, S., Waring, E. and Bode, N. (1991) *Crimes of the Middle Classes: white-collar offenders in the Federal Courts*, New Haven: Yale University Press.

Wen, Jiabao (2004) 'Government work report', at: http://www.chinadaily.com.cn/english/doc/2004–03/05/.

Westerfield, R.R. (1947) *Money, Credit and Banking*, New York: Ronald Press.

World Bank (1995) *Bureaucrats in Business: the economics and politics of government ownership*, Oxford: Published for the World Bank [by] Oxford University Press.

Wu, An-chia (2000) 'State capacity in the RoC and PRC: a comparative perspective', in K. E. Brodsgaard and S. Young (eds) *State Capacity in East Asia: Japan, Taiwan, China and Vietnam*, Oxford: Oxford University Press.

Wu, Chengxi (1936) 'Minguo ershisi nian de zhongguo yinhangjie' (China's banking industry in 1935), *Dongfa Zazhi (The Eastern Miscellany)*, Shanghai, 1 April.

Wu, Jinglian (1995) 'China's economic and financial reform', in O.T. Kam (ed.) *Financial Reform in China*, London: Routledge.

—— (2000) 'China's economic reform: past, present and future', *Perspectives* 1 (5).

—— (2004) 'Zhizao jinrong heidong de jizhi bingwei xiaoshi' (The mechanism of creating financial black holes has not disappeared), *Caijing*, 5 August.

Wu, Qing (2001) 'The challenges facing China's financial services industry' in P. Nolan (2001) *China and the Global Business Revolution*, Basingstoke: Palgrave.

Xie, Ping and Lu Lei (2005) *Zhongguo Jinrong Fubai de Jingjixue Fenxi: tizhi, xingwei yu jizhi sheji* (*The Economics of China's Financial Corruption: institutions, behaviour and mechanism design*), Beijing: Zhongxin chubanshe (Citic Publishing House).

Xinhuanet website: www.xinhuanet.com.

Xinong (1922) 'Xinnianlai duiyu yinhangjie zhi xinxiwang' (The new expectation for the financial industry in the new year), Shanghai: *Yinhang Zhoubao* (*Bankers Weekly*) 6 (3).

Xu, Cangshui (1923) *Guonei gongzhaishi* (*Domestic Bond History*), Shanghai: Yinhang zhoubaoshe (Office of Bankers Weekly).

—— (1925) *Shanghai Yinhang Gonghui Shiyeshi* (*The Working History of the Shanghai Bankers Association*), Shanghai: Yinhang zhoubaoshe (Office of Bankers Weekly).

Xu, Hongcai (2000) *Questions and Answers – China's Financial Market*, Beijing: Foreign Languages Press.

Xu, Jiansheng (1996) 'Lun minguo chunian jingji zhengce de fuzhi yu jiangli daoxiang' (The support and guiding roles of economic policy in the early Republic of China), *Xiandaishi Yanjiu* (*Research on Modern History*) 1.

Xu, Meizheng (1998) 'Shangye yinhang chanquan zhidu de gaige' (Reform of property rights of commercial banks), in J. Lou (ed.) *Zhongguo Guoyou Zhuanye Yinhang Shangyehua Gaige* (*The Commercialization Reform of China's State Banks*), Beijing: Zhongguo jinrong chubanseh (China Financial Publishing House).

Xu, Xiaonian (2004) 'Cong zhidu jingjixue de jiaodu kan guoyou yinhang gaige' (The reform of state banks from the perspective of institutional economics), Shanghai: CEIBS (China Europe International Business School) document.

Xu, Yisheng (1962) *Zhongguoj Jindai Waizhaishi Tongji Ziliao* (*Statistical Material on the History of Modern China's Foreign Debts*), Beijing: Zhonghua shuju (Zhonghua Book Co.).

Yan, Pinzhong (2004) *Huaqi Yinhang zai Hua Yueduo Jishi* (*Citibank's Plundering in China*), Beijing: Xin shijie chubanshe (New World Press).

Yan, Zhongping, Xu, Yisheng and Yao, Xiangao (1955) *Zhongguo Jindai Jingjishi Tongji Ziliao Xuanji* (*Selected Statistics on Modern Chinese Economic History*), Beijing: Kexue chubanshe (Science Press).

Yang, Peixin (1985) 'Lun zhongguo jinrong zichan jieji de fengjianxing' (The feudal characteristics of China's financial capitalists), *Xiandaishi Yanjiu* (*Research on Modern History*) 2.

Yang, Ya-Hwei (1994) 'Taiwan: development and structural change of the banking system', in H.T. Patrick and Y.C. Park (eds) *The Financial Development of Japan, Korea and Taiwan: growth, repression, and liberalization*, New York: Oxford University Press.

Yang, Yinpu (1930) *Shanghai Jinrong Zuzhi Gaiyao* (*Shanghai's Financial Organizations*), Shanghai: Shangwu yinshuguan (Commercial Press).

Yang, Yonggang (1997) *Zhongguo Jindai Tielushi Ziliao* (*Historical Material on Modern China's Railways*), Shanghai: Shanghai shudian chubanshe (Shanghai Bookstore Press).

Yao, Linqing (2004) 'The Chinese overseas students: an overview of the flows change', paper prepared for the 12th Biennial Conference of the Australian Population Association, 15–17 September 2004, Canberra, at: http://acsr.anu.edu.au/APA2004/Papers/6C-Yao.pdf.

Yao, Songling (1968) *Zhonghang Fuwu Ji (The Experience of Serving in the Bank of China)*, Taibei: Zhuanji wenxueshe (Biography Literature Press).

—— (1982) *Zhang Gongquan Xiansheng Nianpu Chugao (The Chronicle of Mr. Zhang Jia'ao)*, Taibei: Zhuanji wenxueshe (Biography Literature Press).

Yin, R.K. (1994) *Case Study Research: design and methods*, Thousand Oaks, CA: Sage.

Young, A.N. (1965) *China's Wartime Finance and Inflation, 1937–1945*, Cambridge, MA: Harvard University Press.

—— (1971) *China's Nation-building Effort, 1927–1937: the financial and economic record*, Stanford: Hoover Institution Press.

Zhang, Allan (2004) 'China's leadership rolls out reform agenda', at: www.pwc.com.

Zhang, Haipeng (ed.) (1993) *Zhongguo Shida Shangbang (China's Ten Big Merchant Bangs)*, Hefei: Huangshan chubanshe (Huangshan Publishing House).

Zhang, Jia'ao (Chang Kia-Ngau) (1958) *The Inflationary Spiral: the experience in China, 1939–1950*, Cambridge, MA: MIT Press.

—— (1977) 'Zhang Gongquan xiansheng zishu wangshi dakewen' (Mr. Zhang Jia'ao narrates past events in answer to questions), *Zhuanji Wenxue (Biographical Literature)*, Taibei: Zhuanji wenxueshe (Biography Literature Press) 30 (2).

Zhang, Jianping and Li, An (1997) *Kongshi Jiazu Quanzhuan (Complete Biography of Kung Family)*, Beijing: Zhongguo wenshi chubanshe (China Literature and History Press).

Zhang, Weiwei (2000) *Transforming China: economic reform and its political implications*, Basingstoke: Macmillan.

Zhang, Yulan (1957) *Zhongguo Yinhangye Fazhanshi (A History of the Development of Chinese Banking)*, Shanghai: Shanghai renmin chubanshe (Shanghai People's Press).

Zhang, Zihan (1942) 'Interview with Mr. Zhang Gongquan (Jia'ao)', *Jinrong Zhishi (Financial Knowledge)*, January.

Zheng, Guanying (1893) *Shengshi weiyan (Warnings to a seemingly prosperous age)*, Shengyang: Liaoning renmin chubanshe (Liaoning People's Press), 1994 reprint.

Zheng, Huixin (2004) 'Zhanqian zhongguo jiansheyin gongsi de touzi jingying huo-dong' (The investment activities of China Development Finance Corporation before the War), Issue 1, *Zhongguo jingjishi yanjiu (Research of China's Economic History)*.

Zhou, Jianping (2000) Roots of the financial crisis in Asia and implications for China, in Baizhu Chen (ed.) *Financial Market Reform in China: progress, problems and prospects*, Oxford: Westview Press.

Zhou, Kaiqing (ed.) (1951) *Jingji Wenti Ziliao Huibian (Collection of Materials on Economic Issues)*, Taibei: Huawen shuju (Huawen Book Co.).

Zhou, Xiaochuan (ed.) (1999) *Chongjian yu Zaisheng (Rebuild and Rebirth)*, Beijing: Zhongguo jinrong chubanshe (China Financial Publishing House).

Zhu, Tian (2000) 'Restructuring China's state-owned enterprises: a corporate governance perspective' in Baizhu Chen (ed.) *Financial Market Reform in China: progress, problems and prospects*, Oxford: Westview Press.

Zi, Yaohua (2005) *Shiji Zuyin: yiwei jindai jinrongxue jia de zishu (Century Footprint:*

account by a banker in China's modern times), Changsha: Hunan wenyi chubanshe (Hunan Literature Press).

ZJIB (Zhejiang Industrial Bank) (1921) 'Dongshihui jueyi' (Resolution of the Board of Directors), 11 December, ZJIB file No. 5.

Index